War Termination as a Civil-Military Bargain

War Termination as a Civil-Military Bargain

Soldiers, Statesmen, and the Politics of Protracted Armed Conflict

Shawn T. Cochran

palgrave
macmillan

WAR TERMINATION AS A CIVIL-MILITARY BARGAIN

First published 2016 by
PALGRAVE MACMILLAN

Palgrave Macmillan in the UK is an imprint of Macmillan Publishers Limited, registered in England, company number 785998, of Houndmills, Basingstoke, Hampshire, RG21 6XS.

Palgrave Macmillan in the US is a division of Nature America, Inc., One New York Plaza, Suite 4500, New York, NY 10004-1562.

Palgrave Macmillan is the global academic imprint of the above companies and has companies and representatives throughout the world.

Hardback ISBN: 978–1–137–52796–7
E-PUB ISBN: 978–1–137–52798–1
E-PDF ISBN: 978–1–137–52797–4
DOI: 10.1057/9781137527974

Distribution in the UK, Europe and the rest of the world is by Palgrave Macmillan®, a division of Macmillan Publishers Limited, registered in England, company number 785998, of Houndmills, Basingstoke, Hampshire RG21 6XS.

Library of Congress Cataloging-in-Publication Data

Cochran, Shawn T.
War termination as a civil-military bargain : soldiers, statesmen, and the politics of protracted armed conflict / by Shawn T. Cochran.
pages cm
Includes bibliographical references and index.
ISBN 978–1–137–52796–7 (hardback)
1. War—Termination. 2. Civil-military relations. I. Title.

U21.2.C62 2015
303.6′6—dc23 2015019583

A catalogue record for the book is available from the British Library.

In memory of Fred Charles Iklé, 1924–2011

Contents

Illustrations

Figures

Tables

Acknowledgments

I hold firmly to Einstein's assessment that "what a person does on his own, without being stimulated by the thoughts and experiences of others, is even in the best of cases rather paltry and monotonous." With this in mind, I am deeply grateful to the many individuals who have assisted with this book at various stages, providing valuable assistance, feedback, mentoring, insights, and expertise along the way. I am particularly indebted to Bob Pape, Charles Lipson, Paul Staniland, David Benson, Mike Rosol, John Schuessler, Yasemin Bilgel, John Stevenson, Morgan Kaplan, Yuna Park, Josh Sutton, Chad Levinson, Bernard Silberman, Patricia Shields, Brian O'Connor, Elaine Fan, Alexandra Dauler, Deepa John, Steven Miller, Kelly McHugh, Douglas Porch, Chester Crocker, Stephen Burgess, Lindsey O'Rourke, Ryan Grauer, Casey Lucius, Stephen Chiabotti, Tom Hughes, Joe Panza, Daniel Conway, Richard Gabriel, Petra Groen, Hilton Hamann, Jaap Hoogenboezem, and Thula Simpson.

And to Karen, Isabelle, and Aidan—thank you for your love, patience, and support.

CHAPTER 1

An Unexplained Lacuna of the Politics of War

When Henry VI was crowned king of England in 1429, the Hundred Years' War with France (1337–1453) was already in its ninth decade. Over the next 15 years, English fortunes in the protracted conflict steadily declined. Losing ground to the French while facing a burdensome drain on state resources and growing domestic unrest back in England, the young king brokered a truce in 1444 as the basis for what he hoped would be a permanent peace settlement recognizing English claims to Normandy. In subsequent negotiations, Henry agreed to give up the English-held province of Maine in northern France, but his military commanders had other ideas. Resentful "they had been sold out by politicians and even by their king," the commanders balked at returning the province to the French; or, as Corson notes, they refused to "give up territory they and their forces had captured at great human cost for a political objective they did not share."[1] This set in motion a series of events leading to the resumption of hostilities and culminating in England's defeat and wholesale loss of Normandy. With even a marginal settlement out of reach and the war approaching its ignominious end, the English army and its domestic allies criticized the king and demanded a scapegoat for the debacle. In response, Henry turned on his closest friend and most trusted adviser, the Earl of Suffolk, who was arrested, imprisoned in the Tower of London, impeached by Parliament, and subsequently banished to the continent.

Although banishments have become less prevalent, the above anecdote still hints at two central and enduring facets of war termination politics. First, apart from cases of clear victory or outright defeat, the decision to end a war ultimately reflects a bargain between political and military leadership. And second, this bargain is rarely an easy one. In the classic *Every War Must End*, Iklé writes, "In preparing a major military operation, military leaders and civilian officials can effectively work together . . . By contrast, planning to end a war where victory seems out of reach is not a task on which men can easily collaborate. To search for an exit in such a situation, government leaders can rarely move in harmony."[2]

The problem of war termination can strain civil-military relations to the limit, creating a deep and acrimonious divide. It has pushed historically apolitical and subservient militaries to threaten coup. It has driven political leaders to purposefully bleed their own armies in senseless battles, hoping the chastened soldier might be more amenable to peace. But even if rare, civil-military collaboration can, and does occur; and one can find examples of political and military leadership working in harmony to bring costly, protracted war to a close. Under these circumstances, the domestic politics of war termination looks fundamentally different.

This book examines the domestic politics of war termination through a civil-military lens and seeks to explain the behaviors of political leaders embroiled in protracted armed conflict. Such an approach has surprisingly little precedent. More than 40 years have passed since Halperin published the brief but insightful "War Termination as a Problem in Civil-Military Relations."[3] While the broader topic of war termination has received substantial attention over subsequent decades, there has been little attempt to build upon Halperin's analysis; and his arguments have largely gone unchallenged if not ignored. In a recent review of the war termination literature, Maoz and Siverson note there are "at least three aspects of what transpires within the state that are of interest."[4] The first entails interactions within the governing regime and among political elites. The second is the relationship between the government and the population, particularly in terms of public opinion. And the third is the relationship between the government and the military. Maoz and Siverson find this latter aspect, while potentially offering important insights into how wars end, to be the most understudied of relevant domestic factors. Accordingly, the question of "how the interplay between the military and the political leadership affects the conduct of war and its termination" remains one of the "unexplained lacunas of the politics of war."[5]

With the above in mind, this book addresses both the nature of the interplay between political and military leadership and how this interplay influences war termination decision-making. The central claim is that war termination reflects a civil-military bargain, and this bargain affects relevant policy decisions by altering the dynamics of blame attribution.[6] Specifically, the civil-military bargain moderates the extent to which political leaders risk being "charged with the loss," or held culpable and subsequently punished for a failed war.[7] Political leadership's bargaining position in this sense varies significantly across cases. It can also vary over time and from one leader to the next within a given case. The associated risk of culpability factors into a political leader's wartime calculus, influencing whether he or she will remain committed to fighting a costly, protracted armed conflict or else prove willing to withdraw short of victory. While it may be true nobody wants to lose a war, it is surely the case nobody wants to be *blamed* for losing a war.

The Puzzle: War Termination and the Culpability of (old and new) Political Leaders

States have, with some regularity, become embroiled in wars that turn out longer, costlier, and more difficult than expected at the outset. Under these circumstances, political leadership must choose to either persist in the war effort, committing additional resources in pursuit of the state's war aims, or cede some or all of these objectives and terminate the conflict under less-than-favorable terms. Some leaders dig in their heels despite mounting costs, growing discontent at home, and little hope of victory in the foreseeable future while others, facing a similar scenario, prove more apt to cut their losses and bring the fighting to a rapid end. Still others express a desire to settle but prove unable to do so or else drag the process out for years. This wide variation in behavior, along with the enduring observation that "fighting often continues long past the point where a 'rational' calculation would indicate the war should be ended," presents an interesting and important puzzle as well as a long-standing source of scholarly debate.[8]

The conventional wisdom suggests that losing a war, or the prospect of such, does not affect all political leaders the same way. Some leaders face greater risk of domestic repercussions, and this risk, in turn, influences the willingness to settle short of victory. Croco goes so far to argue that "the *primary* factor in determining a leader's choice between continuation and termination of the conflict is the probability of punishment if he or she accepts any outcome less than a win (emphasis added)."[9] Whether primary or not, fear of punishment likely plays an important part. This necessarily raises the question of why some leaders are more susceptible than others. The prevailing view on susceptibility is that leaders responsible for *starting* a war are most likely to be held culpable, and subsequently punished, if the war ends poorly. These initial leaders, "may want to back down, but their clear ties to the decision to involve the state in the war increase their risk of punishment if they settle for anything short of victory."[10] Wars drag on accordingly. New leaders, being ostensibly free of blame and unencumbered by such pressure to win, are more apt to sue for peace. Given this logic, scholars have long noted political leadership change as an important, even necessary, precursor to the termination of protracted armed conflict.[11]

Political leadership change may, in fact, come close to being a necessary condition. But it is by no means a sufficient condition. War termination generally follows some form of change in political leadership, but most incidents of wartime political leadership change do not result in war termination. Gorbachev's accession is often cited as facilitating the Soviet Union's withdrawal from Afghanistan. Similarly, scholars point to the formation of the Mendès-France government in 1954 as the turning point leading to French extrication from Indochina. But Gorbachev was the fourth Soviet premier to preside over the ten-year Afghan conflict. France experienced no fewer than nine wartime changes of government before Prime Minister Mendès-France was able to "complete the job that no other French politician had the courage to undertake."[12]

In essence, existing domestic politics-type theories of war termination can effectively account for the behavior of initial leaders but have little to say about variation in the behavior of new leaders.[13] Even a more expansive interpretation of *initial* culpability does not fully solve this problem. As an amendment to the basic leadership change model, Croco suggests responsibility for starting a war can be shared, extending culpability beyond the "first leader" to subsequent leaders "directly connected to the decision to involve the state in the conflict" and of the same political party as the first leader.[14] Looking at Croco's database of 355 wartime leaders, those directly linked to the start of the war, whether first leaders or not, generally behave as predicted. The majority, or 62 percent, of these culpable leaders continue the war until they either depart office or achieve a favorable outcome. However, nearly 53 percent of non-culpable leaders behave in the same way as their culpable counterparts.[15] The distinction between leader types may be statistically significant, but this does not obviate the fact that fewer than half of non-culpable leaders, as defined by lack of direct connection to the start of the war, exhibit the willingness and ability to settle under less-than-favorable terms.

The real puzzle, then, has little to do with initial leaders, or even with the difference between initial and new leaders. The real puzzle resides with variation among new leaders. Why do so many of these new leaders, despite lacking culpability in the conventional sense, still struggle to extricate the state from costly, protracted war? Croco argues that for new leaders, the probability of domestic repercussions "will most likely be zero" and thus they "will not face this hard choice" of whether to abandon the war or keep fighting.[16] But new leaders still behave *as if* they face a hard choice. They still behave *as if* they risk being blamed and punished for losing the war or otherwise ending it short of victory. This is the puzzle I find interesting and seek to explain. And I propose the explanation requires a broader conceptual framework of political leadership culpability and an understanding of how civil-military bargaining influences blame attribution within this framework.

Toward a Civil-Military Theory of Blame Attribution and War Termination

While political leadership change often has little observable impact on war outcomes, this does not necessarily imply the absence of significant causal effect.[17] By alleviating responsibility for starting a stalemated or unsuccessful war, leadership change removes an important basis for blame and thus a significant hurdle to war termination. But this does not eliminate political leadership's risk of blame and domestic repercussions altogether. Under certain conditions, political leaders with little culpability in the conventional sense can experience the same types of domestic pressures and constraints as their predecessors.

Political Opposition and Political Narrative

The risk to new political leaders stems in part from society's elevated and emotive response to military defeat combined with the entrepreneurship of the political opposition, whatever form this opposition takes. The trauma of military defeat is too rich an opportunity to pass up, and if presented with the opportunity, the opposition will attempt to capitalize on the failure at the incumbent's expense. Croco claims this applies primarily to those leaders responsible for starting a war, as "the domestic opposition will leap at the chance to target a leader who ends a war he or she had a role in starting with anything less than a total victory."[18] Initial leaders may be easy targets in this sense. But there is little reason to think subsequent leaders will be given a free pass. More often than not, the opposition will leap at the chance to target *any* leader who ends a war short of victory or fails to achieve success at an acceptable price.

New political leaders must also account for the vagaries of collective blame attribution. Studies across multiple disciplines demonstrate the collective assigning of blame rarely reflects an objective or apolitical process. Instead, blame can be highly contingent upon partisan affiliation, framing effects, informational limitations, strategic manipulation, and cognitive biases.[19] This can lead to wide variation in how domestic audiences attribute blame in the event of a poor policy outcome. As Weaver observes, "On one hand, they (domestic audiences) may fail to link policymakers to choices they (policymakers) have in fact made or outcomes to which they have contributed. On the other hand, they may attribute a linkage where the policymaker's influence was really weak or non-existent."[20] The bottom line is that culpability for policy failure, to include a failed war, is not a fact. Instead, it represents a social and political construct contingent upon "frames of reference, scripts, and arguments."[21]

Taken together, these frames, scripts, and arguments coalesce into political narrative, a story constructed by political actors to change the discursive environment, generate shared meaning, and exert influence over the domestic audience.[22] To target the incumbent's wartime decision-making and performance, the opposition will craft and attempt to propagate a narrative of failure that counters any narrative offered by the incumbent, defines the implications and harmful effects, and highlights the incumbent's personal culpability.[23] If relevant, this narrative can malign the incumbent's lack of judgement and competence in starting a war he or she could not win, or at least could not win at an acceptable price. Obviously this type of critique, which falls under what I broadly label the *pretender* narrative, will only resonate if directed at a political leader in office at the start of the war or closely connected to the decision to go to war.[24]

New leaders may not be susceptible to the *pretender* narrative but remain at risk of censure under a number of other distinct narratives unrelated to the decision to go to war. As a well-known historical example, the stab-in-the-back myth or *Dolchstosslegende* emerging from Germany's failure in World War I effectively targeted leaders of the nascent Weimar Republic for capitulating to the Allies despite the German army remaining in place and undefeated on the field of battle.[25] Borrowing from this episode, what I conceptualize as the *backstabber* narrative holds political leadership culpable for prematurely and unnecessarily ending a war that was still winnable and still worth fighting. In contrast, the *sellout* narrative blames political leadership for an inadequate, unjust, or dishonorable settlement whether or not the war is deemed a lost cause. Political leadership can further be charged as a *bungler* or *squanderer,* respectively, for mismanaging the war effort or for wasting the state's blood and treasure in a war that is no longer winnable or no longer worth fighting.

Each of these narratives calls into question political leadership's judgment and competence in some way, and each has potential to prompt domestic repercussions. But only the *pretender* narrative is limited to those political leaders linked to the start of a war. Subsequent leaders remain very much susceptible to blame under the *bungler, backstabber, squanderer,* and *sellout* narratives. This residual risk helps explain why so many new leaders behave like old leaders. New leaders still behave *as if* they risk domestic repercussions because they still risk domestic repercussions. The ouster of political leadership responsible for starting the war has important effects in every case where such change occurs, but these effects will likely remain latent and obscured until new political leadership can (if ever) adequately hedge culpability unrelated to the start of the war. And a political leader's capacity to mitigate blame in this regard hinges in large part on his or her ability to strike an effective bargain with military leadership.

Civil-Military Relations as a Principal-Agent Bargain

To characterize civil-military relations as a form of bargaining is nothing new. Feaver describes the civil-military "bargaining relationship" as a fluid strategic interaction punctuated by military leadership's attempts to prevail in policy disputes.[26] Allison and Zelikow similarly posit military leadership as a central player in the incessant "bargaining games" of governmental politics.[27] This characterization captures the possibility that political and military leaders can effectively work together in some policy areas but clash in others and is consistent with Iklé's assertion that with efforts to terminate a protracted and unsuccessful war, civil-military collaboration is uniquely hard to come by.

Recent scholarship further scopes this fluid interaction in terms of a principal-agent relationship.[28] The principal-agent model is useful in that it accounts for the hierarchical yet specialized nature of civil-military bargaining and highlights the need to consider preferences as well as leverage, although there is debate as to what matters more. Some applications of agency theory assume widely divergent principal-agent preferences and accordingly focus on how the principal employs leverage to overcome this gap. Others point to shared preferences as the basis for an effective relationship given that an agent's compliance gained solely through the plying of leverage is apt to be shallow and unstable.[29] Preferences can, and do, converge; and when this happens, bargaining outcomes reflect "affiliation, cooperation, and accommodation" more than "victories in a test of strength."[30] As Feaver astutely points out, though, like preferences between the civilian principal and military agent do not necessarily engender collaboration, and thus convergence does not *a priori* diminish agency problems.[31] More specifically, political and military leaders may agree on the need to extricate the state from protracted armed conflict but still struggle to collaborate, or fail to move in harmony, toward such an end. Leverage in some way, shape, or form still matters.

At least from the civilian perspective, the "success" of civil-military bargaining applied to the problem of war termination is manifest in the extent to which military leadership's war-related assessments, statements, and actions remain consistent with, and supportive of, a given political leader's preferred policy and relevant justifications. Political leadership works, best case, to secure active civil-military collaboration whether aimed at a policy of persistence or withdrawal. At a minimum, political leadership attempts through bargaining to prevent military leadership from going public with divergent views, colluding with the opposition, or otherwise taking actions to undermine political leadership's preferred course of action. If and when a civil-military gap appears, the opposition will become more assertive in targeting the incumbent, and the associated narrative implicating the incumbent as culpable for a failed war will gain purchase with the domestic audience.

Bargaining with Obstructive versus Facilitative Military Leadership

Political leaders are strategic blame minimizers. They anticipate and, when possible, select out of policies or actions likely to result in blame and domestic repercussions. When faced with the difficult and politically explosive problem of war termination, they recognize the opposition will try to exploit any civil-military gap in order to impart blame and propagate a less-than-complimentary narrative. Because of this, political leaders remain sensitive to the interaction with military leadership and adjust their war termination calculus accordingly.

At a fundamental level, political leadership's bargaining position varies based on whether military leadership is obstructive, facilitative, or somewhere in between.[32] On the obstructive end of the spectrum, military leadership remains committed to the ongoing war and, at a minimum, maintains both the willingness and ability to communicate or otherwise promote this preference. This represents the traditional view of military leaders as "strongly biased toward staying the course," with the armed forces being the "last institution who will want to admit that things aren't going well or recommend getting out short of victory."[33] The quintessential example is that of France in Algeria (1954–62), where for the French Army, "it was the war that, even against the will of God or man, could not be lost."[34] On the facilitative end of the spectrum, military leadership as a collective has determined the war is no longer winnable or no longer worth fighting and thus the best course of action is to get out.[35] Where military leadership falls along this continuum does not determine the results of civil-military bargaining or dictate political leadership behaviors but instead presents political leadership with a different set of opportunities, pressures, and constraints.

With obstructive military leadership, the potential domestic costs of continuing the war decline for the incumbent while the risks of being blamed and punished for terminating the war short of victory become more significant. Political leadership seeking to end the war may still be able to secure military leadership's collaboration, but divergent preferences represent a significant hurdle, and an effective civil-military bargain will be more difficult and require greater leverage. Accordingly, political leadership will be less willing to attempt, and less able to realize, a war ending settlement that fails to achieve the state's war aims. Political leadership may view withdrawal as the best course of action but keep this preference hidden indefinitely or delay the decision and any concrete actions until a more opportune time, attempting to marginalize the civil-military gap along the way. If and when political leadership attempts to bring the war to a close, the process will likely be longer, messier, and more erratic. Conversely, with facilitative military leadership, the potential domestic costs of continuing the war increase while the risks of being blamed and punished for an unfavorable outcome lessen. For political leadership seeking to terminate the war, civil-military collaboration is by no means a given but is easier to achieve and generally requires less leverage. Under these conditions, a political leader will be more willing and better able to pursue a war ending settlement short of a win.

At least this is the case with new political leaders. For those political leaders linked to the start of the war, civil-military bargaining is still germane but only affects war termination calculus on the margins. In contrast, for subsequent political leaders who inherit the war, civil-military bargaining plays a more determinative role.

Why Some New Leaders Behave Like Old Leaders (and others don't)

As described previously, the conventional wisdom delineates between political leaders directly tied to the start of a war and subsequent leaders without such connection. This *initial* versus *new* distinction ostensibly shapes a political leader's choice between continuing and terminating a war because it alters the probability of domestic repercussions if he or she accepts any outcome less than a win. The *obstructive* versus *facilitative* distinction characterizing civil-military bargaining matters in the same way, but the observable effects are generally more pronounced with new leaders. This is because the civil-military bargain can have significant impact on the strength and stickiness of the *bungler, backstabber, squanderer,* and *sellout* narratives but has little sway when it comes to the *pretender* narrative. And again, the *pretender* narrative is uniquely relevant to initial political leadership. Thus, political leaders responsible for starting a failed war remain highly susceptible to blame and domestic repercussions regardless of what military leadership says or does.

This changes when it comes to new political leaders. For new political leaders faced with obstructive military leadership, the risk of blame for ending a war short of victory remains great enough to subsume any benefits gained from not being responsible for starting the war. With obstructive military leadership, then, initial and new political leaders should behave in a relatively like manner. In contrast, with facilitative military leadership, the risk to new political leaders wanes while the risk to initial political leaders remains relatively unchanged. One should accordingly observe a marked difference in the decision-making and behaviors of initial versus new political leaders, with the latter more apt to terminate protracted armed conflict even if this means accepting a loss (see figure 1.1).

The proposed causal logic linking the effects of civil-military bargaining, political leadership change, and blame attribution gets at the empirical puzzle of how political leaders respond once a war has proven longer, costlier, and more difficult than expected at the outset. In particular, it provides explanation for variation in the decision-making and behaviors of new political leaders, suggesting when political leaders with little culpability in the conventional sense will experience the same types of domestic pressures and constraints as their predecessors, and why some new leaders are able to secure a timely exit while others struggle to end a war where victory seems out of reach.

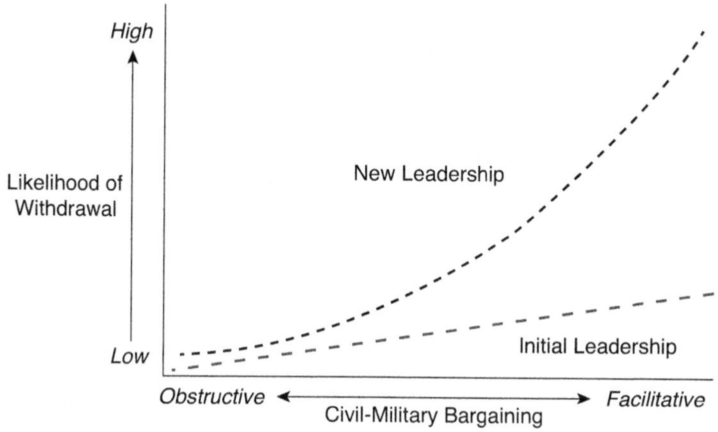

Figure 1.1 Variation in political leadership behavior (proposed model).

Scope and Methodology

In effort to examine the domestic politics of war termination through a civil-military lens, this book purposefully avoids any form of regime-type argument. There is little doubt regime type matters for war termination, and there is insightful scholarly work in this area.[36] But with the focus on civil-military bargaining, part of the intent is to show how a common set of causal mechanisms operates with similar effect across a wide range of political and institutional settings. Of course there are limits. As discussed further in chapter 3, the book's argument still relies on the assumptions that a political leader has domestic rivals and that he or she depends upon a domestic support base of some kind. Further, there must be at least some domestic sensitivity to the costs of war. If a political leader is truly invulnerable to domestic political pressure or constraints, and can wage incessant war abroad without any potential domestic repercussions, then domestic political factors probably do not matter that much, and a domestic politics-type argument probably cannot offer much. But as illustrated with the opening anecdote, even kings are not immune to the domestic pitfalls of protracted armed conflict.

That being said, the scope of this book *is* limited to polities in which there is a professional military establishment distinct from civilian political leadership and in which the military is subordinate to civilian political leadership at least at the start of the war. This excludes any form of military government or military dictatorship. Civil-military bargaining lacks relevance in cases without meaningful distinction between civilian political leaders and military professionals.

Further, while the argument outlined above is not bound by any specific type of armed conflict, the remainder of the book looks primarily at those extended foreign interventions classified as small or asymmetric wars.[37] I propose a civil-military theory of war termination, not a theory of small wars; but I generally apply the theory to the small war context. The question of withdrawal from protracted small war represents a special problem under the broader rubric of the domestic politics of war termination. For the powerful state, failure in small war rarely resembles traditional military defeat. Instead, failure is more often manifest as a political decision to withdraw prior to the securing of state aims and despite maintaining an option to persist. Given the structure of the small war problem, the powerful state almost always has a meaningful political choice. On this phenomenon, Mack observes, "In every case, success for the insurgents rose not from a military victory on the ground, but rather from the progressive attrition of their opponent's *political* capability to wage war (original emphasis)."[38]

An emphasis on powerful state behavior in protracted small war yields useful analytic controls and allows one to better observe and assess the causal mechanisms of interest. There is little, if any, direct threat to the metropole, and thus the stakes of the conflict and consequences of military failure are limited in scope. In particular, political and territorial sovereignty are not at risk. While important strategic concerns certainly remain in play, the domestic political, as opposed to material or existential, repercussions of military failure come to the fore. In a similar vein, the powerful state generally has a meaningful option to maintain or escalate its war effort up until the very end. Without such choice, the significance of political leadership preferences and domestic political debate wanes. Of further note, an emphasis on protracted small war potentially adds to the book's contemporary relevance. There is some veracity to the claim that large-scale conventional war among major powers has become less likely, if not a thing of the past altogether.[39] Recent interventions by the United States in Iraq and by Russia in Chechnya, each exhibiting traits of protracted small war, represent more probable scenarios.

The obvious drawback relates to portability. Even if relevant to protracted small war, does the theory offer explanatory power outside this context? From a theoretical perspective, there is little to suggest limited applicability. As long as domestic politics matter, and political leaders seek to avoid blame for a failed war, civil-military bargaining should still play an important role. And while the book looks to the subset of protracted small wars for theory testing, it draws upon a number of more conventional armed conflicts for theory building to include the Franco-Prussian War (1870–71), World War I (1914–18), and the Soviet-Finnish Continuation War (1941–44).

It is also important to recognize that the category of protracted small war, as employed here, is best defined in terms of asymmetric power relationships among belligerents and lack of direct, conventional threat to the powerful state. Small or asymmetric war does not imply a type of warfare. Irregular or guerilla-style tactics are often a side effect of asymmetry—and such tactics tend to make these wars more protracted—but small war is not necessarily limited to guerrilla warfare or counterinsurgency campaigns. Some of the cases included in this study, while alike in some key criteria, look very different in terms of size, level of violence, and tactics employed.

To weigh the explanatory power of the proposed logic, the book combines a cursory cross-case analysis with more detailed within-case studies. With both the cross-case and within-case analysis, I try to assess the effects of civil-military bargaining on blame attribution and war termination by looking at wartime decisions and wartime behaviors. As an alternative, one could examine postwar punishment, or try to determine the types of leaders most *at risk* of punishment by looking at which leaders were *actually* punished. Other studies employ this latter approach, and it may seem reasonable, but there is a fundamental disconnect. Blame avoidance is both reactive and anticipative. If leaders are conscious of risk and make policy choices in an effort to prevent or reduce punishment, one could conceive of a situation in which the types of leaders at most risk are least likely to experience actual punishment. Observations of actual punishment can thus be misleading, and the resultant findings can be contradictory or uncertain at best. At a minimum, a focus on postwar punishment misses the nonevents, the cases in which at-risk leaders successfully avoid blame.

As a related concern, one cannot always observe or determine the *post bellum* occurrence of punishment. Removal from office may be evident, but domestic punishment extends well beyond whether or not a political leader stays in power. Studies have shown that when dealing with policy failure, political leaders face a broad array of domestic concerns to include standing within the party, the ability to achieve other policy objectives, and even long-term legacy. For a number of reasons, a political leader may not necessarily be at risk of losing office, at least in the short term. Or a political leader could be on the way out regardless due to term limits among other factors. But this same leader may still be very concerned with avoiding blame for a failed war. A focus on actual punishment in the form of loss of power can be misleading in this sense as well. My methodological response, although not without limits of its own, is to assess whether political leaders behave *as if* they are likely to be blamed and punished for a failed war regardless of the actual occurrence of postwar punishment.

Toward this end, the cross-case analysis looks at 28 cases of protracted small war which yield 81 total leader-conflict observations (on the side of the powerful state). Given the nature of the data, this analysis consists of relatively straightforward contingency tables. The utility of the cross-case analysis is limited in that it says little about the theorized causal processes and mechanisms.[40] Still, it serves the important purpose of establishing a pattern of political leadership behavior consistent with the proposed logic. It does not explain this pattern but instead builds confidence in an empirical regularity in need of explanation. The cross-case analysis thus validates the need for and guides the within-case analysis.

The within-case analysis includes case studies of Israel in Lebanon (1982–85), the Netherlands in Indonesia (1946–49), and South Africa in Namibia (1966–89). Case selection was partly based on three general criteria. First, the cases are diverse in terms of providing significant cross-case and within-case variation on political leadership's bargaining position and the consequent civil-military dynamic. Second, each conflict lasted well beyond the point of being more costly and more difficult than expected at the outset while ultimately ending in failure, or at least a lack of clear success, for the powerful state. Accordingly, there is meaningful within-case variation in terms of outcomes of persistence versus withdrawal. Finally, being more obscure than others in the existing literature (i.e., the United States in Vietnam, France in Algeria), these cases were easy to exclude from theory building and thus provide a relatively clean slate for theory testing.

Beyond the general characteristics, I chose each of these cases for a specific reason, and each adds leverage to the analysis of the proposed logic in different ways. Israel in Lebanon was selected in part because it allows for effective comparison between the proposed logic—which eschews a regime-type argument—and what is arguably the leading theory of how democracies behave in protracted small wars, as the case comes close to being a *most-likely* test for each theory.[41] This is the one case study where I make such an explicit comparison. The Netherlands in Indonesia is a more difficult case because it represents a "failure" of the proposed logic within the framework of the cross-case analysis. On the surface, it not only fails but fails in a big way and thus represents a type of *deviant* case.[42] I selected the case for further study in part for this reason. Understanding why a case fails vis-à-vis a theory under investigation is often just as useful as understanding why a case succeeds. Instead of undermining a theory, such analysis can provide new insights into how the underlying mechanisms operate in unique circumstances and interact with other factors outside the scope of the theory. Finally, I chose South Africa in Namibia for further study in part because, out of the designated population of protracted wars, it represents an *extreme* case in terms of duration. This book purports to offer insights into the persistence and endings of protracted wars. In this sense, the case of South Africa in Namibia, the most protracted of the protracted wars, provides a unique opportunity to assess the causal mechanisms at work.

For both the cross-case and within-case analyses, I draw upon primary source materials to include governmental transcripts, diplomatic communications, intelligence reports, defense white papers, contemporary media accounts, memoirs, interviews, and historic polling data. The relevant materials come from a range of countries to include Australia, China, Ethiopia, France, Great Britain, India, Israel, the Netherlands, Portugal, Sri Lanka, South Africa, the Soviet Union, and the United States. For the case studies, I also received generous assistance from some of the world's leading experts on the relevant conflicts. With the case of the Netherlands in Indonesia, this involved working with Dutch historians as well as the chief biographer of key Dutch military leaders. The other two case studies benefited from my personal correspondence with diplomats, scholars, and journalists who had near-unlimited access to, and who conducted extensive interviews with, Israeli and South African political and military leaders during and/or immediately after the respective armed conflicts. Because such access is no longer practical or even possible, this assistance proved invaluable to my efforts to assess the perspectives, motives, and roles of leaders across the civil-military divide.

Overview of the Book

The remainder of the book proceeds as follows. Chapter 2 looks more closely at civil-military bargaining apart from its impact on war termination outcomes. Concerning the alignment of civil-military preferences, the chapter looks primarily at how military leadership preferences associated with war termination vary. I perceive this part of the equation to be the least understood and contend that military leadership preferences vary more than is commonly thought. As the basis for this claim, I go beyond traditional conceptions of bureaucratic interest and emphasize military leadership's concerns with preserving institutional legitimacy. This "legitimacy motive" not only helps explain a wider range of military leadership preferences but also suggests why the gap with political leadership can become so intractable. The chapter addresses in particular how the motive applies to the context of protracted small war. The chapter then turns to the requirement for political leadership leverage, elaborating upon key elements of leverage that can vary over time and from one leader to the next.

Chapter 3 addresses how civil-military bargaining affects the domestic politics of war termination. There is little doubt the military can, in extreme circumstances, intervene and shape outcomes directly; but the aim of this chapter is to explain how the interplay between political and military leadership affects more "normal" political processes of blame attribution and blame avoidance. Toward this end, it elaborates upon the five distinct narratives of failure relevant to the context of protracted war and explains how military leadership is uniquely situated to influence the strength and stickiness of these narratives. The chapter then describes in more depth the domestic constraints and expected political leadership behaviors under various civil-military bargaining scenarios and concludes with the findings of the cross-case analysis.

Chapters 4, 5, and 6 make up the within-case analysis. The primary aim of the three case studies is to assess the causal linkages between civil-military bargaining, blame attribution, and war termination outcomes. Although each case is unique and adds leverage to the overall analysis in different ways, I ask three baseline questions of each. First, does political leadership risk domestic repercussions for losing or failing to win the war despite having little to no responsibility for starting the war? Second, does political leadership's interaction with military leadership either exacerbate or mitigate this risk? And third, does this dynamic affect the direction and/or timing of political leadership's war termination decision-making? As a lesser aim, the case studies also look tentatively at the relevance and utility of the "legitimacy motive" introduced in chapter 2. The concluding chapter summarizes the book's empirical findings and theoretical implications, and then touches briefly upon the relevance to ongoing US military endeavors in Afghanistan.

CHAPTER 2

The Civil-Military Variable and How It Varies

This chapter looks in more depth at the contours of civil-military bargaining, focusing on military leadership preferences and political leadership leverage, apart from any effects on war termination outcomes.[1] It provides a foundation for understanding how political leadership's bargaining position can vary across cases and over time within cases of protracted war, to include from one political leader to the next within a given case. This preliminary discussion is useful for at least three reasons. First, the proposed view of what drives military leadership preferences, and thus the basis of either convergence or divergence with political leadership's policy, differs from the traditional conception found in the bulk of the relevant literature. While this alternative perspective does not necessarily add predictive value, it does suggest a greater range of preferences, and a more dynamic interplay between political and military leadership, than is generally thought. This warrants explanation. Second, understanding how these preferences vary and what makes for effective political leadership leverage, in turn, provides clues as to why the civil-military gap can become so intractable and the conditions under which political and military leaders are able to collaborate in bringing protracted war to a close. And third, the discussion provides opportunity to illustrate what the abstract concept of civil-military bargaining might look like in actual cases of protracted war.

The Bases of Military Leadership Preferences

Civil-military bargaining associated with war termination revolves around the basic policy question of persistence versus withdrawal.

Existing scholarship assumes a wide range of political leadership preferences tied to this policy question but generally does not consider or allow for such variation when it comes to military leadership. This limited view, in turn, stems from an underlying conception of military leadership as narrowly focused on bureaucratic incentives.

The Traditional View: Military Leaders as Armed Bureaucrats[2]

Scholars of civil-military relations have long problematized the assumption of the professional military as a loyal and obedient servant, thus calling into question Huntington's idealized claim that professionalization leads to an apolitical officer corps ready to carry out the wishes of civilian government without hesitation.[3] Representative of this widespread critique, Finer argues, "The very nature of the professionalism by which Huntington sets such store, and which he regards as politically sterile, in fact often thrusts the military into collision with civil authorities."[4] There is also broad consensus on what motivates the military and thus what drives these civil-military disputes, with most studies privileging the role of bureaucratic or corporate interests.[5] Adopted wholesale from organization theory and applied to the study of the armed forces for decades, the bureaucratic paradigm characterizes large organizations, particularly those associated with government, as functioning in accordance with standard patterns that best serve to minimize uncertainty and maximize influence, resources, and autonomy.[6] According to this view, the military, far from being unique, is best described as equivalent to other bureaucratic organizations; and the key to understanding military leadership preferences and behaviors is to recognize that "militaries promote and defend themselves like other bureaucracies."[7]

The bureaucratic paradigm underpins the prevailing conception of military leadership and war termination. As a leading proponent of this paradigm, Halperin argues the imperative to maximize resources and protect bureaucratic turf "cannot help but influence their (military leadership's) attitude toward war termination issues."[8] Any admission of failure or acceptance of an unfavorable outcome can ostensibly result in curtailed resources, more intrusive political oversight, and loss of mission area responsibility to an organizational rival. Halperin concludes that, given the weight of bureaucratic interests, the initiative to terminate a war short of victory will almost always come from political leadership; if left to its own devices, military leadership will obstruct such a move. Military leadership may eventually shift its view and come to support a policy of withdrawal, but such change comes *after,* and in response to, a similar shift by political leadership, and after the *least military* of military leadership has adopted the *civilian* perspective.[9]

Although well entrenched, this conception of military leadership as rigidly obstructive remains underdeveloped and largely unsupported, with advocates citing the same handful of cases as evidence (i.e., France in Algeria).[10] It is certainly true military leaders do not like to lose, and one can readily locate examples of obstructive behavior. But this does not necessarily imply military leadership preferences associated with war termination cannot flex absent civilian pressure, and there is no reason, *a priori,* to suggest the impetus to end a war will by rule come from civilians. Halperin notes that political leaders view the question of war termination largely through the lens of domestic political constraints, that they will "be concerned with the impact which various kinds of war termination conditions will have on the post war politics of their country" and particularly "with the impact of war termination conditions on elections."[11] But he provides no explanation of why such concerns will necessarily prompt a shift by political leadership prior to, and in the absence of, any similar shift by military leadership. This reflects a dubious assumption that domestic pressures and constraints drive political leadership preferences to fluctuate while military leadership preferences remain relatively fixed. Such an assumption, in turn, has prompted others to argue that wars will be more protracted in states with weak civilian control.[12]

Evidence of a Facilitative Military

Theory aside, there is anecdotal evidence that at least problematizes the assumption of an obstructive military, or that hints at a wider dynamic in the interplay between political and military leadership. By early 1954, the French government was stalemated in its policy toward the ongoing conflict in Indochina (1946–54). Despite a growing sense the war had become "a bottomless pit, a pointless adventure," the politicians proved unable and unwilling to take meaningful steps to end it; and up to that point, French military leaders had remained relatively optimistic and lobbied to keep fighting.[13] But from late February to early March, General Ely, the Chairman of the Chiefs of Staff Committee, General Blanc, the Chief of Staff of the Army, and General Fay, the Chief of Staff of the Air Force, conducted extensive analyses of the situation in Indochina and simultaneously determined, "No military solution could be achieved, in spite of the scale of air, ground, and sea forces at General Navarre's disposal. Not even heavy reinforcement of the Expeditionary Corps could influence the outcome in any way. France had reached the limits of its military effort."[14] The findings were briefed to the National Assembly and then circulated widely throughout the government and other political circles. General Blanc was particularly outspoken in arguing the need to extricate French armed forces from Indochina given the increasingly intolerable costs. The result, Devillers and Lacouture explain, was that the conclusions reached by the military leaders "convinced the government that there was no time to lose. France had to demonstrate its willingness to end the war without further delay."[15]

With the case of the USSR in Afghanistan (1979–89), Porter finds the Soviet exit "would seem to have provided ample cause for civil-military discord, either over the policy of withdrawal itself or over its execution . . . But to the contrary, there is evidence suggesting that the military was as disillusioned with the war as were the civilian leaders, and therefore supported the policy of withdrawal."[16] But what Porter and others fail to recognize is that Soviet military leadership did not just support the policy of withdrawal but also prompted political leadership to adopt this policy in the first place. When Gorbachev came to power in March 1985, there was little indication the new premier intended to abandon Afghanistan. Over his first year in office, Gorbachev raised the number of Soviet troops in country to peak levels and substantially increased the number and scope of military operations.[17] Arnold makes the critical point that "Although Gorbachev is credited with having engineered the Soviet withdrawal in 1988–89, this was not necessarily his initial impulse . . . the evidence contradicts what seems to have been a later effort to portray Gorbachev as always having sought a peaceful solution to the conflict."[18] At what would prove a pivotal Politburo meeting in November 1986, however, Army Chief of Staff Sergei Akhromeyev countered Gorbachev and other civilian party officials by presenting a relatively gloomy view of military progress and prospects in Afghanistan. Akhromeyev stated that despite the recent troop increases, escalation of operations, and extensive support provided to local allies,

> Military actions in Afghanistan will soon be seven years old. There is no single piece of land in this country which has not been occupied by a Soviet soldier. Nevertheless, the majority of the territory remains in the hands of rebels. The government of Afghanistan has at its disposal

> a significant military force... and yet there is still no result. We control Kabul and the provincial centers, but on occupied territory we cannot establish authority. We have lost the battle for the Afghan people. Our army... is now in a position to maintain the situation on the level that it exists now. But under such conditions the war will continue for a long time... I repeat that we can maintain the situation at the current level, but we need to look for a way out.[19]

A more extreme incident of military leadership "facilitating" the end of protracted war is seen with the case of Portugal in the African Territories (1961–75). In mid-1974, a group of mid-level Portuguese officers known as the Armed Forces Movement (MFA) successfully staged a near-bloodless coup overthrowing the civilian Caetano regime. The conspirators had little desire to seize and hold political power. Instead, the coup was motivated explicitly by a desire to withdraw from Portugal's three wars being waged simultaneously in the overseas territories of Angola, Mozambique, and Guinea. Such sentiments were not confined to the more radical MFA. General Antonio de Spinola, an officer of impeccable conservative credentials and Portugal's most decorated and revered war hero, met with Prime Minister Caetano several times in private throughout 1973 to express the need to end the wars through negotiated settlement. Caetano rebuffed these appeals, and in response, Spinola collaborated with Army Chief of Staff Francisco da Costa Gomes in early 1974 to release a publication in which he "dared say that a military solution to the problem of insurgency in the African territories is impossible."[20]

Such anecdotes point to the possibility that military leadership will, under certain circumstances, shift to a preference of withdrawal prior to, and independent of, any similar shift by political leadership. In such cases, one may still observe civil-military conflict, but military leadership plays a facilitative as opposed to obstructive role in the war termination process. The staying power of the conception of military leadership as rigidly biased toward persistence stems in part from the fact that the underlying bureaucratic paradigm has, itself, gone largely unchallenged outside the niche field of military sociology. The bureaucratic paradigm does seem to offer significant purchase when it comes to questions of peacetime preferences and peacetime decision-making. However, it has proven less useful for understanding the wartime context.[21] In particular, it does not appear adequate for capturing the wide range of military leadership preferences, and thus the diversity of civil-military interaction, linked to war termination.

An Alternative Basis of Military Leadership Preferences

The concept of institutional legitimacy provides the foundation for an alternative model of military leadership motives. What can be termed the professional-institutional paradigm takes bureaucratic interest into account but also considers institutional legitimacy an analytically distinct, and hierarchically superior, basis of military leadership preferences. This alternative paradigm is highly relevant to the context of protracted war and the question of war termination. It thus, at a minimum, serves as a useful supplement for understanding military leadership preferences of persistence versus withdrawal.

Neo-institutionalist theory characterizes the organizational actor as embedded within a broader social environment and, even if exercising a high degree of autonomy, as being deeply affected by this environment.[22] Because of this "embeddedness," organizational dynamics cannot be assessed solely in terms of bureaucratic or material imperatives. Instead, one must also account for the organization's legitimacy in terms of "a generalized perception or assumption that the actions of an entity are desirable, proper, or appropriate within some socially constructed system of norms, values, beliefs, and definitions."[23] While not applicable to all organizational actors to the same extent, the preferences of some actors in some contexts are influenced heavily by the legitimacy motive, with specific behaviors aimed at preserving or enhancing collective legitimacy. The notion of a legitimacy motive thus provides "an anchor-point of a vastly expanded theoretical apparatus addressing the normative and cognitive forces that constrain, construct, and empower organizational actors."[24]

This "theoretical apparatus" has significant implications for how one conceives of military leadership and its preferences. According to Dutch sociologist Jacques van Doorn, the military as a collective exhibits traits and maintains interests similar to those of other organizations within the governmental bureaucracy but also represents "an excellent and possibly unique" example of the integration of bureaucratic organization and professional institution.[25] Even among the latter, the military is so exceptional that it "differs sharply from other institutions which ensure the continuity of society."[26] This distinction stems from the role of violence in defining the purpose and identity of the professional armed forces. Although essential to the security and even preservation of society, the function of the armed forces is, absent the imprimatur of the relevant political community, considered criminal or antisocial. The consequence is a collective aspiration for legitimacy that runs deeper than seen with most other governmental, economic, or social actors. Thus, for those specialists entrusted with the management and practice of violence in the service of the state, "their reward lies in the general recognition of their legitimacy and in the special status that is granted to them."[27]

Building on this theoretical framework, the present study takes institutional legitimacy to mean *the extent to which the relevant political community recognizes the professional military establishment as meeting socially defined standards of effectiveness and appropriateness.* The military must not only demonstrate the necessary functional capacity and expertise but must also be perceived as upholding the values and normative expectations of the political community it serves.[28] Recognition of effectiveness and appropriateness is rarely formalized or explicit. Instead, this recognition is best thought of in terms of the "public confidence and esteem" and "public support and political trust" shown the armed forces.[29] The relevant political community, or the group empowered to confer legitimacy upon the armed forces, will necessarily vary across time and place; but the legitimacy motive holds sway across a wide range of polities, from liberal democracies to right-wing totalitarian systems.[30]

The key implication is that the armed forces as a collective is motivated by a desire, beyond traditional bureaucratic incentives, to preserve and enhance its institutional legitimacy; and military leadership preferences and behaviors tied to war termination reflect this motive. None of this suggests national interests and security issues to be immaterial, but the legitimacy motive provides a powerful lens through which these often debated concerns are interpreted. And none of this means bureaucratic interests and incentives are unimportant. In theory, as long as institutional legitimacy goes unchallenged, military leadership preferences should mesh with the demands of bureaucracy to include the push for resources, autonomy, and governmental influence. However, if military leadership perceives institutional legitimacy to be at risk, the basis of its preferences will shift accordingly. When it comes to the question of war termination, the demands of legitimacy may point in a similar or fundamentally different direction than the demands of bureaucracy.

Institutional Legitimacy and Protracted War

The types of costly, protracted wars of interest to this study tend to bring the question of legitimacy to the fore, and the problem becomes uniquely acute in protracted "small" war where the threat to the state remains indirect or ill-defined.[31] This does not imply military leaders will necessarily favor persistence over withdrawal or vice versa. The legitimacy motive does not, by rule, push toward one outcome or the other. The assertion here is that the experience of protracted war, and especially protracted small war, imposes unique demands upon the professional armed forces in terms of recognition, effectiveness, and appropriateness; and military leadership preferences regarding war termination are shaped by these demands. The legitimacy motive can prompt a wide range of military leadership preferences and thus wide variation in how military leadership preferences align with political leadership's policy. Such is true not only with the direction but also the intensity of these preferences. Whatever the direction, preferences spurred by the legitimacy motive can run deeper than those based on bureaucratic incentives, a characteristic that provides some clue as to why civil-military disputes over the question of war termination can become so acrimonious and intractable.

The Special Case of Protracted Small War

Military leadership's aversion to defeat likely stems just as much, if not more so, from the legitimacy motive as it does from bureaucratic interest given that losing a war can have a profound impact on perceptions of effectiveness. In small war, the powerful state may not face the specter of traditional defeat, but for a modern, professional army, the inability to succeed against an inferior opponent can sting just as bad. Discussing the US armed forces in Vietnam, Schwab explains, "The JCS could not conceive of fighting a war to lose... The loss of Indochina, after the commitment of large US forces, was anathema to the professional armed forces. It challenged the legitimacy of their profession."[32] On the implications of a Soviet loss in Afghanistan, Porter similarly notes, "Such a development must have been of profound concern to the Soviet officer corps, the one group whose prestige and legitimacy had been recognized by virtually every sector of Soviet society in the past."[33]

For military leadership, there will always be an impetus to keep fighting until securing victory or at least a reasonably favorable outcome. But the experience of protracted small war, apart from any outcome, can also impinge upon institutional legitimacy in a number of ways. Institutional legitimacy is closely linked to conceptions of the appropriate use of force and, in turn, the appropriate role of the armed forces. Again, small war is defined primarily in terms of asymmetric power relationships and does not, by rule, have to involve irregular or guerilla forms of warfare. But given the inherent asymmetries, such forms of warfare often come to characterize these wars. Military leadership, and even society as a whole, may idealize conventional war and decisive battles, or link the military's prestige to certain advanced technologies or to how the military stacks up with its counterparts in other modern states. Fighting a war using irregular means against irregular forces can thus cause dissonance. Worse yet, the war may be labeled a "police action," discounting the unique role and status of the professional armed forces altogether.

Along these lines, a common complaint emanating from military leadership is that extended involvement in small war comes at the cost of training and equipping for other, typically more conventional, roles and missions. As illustration, Indian military leaders saw operations in Sri Lanka (1987–90) as detrimental to India's posture vis-à-vis Pakistan. Portuguese officers chafed at having to decimate Portugal's military commitment to NATO in order to fight colonial "bush wars" in Africa. While such concerns do not relate solely to legitimacy, the legitimacy motive can play an important role. For the Portuguese armed forces, participation in NATO was arguably just as much about the associated status as it was about state security. In contrast, the French army in Algeria came to identify itself with small war, linking its perceptions of legitimacy to the doctrine of *guerre révolutionnaire*.[34]

Regardless of whether military leadership idealizes or eschews waging small war, this type of armed conflict can generate pressures to employ means that open up the armed forces to societal critique. Battle lines and combatants are typically ill-defined, and the fighting can exhibit unconventional, and often particularly brutal, forms of violence as the armed forces of the powerful state must find ways to counter an adversary that operates outside of accepted norms. The resultant pattern of violence can alter society's perception of the armed forces, with the associated methods increasingly viewed as illegitimate.[35]

That such methods do not generally yield timely and measurable results on the battlefield only exacerbates the problem. Any progress made with counterinsurgency or antiguerilla operations can be frustratingly slow despite the marked asymmetry of resources and power, resulting in unwarranted critiques of military inefficiency and setbacks. And public perceptions of military effectiveness and appropriateness are inherently intertwined. Success tends to encourage a "blind eye" toward harsh methods, but as the war effort stalls, critique directed at the conduct of the war will likely build.

Overt societal critique, particularly in the form of war protest activity, is perhaps the most obvious indicator that the armed forces' legitimacy might be at risk, and military leadership remains sensitive to such critique. But it is important to recognize that while antiwar movements generally garner a great deal of publicity, they do not always mirror the sentiments of the majority. Also, public disapproval of war policy does not necessarily translate to public pressure to end a military intervention or a lack of support for the armed forces.[36] Although less obvious than overt critique, the threat of societal abandonment may be of equal or even greater concern. Small war rarely requires a total commitment of resources and national effort by the powerful state. And absent a clear threat, these wars may not exhibit the rallying effects seen with other wars. Small wars can thus go on for years and receive little attention back home, or the public may experience war weariness and grow disinterested. Political leaders may become embarrassed by the quagmire and its manifestation as a "dirty war" and thus ignore or conceal the armed forces' ongoing efforts and sacrifices.[37]

With memories of World War II victories still fresh, the US army found itself bogged down in a stalemated, limited armed conflict in Korea. Military historian T. R. Fehrenbach describes how over the final year of the Korean War (1950–53), American soldiers of all ranks became "haunted by the sense of being forgotten" given a pervasive belief the public back home "preferred to put the unpleasantness out of mind."[38] Likewise, after celebrated victories over French and American imperialists, the Vietnamese army found itself in a very different situation following its 1979 invasion and occupation of Cambodia. Essentially, the "shoe was on the other foot" as Vietnam assumed the role of the foreign power in a decade-long campaign against Khmer Rouge fighters (1979–89). This protracted war was unpopular back home in Vietnam, and as Doyle describes, "Unlike Vietnam's wars against the French and Americans, the intervention was downplayed to the Vietnamese public... When soldiers returned from Cambodia without the fanfare of previous wars, veterans felt they had been forgotten."[39] Reflecting on a similar lack of recognition for the Indian army during its intervention in Sri Lanka, a senior Indian officer laments, "All the basic motivations—psychological or material—for the troops, who were in the eventual analysis meant to lay down their lives, were not there. What was worse, for the people who mattered, the political leadership, these men were just statistics, a bit embarrassing, but still just statistics."[40]

Protracted war does not just impose a drain on states resources. It can also levy a toll on the military in terms of waning perceptions of effectiveness and appropriateness. Even if the negative effects are not yet felt, the danger always lurks. Accordingly, there are scenarios under which the demands of legitimacy might be better served by accepting a loss than by continued pursuit of victory, even if victory remains within reach. Military leaders can face countervailing pressures to either stay the course or get out. A shift in preferences can be triggered by a single big event or several smaller but cumulative effects. The timing of a shift, and whether it even occurs at all, also depends upon the viability of "legitimation" measures to include efforts by military leadership to mitigate blame.

Legitimation Measures and Blame Avoidance

Collective efforts to preserve or enhance institutional legitimacy, while taking many forms, generally consist of substantive and symbolic legitimation measures. Assuming a status quo preference of persistence, a shift by military leadership to a preference of withdrawal would constitute substantive legitimation, an approach that "involves real, material change in organizational goals."[41] Conversely, military leadership could remain committed to fighting the war while addressing threats to legitimacy through symbolic means. In contrast to substantive measures, Ashforth and Gibbs explain, "Rather than actually change its ways, the organization might simply portray—or symbolically manage—them so as to appear consistent with social values and expectations."[42] Symbolic legitimation, including efforts to manage the flow and interpretation of war-related information, may accompany or be employed in lieu of substantive measures. As a tentative rule of thumb, though, military leadership will employ symbolic measures first and then turn, if at all, to substantive measures only after symbolic measures are deemed insufficient. Accordingly, any shift by military leadership to a preference of withdrawal will likely be a drawn-out affair and hard to pinpoint. But this in no way implies such a shift will come about only after, and in response to, a similar move by political leadership.

Once embroiled in protracted war, military leadership, like its civilian counterpart, is very much attuned to the dynamics of blame attribution. Writing in late 1961 to the Chairman of the Joint Chiefs of Staff, the Chief of the Military Assistance Advisory Group (MAAG) in Saigon General McGarr warned that the United States might very well fail in Vietnam and further observed, "The military will be blamed for a situation here which is not of its own making and for which it has not been adequately supported by our country. As I am jealous of the professional good name of our Army, I do not wish it to be placed in the position of fighting a losing battle and being charged with the loss."[43] In early 1965, Admiral McDonald, Chief of Naval Operations, similarly complained to an aide that when the war was over, the civilians responsible "will no longer be in office and the only group left answerable for the war will be the military."[44] When Prime Minister Caetano refused General Spinola's appeals to end Portugal's wars in Africa through negotiated settlement, Spinola became convinced Caetano was setting up the armed forces to take the fall for an eventual loss.[45]

Military leadership's activities aimed at deflecting or mitigating blame for poor wartime performance or an unfavorable outcome represent a form of legitimation and seem to follow two distinct patterns. The first, a substantive measure seen with Portugal in the African Territories, Russia in Chechnya, and the USSR in Afghanistan, is to push for withdrawal before the situation can further deteriorate. In this sense, blame avoidance affects a shift in preferences or change in organizational goals. The attractiveness of this approach hinges in part upon the perception that further failure or stalemate on the battlefield will open the military up to even greater scrutiny and critique while negotiated settlement shifts the onus of withdrawal to political leadership.

As a second pattern, military leadership remains committed to a failing or stalemated war but hedges this bet by shifting blame for poor performance or covering itself in the event of a loss. This pattern, best categorized as symbolic legitimation, is evident in the case of the United States in Vietnam. Buzzanco describes, "The military, sensing early on that conditions in Vietnam were not conducive to American success, looked for ways to avoid responsibility for what they saw as a likely disaster there." This dynamic was subtle at first, but "as the war continued on, without appreciable improvement, in 1967 and thereafter, civil-military jockeying to avoid blame for the war intensified."[46] As part of this maneuvering, US military leadership began to purposefully ask for more resources and leeway than political leadership would grant, thus laying the groundwork for the argument the armed forces had been forced to fight shorthanded. Along these lines, Admiral Sharp, Commander of Pacific Forces, urged General Westmoreland in a 1967 message to "continue to state your requirement for forces even though you are not going to get them."[47]

Symbolic legitimation of this kind can continue long after a war has ended. In 1940, the Netherlands surrendered to Germany after five days of fighting. By most assessments, the Dutch army may, best case, have been able to hold out a few days longer; but the loss was inevitable. Still,

Dutch military leaders were driven by a need to preserve the honor and professional good name of the army. Schoeman describes how Dutch military leaders worked well into the postwar decade to foster the "myth of 1940" as a vehicle to shift culpability and save face:

> The military... created the myth of a Dutch army that, despite numerous heroic acts of individual soldiers, never had a chance because of the overwhelming superiority of the Germans both in numbers and in equipment... The Dutch government had proven itself to be short-sighted during the interbellum because the need to reinforce the armed forces was recognized too late... The war of May 1940 had been lost during the 1920s and 1930s, and the armed forces were not to blame for the defeat.[48]

Political Leadership Leverage

The foregoing discussion hints at a critical impediment to effective civil-military collaboration when it comes to the problem of bringing costly, protracted war to a close. With any form of policy failure, there is a natural tension between those responsible for crafting the policy and those responsible for executing the policy.[49] When faced with an unsuccessful war, neither political nor military leadership wants to take the blame; and there is an inherent tendency, or built-in pressure, to direct blame at and scapegoat the other. This is why, even if political and military leaders agree on the need to terminate the war, collaboration can still be difficult and leverage still matters.

The leverage required for an effective civil-military bargain will differ in every case, and what this leverage looks like necessarily depends upon regime type, civil-military structures, political and legal institutions, and historical juncture among numerous other factors. Some of these factors vary state to state but remain relatively constant over time within a given state. Of greater interest are those factors that can vary from one leader to the next within the same case. Empirically, it is not difficult to find cases in which there is a marked difference between a given political leader and his or her predecessor in terms of dealings with the military. In the case of France in Algeria, for example, there was a clear distinction between Charles de Gaulle and his predecessor Pierre Pflimlin, with De Gaulle exhibiting far more clout and influence with the French army. Likewise, in looking at the case of South Africa in Namibia, there was a marked contrast between P. W. Botha and his predecessor John Vorster. Vorster consistently clashed with military leadership over war policy while Botha subsequently established a strong, mutually supportive relationship with his generals that was "arguably the most intimate in South African civil-military history."[50]

Relevant factors that can vary from one leader to the next include, but are certainly not limited to, political leadership's previous military experience, the nature of domestic political coalitions and alliances, the availability of meaningful side payments, and political leadership's reputation for scapegoating.[51] The first two factors affect civil-military bargaining more indirectly and tie into political leadership's relationship not just with the military but with the domestic opposition and public at large.

As an example of previous military experience that seems to have made a difference, Eisenhower became president and inherited the Korean War in 1953 having retired from active military service in May 1952 as one of the United States' most well-known and prestigious military leaders. The new president could thus go toe-to-toe with any active military leader in terms of status and credibility, a trait that bolstered his leverage in dealings with military leadership. But perhaps of greater importance, as a "war hero Republican president," Eisenhower could also ride herd on much of the right-wing opposition; when moving to end the war, "Eisenhower's prestige as a soldier was great enough that only a very few hardliners accused him of appeasement."[52] Similarly, in 1944, with the Soviet-Finnish Continuation War stalemated, the commander of Finnish Armed forces Marshal Carl Gustaf von Mannerheim was named President of Finland following Risto Ryti's resignation. The new president took office with the intent of extricating his country from the war through negotiated settlement. Like Eisenhower, Mannerheim was a national military hero, having led the dramatic defense of Finland against the Soviets in the preceding Winter War. He not only held the confidence of the Finnish people and clout across the political spectrum but also maintained a tight rein on the officer corps. Because of the latter, he could assure the rest of the government of the unfettered cooperation of military leadership in adopting a sharp policy change and ending the war under less than favorable terms.[53] The result, according to Iklé, was that "a political miracle happened in Helsinki . . . The Finnish government managed to make a 180-degree turn without impairing the cohesion of the army or provoking a coup."[54] Also of significance, and like Eisenhower, Mannerheim was ostensibly "the man who could least be accused of treason" given his military credentials.[55]

Again, a political leader's previous military experience shapes his or her relationship not just with the armed forces but with the domestic audience to include the political opposition. The additional factors of side payments and reputation apply more directly and more narrowly to the relationship between political and military leaders. These latter two factors are discussed in more detail below.

Side Payments and Issue Linkage

The use of side payments, broadly defined, includes inducements offered to military leadership, as well as efforts to link the question of war termination to another issue military leadership cares about, with the aim of securing collaboration.[56] The most readily available inducements generally relate to bureaucratic interests. Coletta and Feaver, for example, describe political leadership's efforts to ply the military with greater organizational autonomy in the form of less intrusive monitoring schemes.[57] However, if military leadership preferences derive from the legitimacy motive, the efficacy of bureaucratic inducements will remain limited. Side payments that somehow bolster institutional legitimacy will be more effective, but these may also be more elusive.

With the Nixon administration looking for a way to extricate the United States from Vietnam, Secretary of Defense Laird came to recognize that "to get the Pentagon brass to accept *anything* in the way of meaningful withdrawals was going to demand all the President's and his own powers of persuasion (original emphasis)."[58] The concomitant attempts to persuade emphasized a budgetary trade-off between continuing the war effort and the acquisition of new weapons and equipment. Laird made clear to military leadership that budget cuts were coming and "told the Chiefs if they wanted new weapons, the United States had to withdraw from Vietnam—the sooner the better... The money being used to pay for the war could and should go toward purchasing new weapons that all of the services desperately needed."[59] As US Secretary of State Henry Kissinger describes, Laird unambiguously "sought to guarantee his preferred course by gearing the withdrawal rate to the defense budget in such a way that any slowdown of withdrawals was bound to reduce procurement—thus enlisting the support of the services for rapid withdrawal by threatening their cherished new projects."[60] Laird thus worked to secure military leadership's collaboration through budgetary sticks and carrots. Results were mixed.

The case of France in Tunisia (1952–55) provides a more explicit example of issue linkage. By 1954, France had been battling nationalists in Tunisia for over two years without clear progress. In July, French Prime Minister Mendès-France flew to Tunisia and, signaling a marked shift in French policy, publicly pledged to cede to nationalist demands and grant Tunisian autonomy. While this "Carthage Declaration" did not come as a complete surprise, observers in France were shocked to see French Marshal Alphonse Juin at the prime minister's side providing at least an appearance of endorsement. At the time, Juin "enjoyed a unique status as France's only living Marshal, giving him considerable influence in political conditions already unstable."[61] He was not only "France's military hero, an idol of the officer corps" but had also shown himself perfectly willing to publicly oppose and lobby against political leadership's policies.[62] In particular, Juin was firmly against any French retreat from North Africa and served as a powerful ally of the North Africa Lobby within French political circles. Accordingly, Giles writes, "Mendes had shown remarkable skill and powers of persuasion in courting Juin and getting him to give, by his presence, tacit approval to the Carthage declaration."[63] Juin later inferred this inducement included not only an agreement by the prime minister to allow the army to continue to occupy key strategic positions in Tunisia, but also assurances that France would hold firm against the emerging nationalist threat in Algeria.[64]

With the above case, political leadership ostensibly secured military leadership's collaboration despite divergent preferences by linking withdrawal from Tunisia to French policy in Algeria. For the French armed forces, the latter was the priority and of greater relevance to its conception of institutional legitimacy, with "military honor, prestige, and self-esteem . . . heavily invested in the defense of French Algeria."[65] De Gaulle's later use of side payments and issue linkage to gain the army's acquiescence to a withdrawal from Algeria accordingly provides an example of leverage *par excellence*.

In the spring of 1958, the newly formed French government under Prime Minister Pflimlin made known its plans for negotiations with the insurgent FLN and eventual Algerian self-determination as a basis for ending the protracted war. This did not sit well with French military leaders. The resultant civil-military crisis, to include a threat of military coup, resulted in the dissolution of the government and fall of the Fourth Republic. With the blessing of the army, De Gaulle assumed the reins of power but then hinted at his own plans for Algerian self-determination in September 1959. This sparked a new wave of protest from military leadership and led to the army-backed "Barricades Week" insurrection in Algiers. De Gaulle survived this episode but was reportedly astonished by the level of backlash from military leadership and subsequently came to realize that "peace in Algeria would only come about through peace with the army."[66]

De Gaulle backed off from his plan to terminate the war and spent the next year and a half working to bring military leadership in line with his views on Algeria. Beginning with the *tourneé des popotes* in March 1960, the president travelled extensively throughout Algeria and Europe meeting with and attempting to propagandize the French officer corps. His message had little to do with resources, organizational autonomy, or bureaucratic influence. Instead, De Gaulle sought to secure military leadership's collaboration through an appeal to national *grandeur* and the honor of French arms.[67] He preached to a captive, but at first skeptical, audience that "a great nation must have great missions . . . a nation summoned to a leading role in the world stage must have military missions global in their inclusiveness."[68] France was destined to once again be a world power, and withdrawal from Algeria was necessary in order to assume this role. Thus, according to De Gaulle, the army would "not continue indefinitely to be in effect a garrison army in colonial territory" but, instead, "higher things were in store for it one day."[69] Of note, De Gaulle offered the military the prestige associated with becoming a nuclear power through the development of the *force de frappe*.

Reputation for Scapegoating

The availability of meaningful side payments increases civil-military bargaining space and can help minimize the effects of divergent preferences. Conversely, a political leader's reputation for scapegoating can shrink this space. Past actions affect the level of trust between military and political leaders and weigh upon the credibility of political leader assurances. Military leaders will be less prone to collaborate in ending a protracted war if they expect the politicians will try to hang the armed forces out to dry for poor wartime performance or an unfavorable outcome. Gauging political leadership in this regard, military leaders are sensitive to various "scapegoating signals" over the course of a war to include political leadership that is quick to fire senior military leaders or that bows to demands for investigations into the armed forces' conduct of the war.

As an example of the former, Indian military officers viewed service in Sri Lanka as a major career risk. All nine division commanders assigned to the operation were fired. Further, of the ten major generals who participated in the operation, only one was promoted to the next higher rank of lieutenant general.[70] The consternation with this trend was exacerbated by a perception that the politicians were not willing to take the actions necessary to bring the conflict to a successful conclusion. In particular, the government balked at targeting Tamils in southern India who were training and supplying Tamil insurgents in Sri Lanka.[71] When operations in Sri Lanka subsequently stalled and Indian forces continued to experience heavy casualties, these same politicians chastised the military commanders and called for their dismissals. In contrast, almost every Soviet military leader known to have played a major role in the planning or execution of operations in Afghanistan received one or more promotions. According to Porter, this pattern served as "a striking manifestation of civilian support for the military, an indication that civilian authorities would not seek to blame the military for the conflict."[72]

Reputation in this sense can be associated with a specific leader, a political party, or civilian leadership in general. And while political leadership's actions during an ongoing war matter, a reputation for scapegoating is hard to shake and can linger from a previous conflict. There are hints of this with what is known as the "Tbilisi Syndrome" in Russian military circles. The term relates to the waning days of the Soviet Union during which the government used the army to quell various nationalist uprisings and then, after the bloody results caused a political storm, the "military commanders, and the army generally, were left to bear the responsibility alone."[73] Senior military leaders critical of Russia's subsequent war in Chechnya (1994–96) pointed to this previous episode of scapegoating as justification for opposing the government's current policies. In a media interview, General Alexander Lebed made clear, "Every time, the orders were explicit and came from the highest level . . . And every time, when we had done their (the politicians') dirty work for them, they ran away and left us to take all the blame . . . Believe me, the army will never allow that to happen to it again."[74]

The case of Portugal in the African Territories likewise illustrates how political leadership's past actions can constrain civil-military bargaining years removed. In 1961, shortly after hostilities erupted in Portugal's colony of Angola, India demanded that Portugal cede its Goa enclave in South Asia, threatening the use of force if necessary. Prime Minister Salazar (Caetano's successor and political mentor) refused the demand and, on the eve of the Indian attack, ordered his military commander General Silva to fight to the last man. Facing a heavily mechanized Indian army of 30,000 supported by modern attack aircraft, however, the Portuguese force of 3,000 lightly armed troops surrendered after a mere skirmish. Political leadership denigrated the outcome as a national disgrace, and after a drawn-out and highly publicized process, Silva and most of the other officers involved were dismissed from the army and charged with cowardice. The episode created an "emotional shock" within the military establishment where it was widely perceived the regime was trying to "shift blame for the loss of Portuguese India to the military."[75]

This was not forgotten as Portugal became increasingly involved in the three separate wars in Africa. Cann elaborates, "The military at large was resentful at the unjust punishment and at making soldiers the scapegoats for civilian mistakes. The armed forces carried into the African campaigns this ominous message that the government was prepared to manipulate and sacrifice them in hopeless missions and to court-martial virtually all survivors."[76] As the wars in Africa dragged on, the earlier Goa debacle emerged as a dominant theme among military dissenters. Reflecting on political leadership's unwillingness to consider a settlement, General Spinola observed, "This lack of realism raised the specter of Goa before the military and at the same time planted in them the conviction of the complete political incompetence of the government."[77] And once word of Caetano's rebuff of Spinola spread throughout military circles, the perception grew that political leadership was again looking to scapegoat the army as had been done in 1961. In the words of another Portuguese officer, "We could see that the African policy would lead to another Goa, the disgrace of the Army, especially for the officer corps."[78] Political leadership's efforts to bargain with military leadership in this case did not go very well.

Why Firing Military Leaders Does Not Always (or even usually) Work

Civilian leadership generally retains the option of firing recalcitrant military leaders. The civil-military literature emphasizes this option as one of political leadership's most effective means of exercising leverage over the military, or as an important tool for bringing military leadership in line with civilian preferences. In reference to war termination and the specific problem of obstructive military leadership, Halperin contends, "The most potent maneuver which civilian leaders have in dealing with a military leader . . . is to replace him."[79] The option of relieving and replacing military leaders may provide political leadership significant leverage in some situations, and political leaders have certainly exercised this option in the past. Perhaps the most famous example in US history is President Truman's much-publicized dismissal of General MacArthur during the Korean War. But it is wrong to assume such actions are without costs or risks to political leadership, and astute political leaders remain wary of such risks.

Even with MacArthur, Truman remained hesitant to dismiss the well-known general and was subjected to intense political and public criticism after the action. One of the most striking facets of Truman's firing of MacArthur is that it did not happen much earlier.[80] And according to Mueller, the firing had a significant negative impact on the president's public approval rating and also bolstered opposition to the president's war policy. He explains, "Truman's dismissal of MacArthur was a major factor in the politicization of the war as Republicans took the General's side and echoed his complaints that it was the president's meddling in policy that was keeping the war from being won ... The public was strongly inclined to support General MacArthur in the dispute."[81] Although politically costly, MacArthur's firing did eventually have the desired effect. MacArthur's replacement, General Matthew Ridgway, was more amenable to a negotiated end to the war given his recognition that victory against the Chinese was likely impossible at an acceptable price.[82] In this sense, MacArthur's removal may not have helped Truman but did matter for President Eisenhower, Truman's successor.[83]

There are a number of reasons the firing of military leaders can backfire and make matters worse for a political leader. For one, a retired military leader, potentially less bound by legal and normative constraints, may be more open with his or her critique of political leadership's war policy and have access to more effective avenues of dissent; at the same time, these retired military leaders can retain the credibility of their active duty counterparts. Buzzanco notes that of all the elites involved in critiquing US involvement in Vietnam, "few, if any spoke with the experience, authority, and legitimacy" of retired generals who "were arguably the most respected and influential military figures of their time."[84] Senator J. William Fulbright, a leading opponent of US involvement in Vietnam, turned repeatedly to this small but influential group of "anti-war military brass" to testify at Senate Committee on Foreign Relations hearings.

Along these lines, near the start of Russia's war in Chechnya, President Yeltsin relieved General Lebed, commander of the Russian 14th Army in Moldova, for expressing misgivings about the Russian intervention. Being an Afghan war veteran, Lebed had complained that "step by step the Afghan war experience is being repeated in Chechnya" and vowed publicly that none of his troops would go to Chechnya "under any circumstances."[85] Once stripped of his command, Lebed decided to retire and subsequently became far more politically active and also more aggressive in his efforts to undermine Yeltsin's war policy. Capitalizing on his military credentials, Lebed built up a sizable political following and stoked widespread antiwar sentiment. He also maintained close ties with Russian commanders in Chechnya. Working with these commanders, Lebed blocked Yeltsin's efforts to further escalate the conflict and soon moved to facilitate Russia's military withdrawal "with absolutely no support from Yeltsin, who according to his usual pattern tried to distance himself both from the bloodshed and from the moves to end it."[86] In the end, Lebed dealt directly with Chechen leadership to negotiate a peace deal and more or less presented Yeltsin with a *fait accompli*.[87] Yeltsin rebuked Lebed for the unauthorized moves but grudgingly agreed to the deal given a lack of political capital to do otherwise.

The firing of senior military leaders can also sow widespread suspicion of political leadership within military circles. As noted previously, firings serve as an indicator political leadership may try to scapegoat key military leaders or the armed forces as a whole down the road. This in turn has the counterproductive effect of eroding trust and weakening political leadership's bargaining position. Further, the firing of key military leaders serves as an important signal to the opposition and domestic audience at large that political and military leadership are at odds over war policy, particularly as it relates to war termination. As discussed in the following chapter, any appearance of a civil-military gap in this regard can have damaging ripple effects and present political leadership with a difficult dilemma.

The Blurred Line between Leverage, Preferences, and Collaboration

The characterization of political leadership's bargaining position as a mix of preferences and leverage is consistent with existing civil-military relations scholarship and broader agency theory, and it is generally useful for depicting civil-military bargaining associated with war termination. However, the characterization does not fully capture the fluid interaction and blurred lines between the two facets of bargaining. In practice, the effects of preferences and leverage can be indistinguishable. When there is observable civil-military conflict marked by divergent preferences, one can readily draw the line between preferences and leverage, and also observe leverage at work. But with tacit agreement or even active collaboration, it is difficult to tell how much is a product of shared preferences and how much is the result of applied leverage. This raises the very real possibility of hidden preferences and/or unobserved influence. Along these lines Colton elaborates, "The absence of actual and observable conflict cannot always be read as proof that power and influence are not being exercised... Political winners in many countries use their resources, not only to resolve open disagreements in their favor, but to keep potential grievances from being voiced."[88] This is relevant to scenarios where civilian leadership is exercising power and influence in relation to military leadership as well as those where military leadership has the upper hand.

On a related note, preferences and leverage are not fully independent of each other, and preferences are not wholly exogenous to the bargaining process. Preferences are necessarily constrained and even shaped by realistic and available alternatives, representing "the best means of satisfying the agent's desires given his beliefs about the available options and their consequences."[89] Leverage inherently affects what options are available and their potential consequences, and preferences anticipate bargaining outcomes.

Given this blurring, one may not always be able to determine the true nature of political and military leadership preferences or why civil-military bargaining plays out the way it does. The obstructive versus facilitative distinction introduced in the preceding chapter and employed throughout this book emphasizes military leadership's observable stance on the question of war termination, but this distinction inherently encompasses the element of leverage as well. What ultimately matters, though, is that political leadership's bargaining position can vary, and does vary, greatly across cases and over time within cases of protracted war, with observable effect ranging from close civil-military collaboration to extreme civil-military conflict. This dynamic interplay between political and military leadership helps determine whether a given political leader will opt to keep fighting in hopes of securing a positive outcome or else prove willing and able to terminate a protracted war under less-than-favorable terms. At least such is the case when it comes to new political leaders. The following chapter explains why this is so.

CHAPTER 3

Civil-Military Bargaining and the Politics of Blame

This chapter explains why civil-military bargaining matters and how it influences war termination decision-making. The domestic context has significant bearing on political leadership's response to the problem of protracted war and question of war termination, but no single domestic factor can account for all, or even most, of the variation in political leadership behavior let alone suggest how long a war will last. That being said, the "civil-military variable" is not just one factor or one cause among many. Again, Maoz and Siverson parse the domestic politics of war termination as three distinct relationships to include political leadership's dealings with other political elites, with the populace, and with the military. Such a division is useful but is also artificial and obscures important interaction effects. Of particular note, the interplay between political and military leadership is not just about political and military leadership. The civil-military aspect has deep implications for other domestic political factors. In extreme cases, the army may intervene directly in the political domain, applying explicit pressure, threatening mutiny, or even employing force against its own government in order to end a war or keep a war going. But civil-military bargaining also acts as a moderator, altering the direction and intensity of the relationship between other causal factors and the outcomes of interest.[1] By moderating the effects of other "aspects of what transpires within the state," civil-military bargaining can have a powerful and far-reaching, even if more subtle, impact on the "normal" politics of blame attribution and war termination.

Addressing these latter effects, the chapter offers and links four broad claims. First, the domestic politics of war termination, along with relevant decision-making, centers on blame; and contrary to the conventional wisdom, susceptibility to blame for a failed war extends well beyond political leaders responsible for starting the war. Second, the collective attribution of blame depends on how a given narrative of failure resonates with the domestic audience, and as the agent tasked with fighting the war, military leadership is in a unique position to affect the stickiness of the narrative in this sense. Such holds true whether military leadership actively engages in, or remains on the sidelines of, the domestic political fray. Third, once a war has become longer, costlier, and more difficult than expected at the outset, a political leader's decision to either end the war or continue fighting reflects his or her bargaining position vis-à-vis military leadership. Finally, the effects of civil-military bargaining, as manifested in political leadership's policy choices and behaviors, are more pronounced with new political leaders, those with little to no responsibility for starting the war.

Blame Attribution and the Narrative(s) of Military Failure

The above reference to "normal" political processes should not be interpreted as privileging any specific regime type. In particular, the preceding argument does not imply the presence of democratic institutions or mechanisms. It does, however, align with and assume three basic tenets of the logic of political survival. To start, every political leader has domestic rivals and faces the challenge of how to maintain his or her position.[2] Next, every political leader relies upon and answers to a domestic audience of some kind so that, "No leader rules alone . . . even the most oppressive dictators cannot survive the loss of support among their core constituents."[3] And further, political leadership's policy decisions are shaped in large part by the imperative to fend off political rivals and maintain domestic support, with the ultimate goal of retaining political power in terms of both political office and political influence.[4]

Why the Politics of War Termination Equates to the Politics of Blame

The logic of political survival dictates that leaders maximize credit for policy successes and minimize blame for policy failures. This is particularly the case during times of war. War, especially costly but unsuccessful war, Tilly explains, "stimulates collective attributions of credit and blame more often than any other human activity. Even revolutions, bungled natural disasters, political corruption, and economic crises produce less collective pointing of fingers."[5] A political leader's wartime performance stands out as a key, albeit imperfect, measuring stick of broader executive qualities and competencies. Decisions related to the initiation, management, and termination of armed conflict tend to garner elevated attention from the domestic audience; and domestic reactions to wartime success and failure tend to be exaggerated.[6] At a basic level, political leadership will strive to garner credit for winning a war and avoid blame for losing a war. But when the state is embroiled in a costly quagmire, ending war short of victory can also represent policy success. Withdrawal can thus present political leadership with credit claiming opportunities but also simultaneously open the door to blame. Reflecting on the end of the Vietnam War, for example, Kissinger observed, "Everybody wanted some credit for the withdrawal program; nobody desired the blame for failures or defeats it might produce."[7]

Credit claiming and blame avoidance imperatives are always present but do not necessarily carry the same weight. Suggesting a negativity bias pervasive to domestic politics, numerous studies indicate domestic audiences are more likely to blame a leader for a negative outcome than credit the same leader for a positive outcome. As result, "When push comes to shove, most officeholders seek above all not to maximize the credit they receive but to minimize blame."[8] This holds true with the domestic politics of war termination, and the overriding imperative to avoid blame rather than earn credit can generate a unique pattern of behaviors and policy outcomes. Specifically, blame avoidance fosters policy inertia, and even when unsuccessful, in-place policies are difficult to change. Such inertia is evident in the protracted nature of protracted wars and in the hesitancy of political leaders to take steps to end a war even if they recognize further fighting will do little good.[9]

The greater the risk of blame for terminating a war short of victory, the greater the chance a political leader will adopt a jump-on-the-bandwagon strategy, electing to fund, endorse, or prop up a failing war that he or she might otherwise seek to end.[10] Or else a leader may delay the decision to withdraw or refrain from taking concrete actions until a politically more opportune time. Along these lines, Kenneth O'Donnell, one of President Kennedy's top civilian advisers, describes an (alleged) meeting between himself, the president, and Senate Majority Leader Mike Mansfield in the spring of 1963:

> The President told Mansfield... that he now agreed with the Senator's thinking on the need for a complete military withdrawal from Vietnam. "But I can't do it until 1965—after I'm re-elected," Kennedy told

> Mansfield. President Kennedy felt, and Mansfield agreed with him, that if he announced a total withdrawal of American military personnel from Vietnam before the 1964 election, there would be a wild conservative outcry against returning him to the Presidency for the second term. After Mansfield left the office, the President told me that he had made up his mind that after the re-election he would take the risk of unpopularity and make a complete withdrawal of American forces from Vietnam.[11]

And once a political leader has committed to and initiated a policy of withdrawal, the withdrawal process is likely to be lengthier and more fitful than if he or she did not fear culpability. So-called exits can take years and cost a great deal in terms of blood and treasure.

A political leader's efforts to avoid blame are complicated by the fact that losing a war and failing to win do not always mean the same thing. While a leader can be charged with a loss if withdrawing short of victory, the same leader, if electing to continue the fight, can be blamed and punished for managing the war poorly, for dragging the war out unnecessarily, or for the exorbitant and unjustifiable expenditure of state resources in a lost cause. The upshot is that once a state is embroiled in military quagmire, political leaders often fear the domestic fallout of defeat but also struggle to justify the costs necessary to secure victory. They can ill-afford to either win or lose.[12] While the incumbent navigates this domestic minefield, the political opposition will exploit any and all opportunities to point the collective finger at the incumbent for his or her lack of success.

The Five Narratives of Military Failure

To target the incumbent's wartime performance, the opposition will craft and attempt to propagate a narrative that counters any narrative offered by the incumbent, defines the implications and harmful effects of the failed war policy, and highlights the incumbent's personal culpability. Again, there are at least five broad narratives associated with military failure that call into question political leadership's judgment and competence and can thus prompt domestic repercussions. These narratives—labeled the *pretender*, the *bungler*, the *backstabber*, the *squanderer*, and the *sellout* as ideal types—are described in more detail below.

As a *pretender*, political leadership demonstrated a lack of competence by starting a war he or she could not win, or at least could not win at an acceptable price. The decision to go to war was misguided and based on faulty assessments. Any bellicose statements or assurances of success made at the outset have been exposed as little more than a façade. By dragging the state into an unsuccessful war, political leadership damaged the state's reputation and incurred other economic and geopolitical costs. The emphasis with the *pretender* narrative is political leadership's selection into the failed war. This most readily applies to foreign military interventions or other wars of choice. However, the narrative does not necessarily require that the losing state acted the aggressor. Even if the losing state was truly the victim of an unjustified and unprovoked attack, such attacks rarely come as a complete surprise. Initial leadership can still be blamed for failing to recognize the danger and preempt the attack, or for failing to effectively negotiate with or deter the aggressor in order to avoid war altogether.[13]

As a *bungler*, political leadership showed a lack of competence by failing to effectively prosecute or manage the war. Whether responsible for starting the war or not, political leadership remained intent, at least for a time, on winning the war or salvaging a favorable outcome, thus expending additional resources and incurring a sense of ownership. However, political leadership made poor decisions along the way in terms of strategy, tactics, resource management, alliances, or other critical matters that exacerbated costs, fostered stalemate, or ultimately derailed the war effort. Relevant charges relate to inadequately resourcing the military, tying the military's hands, and otherwise adopting a "no win" approach. Along these lines, shortly after India's Less-than-successful intervention in Sri Lanka had ended, one Indian officer complained, "It appeared that there were segments in the Government who were keen that this effort by the Indian Armed Forces failed," while others described the experience as "a politician's war fought by soldiers with one arm tied behind their backs."[14] Taken broadly, the emphasis with the *bungler* narrative is on political leadership's poor wartime performance as opposed to the decisions and actions leading to the war in the first place. It is relevant regardless of whether a leader has determined to end the war short of victory or else remains committed to the war but has yet been able to secure victory.

As a *backstabber*, political leadership demonstrated a lack of competence by prematurely and unnecessarily terminating a war that was still winnable and still worth fighting. Victory, or at least a reasonably favorable outcome, remained within reach. Nonetheless, because of a dearth of courage, patriotism, resolve, or commitment, political leadership determined to pull the plug before the military could finish the job and thus snatched defeat from the jaws of victory.[15] There is some overlap with the *bungler* narrative in that a political leader can be charged as a *backstabber* if he or she drastically cuts the resources necessary to continue the war. But the *backstabber* narrative is less about resource management. Instead, it hones in on political leadership's policies aimed at terminating or curtailing military involvement prior to the achievement of the state's war aims. At a minimum, political leadership is characterized as weak and vacillating. At the extreme, this can turn to charges of treachery and betrayal. Unlike the *bungler* narrative, the *backstabber* narrative does not require that a new leader take ownership of the war in order to take ownership of the loss. A new leader can make clear from day one an intent to withdraw and still be charged as a *backstabber*. The *backstabber* narrative does, however, hinge upon belief that the war was still winnable. A leader who inherits an unwinnable war cannot reasonably be blamed for losing the war or for robbing the nation and the armed forces of deserved victory.

As a *squanderer*, political leadership exhibited a lack of competence by failing to recognize or admit when victory was out of reach, when war-related costs had exceeded potential gains, or when continuing the war was otherwise no longer in the best interest of the state. Accordingly, political leadership proceeded to "throw good money after bad," squandering the state's blood and treasure unjustifiably. The offending leader is castigated for arrogance, adventurism, stubbornness, war mongering, and a lack of realism. He or she may be accused of acting in accordance with personal interests or a narrow political agenda as opposed to what is best for the state. The *squanderer* narrative essentially represents the flipside of the *backstabber* narrative. The latter privileges the costs of losing and holds political leadership culpable for terminating a war that was still worthwhile *and* still winnable. The former latches on to the costs of fighting and casts blame on political leadership for *continuing* a war that was no longer winnable *or* no longer worthwhile. In the case of Portugal in the African Territories, General Spinola argued that both applied, that the war was neither winnable nor worthwhile. Contradicting the government, his message was plain: "Portugal could not continue spending almost half its annual budget fighting an unwinnable war for indefensible principles."[16]

As a *sellout,* political leadership demonstrated a lack of competence by failing to procure or salvage the best possible settlement. Even if victory was unattainable or the war was no longer worth fighting due to mounting costs, the impact of the loss did not have to be as severe. Political leadership traded away the sacrifices of the nation and its armed forces at the negotiating table, or through other means of settlement, for an unfair, unworthy, or dishonorable peace. Further, political leadership may not have done everything possible during the war, even in a losing cause, to save face and/or posture the state for the best possible outcome at the negotiating table. The *sellout* narrative emphasizes the terms of settlement, and how political leadership manages the consequences of a Less-than-successful war, as opposed to the causes of failure or the decision to end the war; but these elements blur in practice. A key distinction between the *backstabber* and *sellout* narratives is the latter does not require a perception the war was still winnable. Under the *sellout* narrative, a new leader can inherit a war widely viewed as a lost cause and still be blamed for the outcome. Specific charges can relate to objective measures of future security and economic welfare but may also draw upon the more visceral notions of honor, sacrifice, and fairness. Accusations of treachery and betrayal come into play here as well. And there is a fine line between peace with honor and betrayal.

To illustrate the sellout dynamic, when Harold Macmillan took the job of British prime minister in January 1957, he inherited the Cyprus Emergency, or the "Cyprus Tangle" as the new leader referred to the conflict, which had been ongoing for more than two years. After three months in office, Macmillan noted in his diary, "I am anxious as anyone to get clear of Cyprus... I am not persuaded that we need more than an airfield (on Cyprus) ... on long lease."[17] The new prime minister was thus, in theory, amenable to pursuing a settlement well short of the original aim of maintaining British control over the entire island. In private memorandums, however, he expressed fear of domestic repercussions for "selling out in Cyprus" and accordingly made permanent British sovereignty over a number of military enclaves in Cyprus the cornerstone for any settlement plan.[18] Personally, neither Macmillan nor British Colonial Secretary Alan Lennox-Boyd viewed the sovereignty issue as critical to British interests, but their obstinacy on the matter complicated negotiations and delayed resolution of the ongoing conflict. Holland explains, "Imprisoned by their own domestic political timetable, they (Macmillan and Lennox-Boyd) were determined to retain the option of preventing any settlement of the Cyprus dispute which could not be credibly represented as, in Macmillan's crucial phrase, 'a symbol of success.'"[19]

Each narrative is distinct, holding political leadership culpable in different ways, but they are not necessarily exclusive. Criticism and blame associated with a given war may exhibit elements of two, three, or even all five narratives. A single leader may be subjected to elements of each. The key is that only one, the *pretender*, is limited to the political leader who either starts a war or can be readily linked to the first leader. New leadership, leadership with little to no role in starting a war, remains at risk of blame and domestic repercussions tied to the *bungler, backstabber, squanderer,* and *sellout* narratives.

Why the Civil-Military Bargain Matters

At the initiation of hostilities, political leadership proffers a narrative justifying the decision to go to war. After the war has proven longer, costlier, and more difficult than expected at the outset, political leadership, whether initial or new, must devise an amended narrative justifying the decision to either continue fighting or get out. With either direction, the political opposition will exploit the opportunity to craft and propagate its own narrative targeting the incumbent as culpable in some way. The narrative that sticks, or that gains purchase with the domestic audience, is the one that best incorporates and combines elements of the rational, emotional, and moral.[20] For a narrative to resonate, each of these elements must be present, and they must be linked in a consistent and seamless manner. If the narrative becomes fragmented—if there is dissonance among the narrative's rational, emotional, and moral appeals—the political actor propagating the narrative will lose credibility and influence with the relevant domestic audience. There are many actors within the state capable of affecting one of these elements in an isolated or compartmentalized manner. Some actors may be able to affect more than one. But military leadership is uniquely situated to influence—through its wartime assessments, statements, and actions—a wartime narrative's logical, emotional, and moral appeals simultaneously and also to reconcile these appeals.

Unique Traits of the Military as Agent

Military leadership's uniqueness in this sense is based in part on unparalleled access and exposure to the war zone. That the military has unique access to the war zone may seem obvious, but this simple reality carries profound implications. Political decisions to either continue or cease combat operations are carried out by the state's armed forces. With more extreme civil-military disputes, military leadership can balk at civilian direction and pursue its own preferred course of action. But even in polities with robust civilian control, the military can take actions in the field that undermine political leadership's policy or limit political leadership's options more subtly. Further, unique access to the war zone yields significant information asymmetries relative to the civilian principal, with military leadership serving as an important, sometimes lone, conduit of war-related information for political leadership, the opposition, and public as a whole.[21] This information feeds and underpins a narrative's rational element. And being uniquely situated to act as a gatekeeper—to manage and control the flow of information—enables military leadership to "mediate the process" of wartime debate by "privileging some elites" over others without necessarily taking an overt political stance.[22]

Less well-defined, the impact of the military's unique exposure to the war zone also crosses into the emotional realm. Rational appeal is a necessary baseline but also does little to stir and inspire the masses. For a narrative to take hold with a domestic audience, Simpson explains, "Its rational argument needs to find resonance in human, emotional terms."[23] Emotional appeal thus seeks to add a human face and individual meaning to impersonal and cold logic. In an abstract way, the military serves as a human conduit to the war zone. Soldiers are not just soldiers. They are sons and daughters, mothers and fathers, who have answered the nation's call. The nation experiences the war through their eyes, through their stories, and through their sufferings. Political actors, to include those of the opposition, can be constrained by the need to at least be perceived as admiring and supporting the troops, and as not being profligate with soldiers' lives. This emotive "tax" can distract and subsume objective policy discussions. And it can be exploited by those with a wartime policy agenda.

Apart from the advantages associated with access to the war zone, military leadership exercises epistemic authority based on its unique role in the management of violence. The idea of epistemic authority stems from the "psychology of expertise."[24] Even if information is readily available, there is a natural, psychological tendency to defer to the authority of experts, thus creating a division of cognitive labor between expert and layperson. While always present to some degree with defense-related matters, this cognitive gap widens during times of war and "brings the military to the front of the stage and empowers its presence in public discourse as well as its influence over public opinion due to its expertise."[25] Given this epistemic authority, military leadership not only supplies information about a war, feeding the policy debate, but also provides interpretation, meaning, and context. Military leadership accordingly defines the terms and boundaries of the policy debate, with the upshot being a deeper, more pervasive influence over a narrative's rational appeal. Of further note, as communication technologies improve and the media gains more direct access to the war zone, military leadership's role as an information gatekeeper may wane, but these trends do not diminish its role as an epistemic authority. A flood of information triggers deference to expertise just as much as a dearth of information.

In the wartime context, military leadership also attains what Feaver has termed a "special moral competence." Expanding upon agency theory, Feaver theorizes that the "special case of civil-military relations" adds a critical element to the traditional principal-agent model. Specifically, "The military agent is asked to put his life on the line to protect the civilian. By virtue of his willingness to sacrifice, the military agent may be thought of as possessing a special moral competence, balancing somewhat the political competence of the civilian principal."[26] This asymmetry of sacrifice adds a moral component to the more traditional informational and organizational advantages and further boosts the status and sway of the military agent.

There is a natural connection between this special moral competence and a narrative's moral element, or the narrative's appeal to credibility based on moral standing. Military leadership has a unique capacity to prop up or undermine a narrative's moral appeal. And in many respects, this is military leadership's most important source of influence over the domestic debate. Relative to its other unique traits, the military's "special moral competence" is truly special. This trait cannot be fully replicated or effectively balanced by any other domestic actor. Further, the moral appeal itself carries unique weight. As discussed earlier, a narrative's rational logic will not resonate without emotional appeal. But emotional appeal is inherently unpredictable and unstable given its focus on individualized meaning. As Simpson puts it, emotional appeal is a "centrifugal force" that can readily veer from the narrative's rational logic and thus tear the narrative apart. Moral appeal falls somewhere in between and not only balances but also serves to stabilize the relationship of the narrative's other appeals, acting as a "powerful binding force."[27]

A further relevant attribute of the military as agent is the unique level of cohesion relative to other political and societal actors. Scholars have long noted a superiority in organizational cohesion as providing the military with a marked advantage over civilian groups, with this advantage derived from centralized command, hierarchy, discipline, intercommunication, and *esprit de corps*.[28] Whatever baseline advantage this cohesion provides, the effects can be exaggerated within the context of costly, protracted war, especially when the war is being fought against a weaker opponent. This is not because the armed forces become more cohesive; instead, the relative shift is due to the tendency of such wars to foster elite fragmentation and political stalemate.[29] With the kinds of wars of interest to this study, even big strategic questions are rarely straightforward, and one is likely to observe intense domestic debate over very basic facets of the conflict to include the significance of the threat, the consequences of defeat, the viability of military and political objectives, the import of these objectives relative costs, status in terms of military progress, whether the conflict is winnable at an acceptable price, and even what winning looks like. The resultant elite fragmentation and political stalemate creates a permissive condition in which the effects of the military's informational advantages, expertise, and moral competency, even if normally muted, can become more pronounced. And if military leadership does not actively and purposefully exploit the window, other elites will aggressively seek out military leaders as coalition partners and even drag these military leaders unwittingly into the domestic fray.

How the Military Agent Moderates the Narrative(s) of Blame

Given these traits of the military as agent, political leadership embroiled in protracted armed conflict strives not only for passive consistency and tacit agreement from military leadership, but also seeks active collaboration in pursuing and selling a policy of either persistence or withdrawal. Such collaboration provides the incumbent a hedge against the opposition's efforts to exploit a stalemated or failing war and propagate elements of the *bungler, backstabber, squanderer,* and *sellout* narratives. The greater the observed gap between political and military leadership, the greater the threat one or more of these narratives will resonate with the domestic audience.

The *bungler* narrative, centered on whether political leadership effectively managed the war effort, reflects in part how military leadership frames and reports its resource requirements. In the mid-1960s, for example, Republican Party leaders attacked President Johnson for adopting a "no win" policy in Vietnam. However, these accusations "were continually being undercut by public statements from General William Westmoreland—a man highly respected by the Right—insisting that he was receiving all the support he needed from the president and was getting it as fast as he needed it."[30] But this dynamic changed later in the war. As discussed in the preceding chapter, US military leadership began to purposefully ask for more resources and freedom of action than it knew political leadership would grant in order to shift responsibility for pending failure. President Johnson recognized this intent and, in 1968, complained to his advisers, "I don't want them [military leaders] to ask for something, not get it, and have all the blame placed on me."[31]

Beyond massaging resource requirements, military leadership can affect the *bungler* narrative by how it presents various tactical and strategic alternatives. By putting forth an escalated bombing campaign against North Vietnam as a viable and potentially game-changing option, US military leaders pushed the Johnson administration, whether intentionally or not, to alter its blame calculus. Recommending the action to the president in early 1965, National Security Advisor McGeorge Bundy stated, "We cannot assert that a policy of sustained reprisal will succeed in changing the course of the contest in Vietnam . . . What we can say is that even if it fails, the policy will be worth it . . . At a minimum it will damp down the charge that we did not do all that we could have done."[32] Assistant Secretary of Defense John McNaughton similarly linked the proposed action to "the need to put the best face possible on a defeat that we might not be able to avoid."[33]

For the political leader who remains committed to fighting a war, domestic perceptions of war-related progress also matter, feeding into or hedging against *bungler* charges. These perceptions are often just as much a matter of reporting methods and framing as they are an accurate reflection of battlefield outcomes. As information gatekeeper and epistemic authority, military leadership controls and interprets much of the data relevant to the domestic debate on military progress and prospects. In many cases, military leadership determines the metrics by which its own success is measured and evaluated. Of course there are limits to projecting an image of progress irrespective of battlefield results. But military leaders are generally adept at crafting wartime metrics and framing costs in a manner that highlights, when desired, mission success; and studies suggest that the media and broader public in at least some countries are more accepting than not of these reporting stratagems.[34]

Where the *bungler* narrative emphasizes a political leader's failure to effectively prosecute the war, the *backstabber* narrative targets the decision to withdraw, blaming the leader for giving up on a war that was still winnable and still worth fighting. The viability of this narrative necessarily rests on a widespread domestic perception that the war is (or was), in fact, still winnable. Apart from measures of current progress, military leadership influences the perception of winnability through its assessment of future costs and future outcomes. While generally viewed as credible, such assessments are not always free of bias. According to Iklé, "It requires sternly disciplined detachment for the military leaders to separate their political views about the advisability of further fighting from their evaluation of the military prospects."[35] This detachment may be lacking at times, but to peer through the fog of war and determine future prospects is a highly inexact science. Cognitive biases and underlying policy preferences can easily creep in to these assessments without any purposeful effort to manipulate or mislead. Whether intentional or not, the end result is the same: "Generals and admirals are confident of winning a war they want to fight" but will likely be more circumspect when assessing the prospects of a war "they regard as politically undesirable."[36]

As long as military leadership espouses the view that victory remains within reach, political leadership seeking an exit is at greater risk of blame as a *backstabber*. Conversely, once military leadership has declared a war unwinnable—as seen with General Spinola's claim that a military solution in the African territories was impossible and Marshal Akhromeyev's declaration that the best the Soviets could hope for in Afghanistan was endless stalemate—the *squanderer* narrative gains purchase. Drawing upon the perception a war is no longer winnable and thus no longer worth fighting, the *squanderer* narrative takes advantage of and exacerbates the domestic audience's declining cost tolerance. There are many factors affecting collective cost tolerance during times of war, but from most accounts, the public's expectations of success matter most.[37] If the public believes the military effort will eventually succeed, the public will be far more apt to support an ongoing war despite high and increasing costs. But once the public begins to suspect victory is no longer within reach, political leadership will have difficulty justifying even small costs and avoiding charges of throwing good money after bad.

Beyond the question of winnability, the *backstabber* and *squanderer* narratives also depend on perceptions of whether or not the war is still worth fighting. There is certainly a rational aspect to this equation tied to assessments of future costs, potential gains, and the consequences of failure. But there is also a strong moral element tied to the phenomenon of sunk costs. Viewed through "investment" or "redemption-through-victory" frames, casualties and spent resources are not only costs but also "investments that can be redeemed if the nation prevails in the conflict."[38] Along these lines, opponents of US withdrawal from

Vietnam pointed to the tens of billions of dollars spent and tens of thousands of American lives lost in Vietnam and argued, "If the United States withdraws from Vietnam without achieving its objectives, then all of these undeniably significant sacrifices would be wasted."[39] In this sense, high casualties and high resource expenditures make continued fighting more worthwhile, providing a reason to stay as opposed to a reason to leave.[40]

A sunk cost argument can have powerful appeal. From an economic perspective, this type of argument is considered irrational or illogical. Resources spent and soldiers lost in pursuit of the state's war aims will still be spent and "no less dead" regardless of whether or not the state achieves these aims.[41] But there is a moral imperative and thus a moral logic associated with honoring or redeeming these sacrifices through victory. Simply put, a sunk cost appeal is a moral appeal, and given its special moral competence, military leadership is in a unique position to moderate the strength of any sunk cost argument. If military leadership remains committed to the war, sunk costs are more likely to be seen as investments, and the *backstabber* narrative will consequently hold more sway. However, if military leadership indicates a willingness or desire to withdraw despite past losses, the moral imperative to redeem these losses through victory wanes. And when this happens, the political leader who tries to continue the war effort will be less able to fend off charges associated with the *squanderer* narrative.

Military leadership's special moral competence is similarly germane to the *sellout* narrative. As characterized above, a *sellout* charge hinges upon perceptions of whether political leadership attained the best possible settlement even if the war was a lost cause or no longer worth fighting. The question of what constitutes the best possible settlement short of victory also contains a rational component. The assessment of whether a settlement is good or bad is based in part on whether it accurately reflects the status of belligerents, whether the state could have secured a stronger negotiating position in the future, and how well the settlement addresses future security concerns. Associated debates inevitably draw upon military leadership's informational advantages and recognized expertise. But a good settlement is not only good from an economic or rational standpoint. It must also be honorable, appropriately reflecting both the sacrifices and stature of the losing state. Like the appeal to sunk costs, an appeal to peace with honor is a moral appeal, as are closely related charges of betrayal; and by virtue of his or her willingness to sacrifice, it is the military agent who determines the fair and honorable exchange for this sacrifice (See table 3.1.).

Table 3.1 Five narratives of failure in protracted war

Narrative	Who Is Susceptible?	Blameworthy Actions	Key Themes	Military Leadership Influence
Pretender	Initial Leaders	Fails to win war he or she started	Decision to go to war was misguided and based on faulty judgment	N/A
Bungler	New and Initial Leaders	Fails to win war despite committing additional resources	Leader mismanaged war, inadequately resourced military, tied the military's hands, adopted a "no-win" strategy	• Resource requirements • Viable options • Current progress
Backstabber	New and Initial Leaders	Unnecessarily terminates war short of victory	War was still winnable and still worthwhile; leader betrayed the military and snatched defeat from the jaws of victory	• Future outcomes • Future costs • Imperative to redeem sunk costs
Squanderer	New and Initial Leaders	Continues to fight failed war, wasting lives and resources	War is no longer winnable or no longer worthwhile; leader throws good money after bad	• Future outcomes • Future costs • Imperative to redeem sunk costs
Sellout	New and Initial Leaders	Fails to secure best possible settlement even if war cannot be won	Settlement is unjust and dishonorable; leader traded away sacrifices of the nation and armed forces	• Honorable peace • Status of belligerents • Future negotiating position • Security implications

During World War I, civilian leaders in Germany recognized the value of securing military leadership's endorsement for any compromise settlement. By 1916, Chancellor Bethmann-Hollweg and others had become pessimistic regarding Germany's ability to continue the war effort long term and, over the course of the year, "sought zealously, indeed desperately, to extricate the country from a murderous war that was growing more and more hopeless."[42] These political leaders were prepared to accept a settlement far short of German war aims as a means to bring the conflict to a more rapid end. But they also feared domestic repercussions, to include the overthrow of the Hohenzollern dynasty.

Accordingly, before making any such move, they attempted to secure the backing of key military leaders as insurance. Bethmann-Hollweg believed, in particular, "The glory surrounding Hindenburg's name could be used as a cover for a compromise peace," and, further, "Even the Kaiser can afford to lose the war with Hindenburg... To lose the war without Hindenburg would mean the downfall of the dynasty."[43] This stemmed from the logic that if the prestigious military leader told the people this was the best possible settlement, "they would believe him and accept it."[44] Bethmann-Hollweg's associated attempts to bargain with military leadership failed, and he lost his job in the process. Nonetheless, his replacement Georg Michaelis continued to make similar overtures. Throughout the summer of 1917, the new chancellor corresponded with Hindenburg and other military leaders seeking support for a settlement that, while well short of German war aims, could "still bring Germany an honorable peace rather than one of hunger and appeasement."[45] Michaelis' appeals were no more fruitful than those of his predecessor. Such failure stands in sharp contrast to the successful efforts by civilian leaders in Finland to persuade the prestigious Marshal Mannerheim to help guide the country out of the stalemated Soviet-Finnish Continuation War.[46]

Constraints on the Domestic Opposition

As suggested earlier, the opposition will have varying success in its efforts to propagate a narrative of failure that resonates with the public and is thus constrained by the fact there is no guarantee the narrative will stick. But the opposition itself is not immune to blame, and this risk also has constraining effects. Attacks on the incumbent's war policy, especially when military leadership supports this policy, can backfire and result in the transference of blame along with the associated domestic repercussions. For example, a member of the opposition who pressures the incumbent into curtailing the war effort or withdrawing from the conflict may be indicted as a *backstabber* while the incumbent gets off scot-free.

In a study of the US Congress' role in terminating protracted wars, McHugh argues that as long as the United States has troops engaged in combat (as opposed to merely providing military aid), "Members of the opposition in Congress will be skittish about directly challenging the president."[47] This is because with any move to cut wartime funding or otherwise undermine the war effort, they "risk the public perception that they are complicit in a failing and unpopular policy" and also expose themselves to the "politically explosive charge" of not supporting the troops.[48] As result, the opposition's assertiveness and effectiveness in targeting the incumbent's war policy declines.

The case of the United States in Iraq (2003–11) provides hints of this dynamic. From late 2006, following the near-simultaneous resignation of Secretary of Defense Rumsfeld and landslide Democratic victory in the midterm elections, domestic pressure to end the protracted military intervention had been building; as Feaver points out, "The leadership of the newly triumphant Democrats on Capitol Hill had already determined the war to be irretrievably lost and the only responsible course was to get out as quickly as possible."[49] Pundits accordingly predicted the Congressional hearings scheduled for September 2007 to be a decisive turning point in the war, with the United States likely "heading to the exits in six months or so."[50] In the aftermath of the hearings, however, the Democrats backed down, with the antiwar push clearly losing steam. Senior administration officials credited this marked change to General Petraeus' endorsement of the surge strategy and opined that, given the underlying message that defeat was not inevitable, the "bring them home crowd" risked taking ownership of the war as well as the failure associated with a premature exit. The result, Ricks explains, "would be a prolonging of the war, because it meant the Democrats would ultimately shy away from any confrontation with the Bush administration."[51]

But McHugh is only partly correct in her depiction of these constraints. She assumes, as do most scholars, that military leadership remains committed to the war. This assumption is flawed. The opposition's assertiveness and effectiveness does not just hinge upon whether troops are engaged in combat, but also the extent to which military leadership backs the incumbent's policy and continues to endorse the war as winnable and worth fighting. For the first seven years of France's war in Indochina, the opposition refrained from taking any meaningful actions to curtail the war effort, limiting its efforts primarily to empty rhetoric and critique. Then, as described in the preceding chapter, French military leadership came to the conclusion and made known in public that a military solution was no longer possible. In response, the opposition immediately seized upon the opportunity in the National Assembly to demand a military truce; and, for the first time since the conflict began, the Socialists voted against continued funding for the war.[52] The implication is that the opposition was relatively constrained prior to the shift by military leadership. But once military leadership moved from an obstructive to facilitative stance, the opposition became far less skittish about challenging the government's war policy and making moves to bring the war to a close.

The Absence of Traditional Domestic Opposition: Portugal in Africa

The previously cited anecdotes of Great Britain in Cyprus, the United States in Iraq, France in Indochina, and even Germany during World War I all come from cases in which there is a relatively traditional domestic political opposition. When moving away from the democratic polity, one is less likely to observe opposition in a similar vein. Civil-military bargaining should still matter, though, and have similar effects, as long as political leadership has domestic rivals and also relies on a domestic support base of some kind. Portugal under Caetano represents the least democratic state across the entire population of cases (ranked lower than even China under Mao and the USSR under Stalin).[53] Despite the trappings of a democracy, there were no meaningful elections, an absence of open media, and as Machado describes, "no genuine opposition—definitely not broad, mass-based opposition."[54] The case is thus useful for illustrating how civil-military bargaining might affect the domestic politics of war termination at the extreme end of the regime-type spectrum.

As described in chapter 2, when General Spinola released *Portugal and the Future* in which he "dared say that a military solution to the problem of insurgency in the African territories is impossible," Prime Minister Caetano quickly deduced the book "opened a breech between the Prime Minister and the highest chiefs of the armed forces" that "could not fail to influence the desire of the armed forces to continue to defend the overseas provinces, and to weigh on public opinion . . . reducing the already narrow margin of maneuver open to the government in its foreign policy."[55] This was an accurate assessment. The publication had powerful informational effects, inflicting a serious blow to the credibility of Caetano's war policy. The message was not especially novel. Radical elements linked to the banned Portuguese Communist Party, as well as some of the more liberal elites within the regime, had long called for an end to the protracted wars. But, as MacQueen argues, the importance of the publication "lay only partly in its content . . . It was the author's identity and the timing of publication which gave the book its real political charge."[56] Adding to the shock, up to that point, political and military leadership had collaborated in tightly controlling the flow of war-related information.[57] As result, the country "bought the book in lorry loads," and broad domestic support for the war subsequently began to crumble.[58]

But even more problematic for Caetano was the subsequent collapse of support from economic elites who formed a cornerstone of the regime's power base. Caetano's reference to a "narrow margin of maneuver" hinted at the elite fragmentation that had emerged and progressed over the preceding half decade of war. Caetano's support base remained intact, but this base had become increasingly divided over the regime's colonial policy and the value of persistence in the ongoing armed conflicts. In particular, a number of the prominent economic actors within the oligopolistic core had grown frustrated with the seemingly endless wars and were in favor of a more peaceful approach.[59] They saw Portugal's position in Africa as a liability that was stunting development and hindering economic integration with Europe. Even if the wars could eventually be won, they were no longer worth fighting. But the regime was able to maintain a tight rein over dissenting views and quickly censored periodic calls to get out of the African quagmire.[60]

Detractors of Caetano's war policy within the ruling elite saw in Spinola's message some of their own concerns as well as an opportunity, and they were quick to latch on to Spinola's critique. One of the dominant economic groups even covertly subsidized the publication and distribution of Spinola's *Portugal and the Future*.[61] The resultant "new historical bloc" of economic and military elites placed Caetano in a very tenuous position well prior to the MFA coup, and Caetano was "unable to rally supporters and beneficiaries" to back his war policy and even his continued rule.[62] In many respects, the near-bloodless MFA coup was a formality. Most scholars assess the preceding moves by Spinola and Costa Gomes to be the turning point, and that Caetano, no longer able to defend the regime's war policy among his core supporters let alone the broader populace, would have eventually been forced to pursue a settlement in Africa regardless of the coup. But even here, the shift by military leadership fed into preexisting fragmentation, and bolstered underlying opposition, among civilian elites within the authoritarian regime. In this vein, Machado characterizes the shift by Portugal's military leadership as "a catalyst, an accelerator of events" as opposed to a direct and independent cause.[63] This aligns well with the argument that civil-military bargaining affects the domestic politics of war termination by moderating the effects of "other aspects of what transpires within the state."

Civil-Military Bargaining Scenarios

Every political leader embroiled in costly, protracted war must determine whether to keep fighting in hopes of salvaging the state's war aims or else cut the state's losses and seek to end the war under less-than-favorable terms. And as seen with Caetano, Bethmann-Hollweg, De Gaulle, Nixon, Gorbachev, and others, political leadership faced with this difficult policy decision must interact and bargain with military leadership that either remains committed to staying the course or that has determined the best option is to get out. The domestic politics of war termination looks different under these two broad scenarios, as does political leadership's susceptibility to the *bungler, backstabber, squanderer,* and *sellout* narratives. Political leadership's associated policy choices, timing of these choices, and ability to see these choices through should vary accordingly.

Bargaining with Obstructive Military Leadership

With military leadership committed to staying the course, the potential domestic costs of continuing the war decline while the likelihood of being blamed and punished for an unfavorable outcome increases. For the political leader who opts to keep fighting, military leadership can serve as a potent ally in efforts to convince the public of the importance of war aims, the viability of the war effort, and the need to redeem sunk costs, thus justifying the ongoing war effort and future costs. Military leadership's endorsement accordingly helps political leadership fend off charges associated with the *squanderer* narrative. And given the convergence of preferences, such collaboration is typically not hard to come by. As result, dovish elements of the opposition (typically associated with the left) will be more cautious and less successful in their attacks. Rhetoric along the lines of "we oppose the war but support the troops" may be commonplace, but the opposition will be hesitant to take concrete steps to undermine the war effort.

The more proximate threat generally comes from hawkish elements of the opposition (typically associated with the right), claiming that the incumbent is not doing enough, or lacks what it takes, to win the war. This is where the importance of political leadership's leverage becomes more apparent. Political leadership will seek and rely upon military leadership's endorsement to hedge against these *bungler* accusations. But as the war effort stalls, political and military leaders become more prone to battle over strategy, resource allocation, operational oversight, and tactical limitations, with each side of the civil-military divide tempted to point to the other as responsible for the lack of success. The more acrimonious and unsettled these debates, the more the civil-military conflict plays into the opposition's hands.

Worse case, military leadership will actively collude with the opposition in blaming the incumbent for mismanaging the war and for not providing the military the necessary resources and operational freedoms to get the job done. The lack of an effective civil-military bargain in this sense increases the domestic costs of continuing the war but also makes ending the war more daunting. Given the risks associated with *backstabber* and *sellout* charges, the incumbent is not necessarily more apt to alter his or her war policy and look for a way out. Instead, faced with an alliance between military leadership and the pro-war opposition, the incumbent becomes more likely to "gamble for resurrection."[64]

For those political leaders who have determined that the best course of action is to get out, obstructive military leadership represents a significant hurdle. Many leaders who would otherwise prefer to end the war simply decide to keep fighting or else kick the decision down the road. Actual preferences can thus remain hidden. If and when political leadership opts to withdraw, the *bungler* narrative remains relevant, but political leadership also faces increased risk of blame as a *backstabber* and *sellout*. The threat of blame as a *backstabber* uniquely escalates given that military leadership continues to support the view of the war as still winnable and still worth fighting. Consequently, a political leader attempting a negotiated settlement is at risk of losing office before achieving his or her policy goal. The political leader who terminates the war under less-than-favorable terms is more likely to incur punishment of some kind after the fact. Anticipating these repercussions, political leadership will remain hesitant to advertise an intent to withdraw, or may announce the intent but refrain from taking concrete actions, without first marginalizing the civil-military gap in some way.

Once political leadership has hinted at or initiated a plan to withdraw, obstructive military leadership will be tempted to block, slow, or reverse any movement toward such an outcome. These efforts can be independent of, or in explicit cooperation with, the opposition. Relevant activities include overt propaganda and critique or more subtle informational schemes to shape perceptions of the costs of the war, the likelihood of success, and the consequences of failure. With substantial leverage, political leadership is in a better position to keep the civil-military gap under wraps and also sway key military leaders through positive and negative inducements. If incapable of securing active collaboration or getting military leadership to change its views, political leadership may still be able to achieve at least a tacit agreement with military leadership to refrain from promoting contrary opinions, colluding with the opposition, or otherwise impeding withdrawal.

But even if possible, such a bargain will likely take time and, going back to Secretary Laird's assessment during the Vietnam War, demand all of the "powers of persuasion" a political leader can muster. As the process plays out, political leadership behavior will often appear vacillating and inconsistent. Rhetoric tied to ending the war will not always be met with clear moves in that direction. Firm deadlines will become less firm as the time draws near. Best case, one is likely to observe a highly politicized and drawn-out exit. When De Gaulle came to power in 1958, he was arguably in a much stronger bargaining position than his predecessors, yet it took him "another four years to extricate France from the Algerian imbroglio."[65] At the extreme, the obstructive scenario has prompted political leadership to launch costly but hopeless military actions with the aim of bleeding its own army in order to prove the futility of the ongoing war and make the army as well as the populace more amenable to a negotiated peace. On the surface, such moves may look like a gamble for resurrection, but the underlying intent is fundamentally different.

As illustration, in January 1871, with Paris surrounded by the Prussian army, French leaders of the newly formed Government of National Defense determined that a loss was inevitable and that the only problem was how to arrange a surrender "without losing face too badly and without provoking an insurrection inside Paris."[66] At the core of this problem was the National Guard, the army of citizen-soldiers in Paris, clamoring for a fight and adamant there was still a chance for the French to emerge victorious. At a closed-door meeting, a frustrated member of the government quipped, "When there are 10,000 National Guards lying on the ground, opinion will calm down."[67] Although initially uttered in dark jest, this idea took hold. In his memoirs, French soldier and scholar Maurice d'Irisson d'Hérisson describes, "Little by little, there emerged within the minds of the leaders this cruel, godless, and yet logical thought that the agitators would only settle down once enough had been killed, and that to cure Paris of her fever and reduce her excitement, it was necessary to take some pints of blood... They will not be content until we have shown them... that it is time to lay down their weapons.[68] In another eyewitness account, J. De Bouteiller characterizes the subsequent military operation as "a sort of sham-fight for all those who prepared it... it was in the secret hope that all of this excitement would be converted, under the influence of the needle-guns, into a dejectedness leading to a general claim for capitulation."[69] On January 19, 1871, French leadership launched a *sortie en masse* against the most heavily defended Prussian positions to the west of Paris, well aware that the attack had little chance of success. After being routed by the Prussians in what became known as the Battle of Buzenval, the French army retreated to Paris leaving nearly 4,000 casualties behind (a little short of the 10,000 hoped for). The defeat was decisive, but even still, National Guard officers complained that the politicians were attempting to exaggerate the military failure in order to make the population more amenable to giving up in the near future.[70] The French government in Paris surrendered to the Prussians ten days later.

Bargaining with Facilitative Military Leadership

With facilitative military leadership, the potential domestic costs of continuing the war increase while the likelihood of being blamed and punished for an unfavorable outcome declines. For political leadership pursuing a policy of withdrawal, military leadership's collaboration is by no means a given; but an effective civil-military bargain is easier to achieve and generally requires less leverage. If a political leader opts to persist, he or she will become increasingly susceptible to blame as a *squanderer*, charged with wasting the state's blood and treasure in a war that is no longer worthwhile or no longer winnable.

Once military leadership takes a facilitative stance, endorsing withdrawal as the best course of action, political leadership may or may not elect to follow suit for a variety of reasons. For one, policy change can still be risky, although not to the same degree seen with obstructive military leadership. Given military leadership's view the war is no longer winnable or no longer worth fighting, the incumbent is less susceptible to *backstabber* charges. But the *bungler* and *sellout* narratives are still in play. Even if pushing for an end to the war, military leadership can still prop up a *bungler* charge, suggesting explicitly or more subtly that political leadership's mismanagement of the war effort, and failure to bring the war to a successful and timely close, drove military leadership to the point where it had no option but to seek a way out. Otherwise, military leadership may advocate for withdrawal and then turn around and criticize or undermine the terms of settlement, thus increasing political leadership's risk of blame as a *sellout*. The opposition will be more than happy to exploit any such opportunity.

With sufficient leverage, political leadership opting to persist may be able to keep the gap with military leadership concealed and also sway key military leaders through positive and negative inducements. But this is typically a temporary fix. Any hint to the public or opposition that military leadership has given up on the war can have damaging ripple effects. And as the war effort continues to stall, the façade of a unified civil-military front will likely erode and eventually crack. Once the gap with military leadership becomes evident, political leadership's efforts to justify rising costs and convince the public of the importance of war aims and the viability of the war effort will suffer. The public's cost tolerance will wane. The opposition will jump at the opportunity to castigate the incumbent for fighting a senseless war and for sacrificing the nation's soldiers and resources unnecessarily. If in position to do so, the opposition is apt to cut war-related funding or take other concrete steps to force the incumbent's hand.

Continuing the war under such conditions is tough to say the least. The sooner political leadership recognizes the tenuous nature of domestic support, the sooner political leadership will exploit what leverage it has with the military to change gears and collaborate in pursuing a policy of withdrawal. In this sense, a high degree of leverage can have the somewhat paradoxical effect of increasing the likelihood political leadership will abandon its original preference and align itself with the military. This is because political leadership with greater leverage can make the move with less risk. Given military leadership's collaboration, political leadership can better sell the exit as honorable and generate public support for the terms of settlement, thus marginalizing the pro-war opposition. If necessary, political and military leaders will "circle the wagons" in order to diffuse blame for any perceived policy failure or collude in naming a third-party scapegoat.[71] Moderate pro-war factions, seeing the writing on the wall, will soon jump ship as well. More extreme pro-war factions may refuse to go away, but, lacking broad public appeal, they will not be able to undermine the withdrawal process in any meaningful way. Withdrawal is near inevitable and will also be achieved relatively quickly and at relatively little domestic cost for the incumbent.

Without this collaboration, however, political leadership faces a difficult dilemma. The domestic political costs of continuing the war will rise as the civil-military gap becomes readily apparent; but again, a shift in policy is also risky. Under increasing scrutiny as a *squanderer*, a political leader may fire dissenting military leaders and try to maintain the war effort in order to hedge against *sellout* charges. But this political leader faces a high probability of either losing office or eventually being pushed to end the war anyways. Whereas gambling for resurrection may be a viable option under an obstructive scenario, it is less so under a facilitative scenario given that the domestic audience will be less tolerant of such behavior.

Initial versus New Political Leaders

The linkage between civil-military bargaining and blame attribution elaborated above applies most readily to new political leaders. It is less relevant with initial political leaders, those who are uniquely susceptible to the *pretender* narrative. There has been relatively little discussion to this point about the *pretender* narrative. This is because civil-military bargaining has little impact on this narrative, with marginal effect on the associated risk of blame and domestic repercussions. According to the prevailing view, for an initial political leader, "The probability of punishment if he or she accepts any outcome less than a win ... will almost always be very near one."[72] This assessment is fairly accurate and remains so regardless of the nature of political leadership's interaction with the military.

While initial political leaders are uniquely susceptible to the *pretender* narrative, initial and new political leaders are relatively alike in terms of susceptibility to *backstabber* and *sellout* charges if accepting an outcome less than a win; and under an obstructive bargaining scenario, these like risks are great enough to obscure an initial leader's unique risk associated with the *pretender* narrative. Put differently, the risks associated with *backstabber* and *sellout* charges are enough to push a political leader beyond a certain threshold and alter his or her behavior whether or not the leader is also susceptible to blame as a *pretender*. Adding *pretender* charges to the mix has little observable effect. With obstructive military leadership, then, initial and new political leaders should behave in a relatively similar manner even if the underlying reasons vary.

The distinction between political leader types becomes more pronounced under a facilitative bargaining scenario. Once military leadership has determined the war to be no longer winnable or no longer worthwhile, the *backstabber* narrative, for the most part, becomes irrelevant. Risks associated with the *sellout* narrative can remain but are not as severe as with an obstructive scenario and are also easier to mitigate, while risks associated with the *pretender* narrative remain relatively unchanged. New political leaders are in a better position to capitalize on the shift by military leadership and thus, in aggregate, become more amenable to terminating protracted war short of victory. They are still not given a free pass but the pass is less costly. Initial leaders, on the other hand, remain trapped by their culpability for starting a failed war.

Observable Implications: A Survey of Protracted Small Wars, 1945–2009

The remainder of this chapter assesses the above argument across the population of protracted small wars fought since 1945. Admittedly, the proposed logic linking civil-military bargaining, blame attribution, and war termination decision-making does not lend itself fully to cross-case analysis. Further, civil-military bargaining affects a political leader's war termination calculus—imposing different pressures, constraints, and opportunities—but does not dictate behavior. Still, a cursory cross-case look is useful for establishing a pattern consistent with the proposed logic, with the findings an effective prelude to the case studies in subsequent chapters.

Expectations and Questions Asked

As strategic blame minimizers, political leaders anticipate and, when possible, select out of policies or actions likely to result in blame and associated domestic punishment. According to the traditional leadership-change model of war termination, the initial leader faces substantial, even certain, risk of punishment if accepting an outcome less than a win. Initial leaders are thus more likely to continue fighting despite escalating costs and little hope of victory. For *all* new leaders, the probability of punishment will "most likely be zero," and thus they should be far more likely to withdraw under less-than-favorable terms.

In contrast, flowing from an expanded conceptual framework of political leadership culpability and the logic of civil-military bargaining, the probability of punishment for new political leaders differs based on whether military leadership is best categorized as obstructive or facilitative. The behavior of new political leaders should vary accordingly. Given an obstructive bargaining scenario, the behavior of initial and new political leaders should converge in favor of persistence. Given a facilitative bargaining scenario, the behavior of initial and new political leaders should diverge, with the latter more prone to an outcome of withdrawal. This theoretical distinction is represented graphically as the difference between area α and area β on figure 3.1.

Drawing from these expectations, I ask four basic questions of the cross-case data. First, to what extent can the leadership-change model by itself account for the behavior of political leadership (initial and new)? Second, to what extent can the proposed logic, combining the effects of leadership change and civil-military bargaining, account for

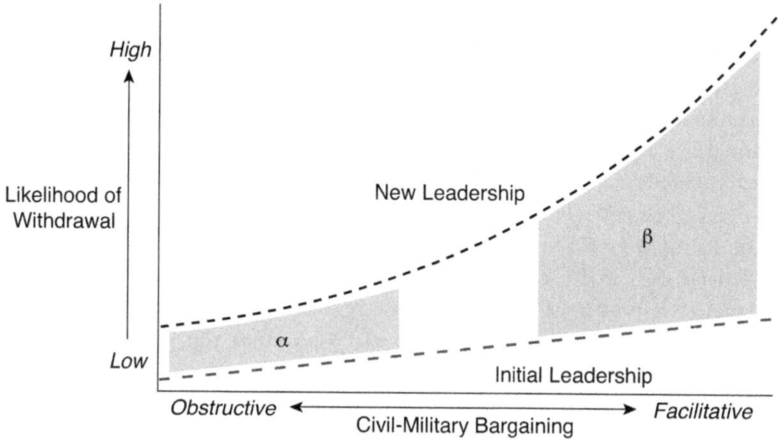

Figure 3.1 Variation in political leadership behavior (cross-case analysis).

the behavior of political leadership (initial and new)? Third, given an obstructive bargaining scenario, does the behavior of initial and new political leadership converge? Finally, given a facilitative bargaining scenario, does the behavior of initial and new political leadership diverge?

Cross-Case Data and Variables

To address these questions across cases, I survey the "best fit" population of protracted small wars fought by external powers between 1945 and 2009. This includes classic counterinsurgency campaigns as well as limited, conventional wars that meet asymmetric criteria. While this type of armed conflict may be relatively prevalent over the past several decades, it is still a rare event. Of 130 cases of external military interventions by powerful states against weaker actors since 1945, only 40 lasted at least one month and resulted in at least 50 deaths for the intervening power. Twenty-eight lasted at least one year and resulted in more than 300 casualties. The cross-case analysis focuses on this latter population of 28 cases, which well-represents the protracted small war phenomena.[73] Twenty of the 28 cases involve at least one wartime change in political leadership, and as a whole, the population yields 81 political leader observations (see appendix).

As the outcome variable, I categorize each leader-conflict observation as ending in persistence or withdrawal. Persistence relates to any observation in which a political leader continues the war until he or she either achieves a successful end-state or departs office. Conversely, for an outcome of withdrawal, the political leader extricates the state without having achieved its primary objectives, or while a credible and immediate threat to these objectives remains.[74] As the two explanatory variables, I characterize political leadership type as either initial ($Pol_{-initial}$) or new (Pol_{-new}) and military leadership, or the civil-military bargaining scenario, as obstructive (Mil_{-obs}) or facilitative (Mil_{-fac}).

Initial political leadership consists of the executive or head of government in power at the outset of a given conflict as well as those second leaders who come from the same party as the first leader and are closely connected to the decision to go to war. In general, "closely connected" implies leaders from the same party who come to power within the first year of the war or who are clearly part of a continuity government. Thus, along the lines of Croco's argument, there can be more than one initial leader in a given case. New political leadership consists of all other executives and heads of government who inherit an ongoing war.

Categorizing military leadership as obstructive or facilitative is more of a challenge. The obstructive versus facilitative distinction is obviously a continuum and involves a collective rather than an individual. In some cases, the distinction is obvious. In others, it is more subtle, and categorization probably remains open to debate. Regardless, I derive the best fit category by focusing on the top echelons of military leadership and weighing the relative prevalence and consistency of a number of common indicators from wartime and postwar assessments, statements, actions, and inactions.[75] If there is a meaningful division internal to senior military leadership, I assess the balance in terms of numbers, public image, political ties, status within the military establishment, and recognized expertise.

Taken together, I employ the variables of leader-conflict outcome, political leader type, and civil-military bargaining scenario to establish and assess a cross-case pattern through a series of contingency tables.

Summary of Findings

Looking first at end-state war outcomes as opposed to individual leader outcomes, the powerful state definitively "wins" in only eight of the 28 cases of protracted small war. This is consistent with other studies that note a markedly low success rate for the powerful state in asymmetric wars since 1945.[76] In none of these cases of powerful state success can one observe any significant civil-military conflict. Political and military leaders remained, at least on the surface, mutually committed to see the war through to a favorable outcome.[77] The remaining 20 of 28 cases end in a loss or at least stalemate for the powerful state, typically reflected in a negotiated settlement short of initial war aims. Out of these 20 losses, political leadership instigated withdrawal in 11 cases, while military leadership provided the impetus for withdrawal in nine, a relatively close split. However, in 5 of the 11 cases of political leadership-instigated withdrawal, military leadership readily aligned itself with and actively supported the move without observably being pushed to do so and thus is best categorized as facilitative. In the other six cases of political leadership-instigated withdrawal, military leadership is best categorized as obstructive, although the degree of observable obstruction varies. Altogether, with the 20 end-state outcomes of withdrawal, military leadership is best categorized as facilitative in 14 and obstructive in six.

Within the population of 28 cases, there are 81 leader-conflict observations, which equate to 37 initial leaders and 44 new leaders. Of the 37 initial leaders, only five elect to withdraw, resulting in a "persist rate" for initial leaders of 86 percent. This aligns with the conventional argument that leaders responsible for starting a war will be unwilling or unable to end the war short of victory. Of 44 new leaders, 15 elect to withdraw. New leaders accordingly exhibit a "persist rate" of 66 percent (or "withdraw rate" of 34 percent). Overall, the basic leadership change model can account for 47 of 81 leader-conflict outcomes (58 percent), and there is a significant association between political leadership type (initial versus new) and war termination outcomes. See figure 3.2. However, most of the weight of this finding comes from the behavior of initial leaders. As expected, leadership change does not account very well for variation in the behavior of new leaders, with more than half acting like initial leaders.

	$Pol_{-initial}$	Pol_{-new}	
Persist	32	29	61
Withdraw	5	15	20
	37	44	81

Fisher Exact Test (2-Tail) $p = .0403$

Figure 3.2 Political leadership type: initial versus new political leadership.

	Pol_{-new} + Mil_{-obs}	Pol_{-new} + Mil_{-fac}	
Persist	28	1	29
Withdraw	5	10	15
	33	11	44

Fisher Exact Test (2-Tail) $p < .001$

Figure 3.3 Civ-Mil bargaining: obstructive versus facilitative military leadership.

Looking solely at new leaders, civil-military bargaining (obstructive versus facilitative) can account for 38 of 44 (86 percent) leader-conflict outcomes.[78] See figure 3.3. Again, political leadership type (initial versus new) can account for 86 percent of initial leader-conflict outcomes but only 34 percent of new leader-conflict outcomes. Merging the effects of political leadership type and civil-military bargaining gives us the best of both worlds, the combined framework more effectively covering the behavior of both types of political leaders. With this combined framework, we should observe an outcome of persistence with initial leadership, or with new leadership *and* obstructive military leadership. Given both new political leadership *and* facilitative military leadership, we should observe an outcome of withdrawal. These expectations hold for 70 of 81 (86 percent) of initial and new leader-conflict outcomes. See figure 3.4.

As two final observations, I assess the expectations that behaviors of initial and new political leaders should converge given obstructive military leadership and diverge given facilitative military leadership. The cross-case data is consistent with these expectations as well. Figure 3.5 reflects the difference in behavior between initial and new political leaders given obstructive military leadership and suggests an insignificant gap (see figure 3.1, area α). In other words, new leaders look a lot like initial leaders. Figure 3.6 reflects the difference in behavior between initial and new political leaders given facilitative military leadership and, in contrast, suggests a significant gap (see figure 3.1, area β), with new political leaders being more likely to withdraw. As noted previously, this distinction gets at the original empirical puzzle of variation in behavior among new leaders and the question of why so many new leaders behave like their "culpable" counterparts.

	$Pol_{-initial}$ + Mil_{-obs}	$Pol_{-initial}$ + Mil_{-fac}	Pol_{-new} + Mil_{-obs}	Pol_{-new} + Mil_{-fac}	
Persist	27	5	28	1	61
Withdraw	1	4	5	10	20
	28	9	33	11	81

Fisher Exact Test (2-Tail) $p < .001$

Figure 3.4 Combined framework: political leadership type and Civ-Mil bargaining.

	$Pol_{-initial}$ + Mil_{-obs}	Pol_{-new} + Mil_{-obs}	
Persist	27	28	55
Withdraw	1	5	6
	28	33	61

Fisher Exact Test (2-Tail) $p < .2048$

Figure 3.5 Obstructive scenario: initial versus new political leadership.

	$Pol_{-initial}$ + Mil_{-fac}	Pol_{-new} + Mil_{-fac}	
Persist	5	1	6
Withdraw	4	10	14
	9	11	20

Fisher Exact Test (2-Tail) $p < .0498$

Figure 3.6 Facilitative scenario: initial versus new political leadership.

Although these findings remain tentative, the cross-case analysis serves its purpose of establishing a pattern of behavior consistent with the proposed logic. The analysis does not explain this pattern but instead builds confidence in an empirical regularity in need of explanation. It thus provides the impetus for and frames the within-case analysis. The utility of the cross-case analysis is necessarily limited to such because it does not capture the multifaceted and constantly evolving nature of civil-military bargaining. It does not depict the fluid interaction between political leaders, military leaders, the domestic opposition, and the populace. And it does not account for the wide range of potential outcomes and effects. More importantly though, the cross-case analysis may suggest an empirical pattern consistent with the proposed logic but says little about the underlying causal mechanisms and processes. For this, we turn to within-case studies.

CHAPTER 4

Israel in Lebanon (1982–1985)

The Lebanon War of 1982–85, generally recognized as the sixth Arab-Israeli conflict, was the longest and most divisive war in Israel's history, producing "a level of polarization in Israeli society not seen since the birth of the state."[1] Israel did not anticipate a lengthy war at the outset nor did this appear likely in the early stages of the conflict. After only a week of fighting, Minister of Defense Ariel Sharon announced to the Knesset Defense Committee, "The job is done in Lebanon," a claim with some parallels to President George W. Bush's "mission accomplished" statement made in relation to Iraq two decades later. Contemporary observers were quick to claim Israeli victory and tout the operation as a military success. Israel Defense Forces (IDF) General Avraham Tamir would later recall, "Nobody in Israel could imagine at that moment that the IDF would withdraw only three years later after what was meant to be a swift operation."[2] Over the next few months, however, Israel became embroiled in a protracted struggle with guerilla forces and terrorists as it tried to translate early military gains into desired political objectives. Pundits labeled the war a "quagmire" and "morass." One popular Israeli commentator likened the IDF in Lebanon to Napoleon's army in Russia. Whatever the reference, apparent by the fall of 1982 was that "Israel was in for a long and dark nightmare from which there was no simple escape."[3]

Israel finally returned its forces to the pre-June 1982 international boundary after three years of war and without having achieved any of its political objectives, perhaps save a marginal increase of security for its northern settlements. Despite the fact the IDF was never beaten in the traditional sense, domestic and international audiences generally viewed the outcome as a loss for Israel, the "Israeli decision to withdraw being taken as a final humiliating admission of the folly and failure of the Lebanese campaign."[4] Not surprisingly, this decision came about only after a change in political leadership. But as illustrated with the cross-case analysis, policy shift under new leadership is not a foregone conclusion. This outcome requires explanation. The question here is how new political leadership, despite facing staunch domestic opposition and an uncertain security situation, was able to achieve a timely exit while garnering broad public support for an outcome assessed as Israel's first military defeat.

The case of Israel in Lebanon provides observations of both initial and new political leaders with facilitative military leadership. It thus allows for comparison between political leadership types. The outcome of each scenario is consistent with the proposed logic. Political leadership responsible for starting the war opted to persist despite a shift in military leadership preferences while new political leadership opted to get out. But the case also aligns with the expectations of the basic leadership change model. Accordingly, there is need to show that political leadership change, by itself, did not eliminate domestic pressures and constraints associated with the problem of war termination. With this in mind, I ask four primary questions of the case. First, did military leadership's shift to a preference of withdrawal increase the domestic costs associated with continuing the war? Second, how did initial political leadership respond to this shift? Next, did new political leadership face possible domestic repercussions for ending the war under less-than-favorable terms? Finally, what was the nature and extent of collaboration between new political leadership and key military leaders, and did this collaboration aid in bringing the war to a close independent of the effects of political leadership change?

I also employ the case to compare the explanatory power of the proposed logic versus what is arguably the leading theory of how democracies behave in protracted small war. The case of Israel in Lebanon is useful for such comparison given that it comes close to being a most-likely case for this competing theory, which I refer to as the Liberal Elite model; further, proponents of the competing theory point specifically to the case of Israel in Lebanon as key evidence. Accordingly, if the proposed logic is shown to offer explanatory power beyond the competing theory, this finding gains added significance.

Background and Case Overview

On June 6, 1982, Israel launched a major ground invasion of southern Lebanon under the name Operation Peace for Galilee. The next day, the navy augmented the ground invasion with the largest amphibious landing in Israeli history. All together, the initial intervention consisted of approximately 80,000 Israeli troops, nearly half of Israel's standing army. At first deliberately vague, Israel's Likud government clarified its four primary war aims after a week of fighting. With the operation, Israel sought to 1) destroy the PLO and PLO infrastructure in Lebanon, thus increasing the security of Israel's northern settlements, 2) remove Syrian forces, and thereby Syrian influence, from Lebanon, 3) facilitate the formation of a new Lebanese government, ideally under Maronite Christian leadership, friendly to Israel and strong enough to maintain its own internal security, and 4) formalize a peace treaty with this new government, which, at a minimum, assured Israel that Lebanon would remain PLO-free.[5]

Early operations went fairly well. Although facing stubborn resistance, the IDF swept through the PLO's territorial base in southern Lebanon in a matter of days, systematically destroying the infrastructure that had taken the PLO more than a decade to build. On June 10, 1982, Israeli armor struck Syrian ground forces in eastern Lebanon, and most of the Syrian forces in the area were soon in retreat or surrounded by the IDF and at the mercy of Israeli air attack. On June 11, Israel and Syria agreed to a ceasefire, and the IDF turned its attention in the direction of Beirut. Two days later, Israeli forces linked up with Maronite militias in the vicinity of the Lebanese capital.[6] At this point, Sharon declared to the Knesset, "The job is done in Lebanon."

Given the IDF's rapid success, the Israeli government perceived itself in position to dictate political terms in Lebanon and that "the stage was set for an end to the war."[7] But the situation began to unravel. Clashes with PLO fighters continued near-incessantly. Israel secured a series of ceasefire agreements with PLO leadership, but each of the agreements broke down within hours. The ceasefire with Syria in the Bekaa Valley generally held, but the IDF continued to engage with Syrian forces around Beirut, along the Beirut-Damascus Highway, and in the Shouf Mountains of central Lebanon. As Sharon would later complain, despite the Israelis declaring the war over, "The other side kept firing."[8] Then there was the problem of West Beirut. The IDF succeeded in expelling most PLO fighters from southern Lebanon, but these fighters simply moved to West Beirut, which had long served as the PLO's headquarters. Altogether, 2,300 Syrian troops and 10,000 PLO fighters entrenched themselves in the city, and few showed any inclination of leaving voluntarily.[9] Israeli leadership never had any intention of using the IDF to clear West Beirut. Instead, Israel expected, or perhaps hoped, that its Maronite allies would assume responsibility for the task. But when the Maronite leader Bashir Gemayel balked, Israel faced a dilemma. Despite Israel's impressive military achievements to that point, failure to evict the PLO from West Beirut, Rabinovich explains, "would constitute a self-defined political defeat and conversely, a distinct victory for the Palestinians."[10] Israel consequently decided to lay siege to the city, combining diplomacy with artillery and air attacks in an effort to oust PLO and Syrian forces. PLO leadership eventually succumbed to the pressure, and under a US-brokered agreement, PLO and Syrian forces departed toward the end of August 1982.[11]

On August 23, 1982, with the siege coming to a successful end, the Lebanese elected Bashir Gemayel as president. Together, the PLO's expulsion from Beirut and Bashir's election suggested that Israel's ambitious war aims were within reach. Once again, however, reality did not live up to expectations. Bashir had already shown himself to be unreliable as a military ally. Meeting with Israeli leadership in early September, he also exhibited shortcomings as a political ally, rejecting Israel's request for a formal peace treaty. At most, the new Lebanese president appeared willing to establish a less substantial system of security and normalization arrangements. This became irrelevant, though, as Lebanese agents acting under Syrian direction assassinated Bashir on September 14, 1982. Fearing a collapse of order in the Lebanese capital and hoping to gain leverage over subsequent political developments, Israeli leadership directed the IDF to occupy West Beirut the very next day.[12]

One of the objectives of this occupation was the removal of an estimated 2,000 PLO fighters who remained in contravention to the siege-ending deal. Most were believed to be hiding in two Palestinian refugee camps, and Israel delegated the task of clearing these camps to the Maronite militia. Despite explicit instructions to avoid civilian casualties during the operation, the Maronites indiscriminately killed up to 800 Palestinian refugees, possibly in revenge for the assassination of Bashir.[13] The Sabra and Shatilla massacre, as the incident became known, sparked a wave of international and domestic condemnation.[14]

Shortly after the massacre, Bashir's brother Amin Gemayel was elected president of Lebanon in Bashir's stead. For Israel, this was not a positive development. Unlike his brother, Amin had never advocated close ties with Israel and was even less likely to cooperate. Further, while Bashir had welcomed the long term presence of Israeli troops, Amin sought to get Israel out of Lebanon as quickly as possible.[15] For its part, the Israeli government made clear any such departure would occur only after four slightly amended conditions were met. The first was the establishment of formal security and normalization relations with the new Lebanese government. The second was the evacuation of all remaining PLO elements from the country. The third was a complete Syrian withdrawal to be accomplished simultaneously with Israeli departure. The final condition was the creation of a southern Lebanon security zone extending 45 kilometers from the Israeli border. The Lebanese army would assume policing responsibility for the zone, and all militias would be disarmed. Further, the zone would be cleared and remain free of artillery and rocket launchers. Taken together, these prerequisites for IDF departure became official government policy on October 10, 1982.[16]

Over the next seven months, the Israeli and Lebanese governments engaged in a series of negotiations while the IDF continued to conduct policing and low-level counterinsurgency operations in Beirut and throughout central and southern Lebanon. The negotiations culminated with the May 17, 1983 Israeli-Lebanese Agreement. This agreement fell well short of a formal peace treaty but still, if fully implemented, would be a strategic gain for Israel and "turn the war into an almost successful enterprise."[17] Accordingly, the Israeli government touted the agreement as one of the main achievements of the war.[18] But in many respects, the May 17 Agreement was stillborn. Syria vehemently denounced the agreement, and the Lebanese government under Amin Gemayel proved both unwilling and unable to carry out its associated obligations.[19] Israel's position was further complicated by growing violence between the Maronites and Druze in the Shouf Mountain region. The underlying conflict between the two communities had existed for more than a century, but Israel found itself in the middle of the latest flare-up and under attack by both sides. In addition, Israel's relationship with Lebanon's Shi'ite population steadily deteriorated. The Shi'a of southern Lebanon had suffered at the hands of the PLO and at first welcomed the Israeli intervention. With the PLO effectively neutralized, however, militant Shi'ite groups with Iranian backing emerged in opposition to both the Gemayel regime and the Israeli occupiers.

At the end of August 1983, the IDF pulled out of Beirut and the Shouf Mountains, repositioning south to a new line along the Awali River. Proponents of the move did not view it as a step toward withdrawal. The Israeli government appears to have abdicated some of its more ambitious aims but still "sought to salvage as much as it could from the Lebanese investment."[20] Most international and domestic observers assessed the shift south as a sign that Israel was settling in for the long term. The Awali River line was ostensibly more sustainable in terms of costs, allowing Israel to build up local allies in the south and pursue its objectives independent of the Lebanese government.[21]

The IDF's departure from Beirut and repositioning to the Awali River line did not prove the panacea advocates of the move had hoped. In February 1984, Druze and Shi'ite militants overran and seized control of West Beirut, essentially returning the capital to its prewar status. The Lebanese army subsequently disintegrated and the Lebanese government collapsed. Of more immediate concern, Israeli forces in the south were routinely targeted with terrorist and guerilla-style attacks. A number of PLO fighters had returned, but these attacks came increasingly from a new enemy using new tactics. General Tamir of the IDF recalls,

> Israeli forces continued to be harassed by systematic terrorist attacks, with a mounting toll of casualties. These attacks came not so much from the PLO groups remaining in Syrian-controlled territory as from elements of the local Shi'ite population. The most dangerous and fanatical group to emerge was the Hezbollah. Some of their actions took the form of suicide missions using vehicles loaded with explosives.[22]

The IDF found itself bogged down in a costly war of attrition. Nonetheless, Israel persisted in its efforts to eliminate the terrorist threat, establish and strengthen local allies, and drive the Syrians out of Lebanon.

The Israeli elections of July 1984 brought to power a new coalition government led by Prime Minister Shimon Peres of the Labor Party. In January 1985, the new government voted in favor of the unilateral withdrawal of all Israeli forces to the prewar international border. The subsequent redeployment, planned in three phases, began the same month and was completed as scheduled in June 1985, roughly three years after the initial invasion.[23] The war accordingly came to an end without Israel having achieved its political objectives. The PLO threat in southern Lebanon was at least temporarily neutralized, but dangerous and fanatical Shi'ite militant groups with close ties to Syria and Iran had emerged in its place; and there was genuine fear that Shi'ite terrorism might follow the IDF into Israel. Syria remained entrenched in Lebanon. Moreover, the Likud's far-reaching goal of a strong Lebanese government, in control of its territory and linked to Israel through a formal treaty, had long since revealed itself a pipe dream.

Military Leadership Preferences

Even before the invasion of Lebanon began, there was a significant, and unprecedented, level of disagreement within IDF leadership as to the wisdom and necessity of the operation. A sizeable element harbored doubts about the worthiness of Israel's war aims and felt "affairs in Lebanon did not affect Israel's basic survival and that the issues involved there did not merit very high costs."[24] Once the war was underway, however, the army fought well, and military leadership for the most part appeared intent on securing Israeli victory.

Still, there were some indications of dissent early in the war, the most prominent being what became known as the "Geva affair." Colonel Eli Geva, commander of the Seventh Armored Brigade, led the initial advance to the outskirts of Beirut in June 1982. Toward the end of July, in the midst of the Israeli debate over whether to assault or lay siege to West Beirut, Geva offered to resign his commission in protest and fight on with his men as a common soldier. Adding emotional appeal to his justification, he submitted, "I do not have the courage to look into the eyes of parents of the soldiers who would be killed going into West Beirut."[25] Despite efforts by the government to downplay the incident, the Geva affair received a lot of attention both in and outside of Israel. And a number of lower profile critiques of the government's war policy emanating from within the IDF soon followed.

But these early incidents were isolated and did not represent the views of the military establishment as a whole, and particularly not of the professional officer corps. Most soldiers were highly critical of others in the ranks perceived as shirking in their duties. And while the reaction of political leadership to occasional protest among the officer corps was relatively muted, senior military leadership responded with harsh and unequivocal measures in an effort to curtail further incidents. Geva, for example, was a rising star with an impeccable military record. He was a hero of the 1973 Yom Kippur War, the youngest and most rapidly promoted brigade commander in the IDF, and even the son of a prominent retired general.[26] Nonetheless, senior military leadership dismissed Geva from the IDF, denied his request to serve in the reserves, and targeted the ex-colonel with a smear campaign. The IDF as a collective remained committed to winning and supportive of the government's war policy. Merom observes, "The army and its officers were conceptually predisposed to side with the government, and had considerable institutional and personal interest in convincing the public that the war was justified and successful... Obviously a failed war threatened to taint the army's image."[27]

Response to the Kahan Commission

The turning point for the IDF came in early 1983 with the aftermath of the Sabra and Shatilla debacle. After news of Sabra and Shatilla broke, Defense Minister Sharon effectively disappeared from public view, leaving the IDF chief of staff and other military spokesmen to answer a deluge of questions. Among senior military leaders, "this was interpreted as an attempt by Sharon to divert responsibility for the tragic affair to the IDF."[28] When Sharon did intervene in an attempt to head off a formal inquiry, he argued that any effort to investigate the massacres would result in blame being directed toward the IDF. This caused further uproar among military leaders who viewed this move, ostensibly aimed at protecting the IDF, as "little more than a cynical attempt to shift the probing public spotlight away from their (political leadership's) own responsibility and failings."[29]

The impact on the IDF of this series of events can only be understood in light of the Yom Kippur War a decade prior. Despite Israel's victory in this previous conflict, intelligence failures and the early success of Egyptian forces resulted in a postwar atmosphere of despondency and anger, as well as a push to assess accountability and assign blame.[30] The Agranat Commission was subsequently formed to investigate the circumstances that had led to the Yom Kippur War and caused the IDF's early setbacks. While civilian leadership was cleared of responsibility, the highest ranks of the army and intelligence service were found culpable of negligence. Essentially, the IDF was to blame, a conclusion that garnered a great deal of bitterness throughout the officer corps. Even Yitzhak Rabin of the ruling Labor Party found the "most startling" aspect of the Agranat Commission report was that "civilian leadership was found blameless," and questioned "the justice of placing the blame exclusively on the military."[31] Thus, in late 1982 as the government moved again toward an investigatory commission, "every officer in the senior command remembered that in the aftermath of the 1973 Yom Kippur War, the Defense Minister came clean out of the final report . . . whereas the army and its officers were thoroughly tainted."[32]

The findings of the subsequent Kahan Commission, released in February 1983, appeared to justify the IDF's concerns. The report found that no IDF personnel had played a role in the massacre. Further, IDF personnel did not have any specific prior knowledge that the massacre would take place and did not learn of the incident until after the fact, when it was too late to intervene. Still, the Kahan Commission issued a scathing indictment of a number of senior military leaders, primarily for failing to predict that a massacre might occur under the circumstances.[33] IDF Chief of Staff Rafael Eitan was charged with breach of duty and pushed into early retirement. And all of this came about despite the testimony of senior military leaders that they had explicitly advised political leadership of the dangers of employing Maronite militias in Palestinian refugee camps.[34]

Political leadership's handling of the Sabra and Shatilla incident "sent a chill through the IDF's professional officer corps" and produced "an unprecedented outpouring of resentment by some of the army's highest ranking officers."[35] More importantly, there was at least a subtle shift in military leadership's perspective on the war. According to postwar interviews,

> Senior officers of the IDF had developed frustrations at an early stage in the war. However, until the massacre... they restricted themselves to anonymous leaks at most, as their collective interest was not at stake. The massacre changed everything. Officers immediately grasped its political significance. They instantly realized that the massacre threatened to tarnish their and the army's image.[36]

This reaction was exacerbated by the memory of 1973 and sense political leadership was once again looking to shift blame to the IDF. The question of whether or not the war was worthwhile, dampened over the first eight months of fighting, again came to the fore of internal IDF debate; and senior military leaders began to seriously consider withdrawal as the best course of action.

The Civil-Military Gap Surfaces

Although these sentiments were pervasive, the effects were not immediately evident. Instead, the observable shift in military leadership preferences emerged over the following year. This delay was at least partly due to the relatively healthy relationship between the IDF and the new civilian minister of defense. In the aftermath of the Kahan Commission, Sharon resigned as minister of defense to be replaced by Moshe Arens. The relationship between Sharon and the IDF had been a rocky one, with Sharon being known for treating senior military leaders with disdain. And this by itself "sometimes led to a dangerous spirit of defiance on the part of a great number of officers."[37] Arens, however, quickly established a strong relationship with military leadership characterized by trust and mutual respect. Despite a growing gap in civil-military preferences, this relationship remained intact and helped keep the gap from public view. Yaniv summarizes,

> The longer the IDF stayed in Lebanon, the greater the objective difference between the minister's perspective and that of the army...Arens steadfastly held on to the conviction that the military fruits of the campaign should not be wasted by a weak political posture ...This position put him in a contradictory position vis-à-vis his subordinates. Thus it seems that only because of the correct, businesslike, and trusting atmosphere that Arens and his team succeeded in injecting into the post-Sharon IDF was he able to prevent this fundamental difference between his preferred policy and the IDF's from surfacing.[38]

But political leadership could only keep this "fundamental difference" from surfacing for so long. Toward the end of 1983, the IDF Planning Division under Major General Einan produced a report suggesting the accomplishment of Israeli aims in Lebanon "may be impossible" and that the continuation of "a military approach was undesirable." Further, the report recommended a unilateral withdrawal to the prewar international border by the earliest feasible date.[39] Although originally meant for internal IDF consumption, the report was soon released to the public. Shortly after this release, IDF Chief of Staff Moshe Levi announced that the recommendation of the Planning Division "had been adopted as the view of the IDF as a whole."[40]

The Basis of Military Leadership Preferences

IDF leadership recognized that unilateral withdrawal would likely be interpreted as a failure. And there was no clear strategic impetus for this course of action. Inevitably, strategic issues were at the core of the debate, but cogent arguments could be made for either persistence or withdrawal. In many respects, the worsening of the situation in Beirut and rise of extremist Shi'ite groups in the south provided impetus for a more lengthy Israeli occupation. Yaniv goes as far as to argue, "The withdrawal, at least on the face of it, made no immediately apparent sense. It would make Israel look weak. It might lead to the buildup of fresh pressures. It could result in renewed attacks on the Galilee. And for all these reasons it ran contrary to the common logic of response to the nation's security dilemma."[41]

Further, there were no compelling bureaucratic or organizational imperatives for the shift. It is true that Israeli journalists noted some negative effects on the IDF as an organization. In mid-1984, Eitan Haber of *Yediot Aharonot* wrote, "The question of whether the war in Lebanon was justified or unnecessary will remain unanswered for a long time, if it is ever answered. To the other question, whether the IDF was hurt as a result of the lengthy stay in Lebanon, the answer is unambiguous: yes, absolutely."[42] Regarding the toll on the IDF's training, readiness, and resources, Zeev Schiff of *Haaretz* similarly observed, "It is first of all a different IDF. It's astonishing and painful. What the people who initiated the war have done to the IDF is unforgivable."[43] But according to military leadership, things were not that bad. While acknowledging some organizational concerns, senior officers argued, "The critics exaggerate the negative impact of the Lebanese experience on the Army... none of the damage is irreparable."[44] Military leadership was primarily concerned with how the ongoing conflict disrupted training and reserve call-up schedules. To make up for traditional training losses, however, the IDF implemented new simulation programs. Although not ideal, military leadership assessed that, in terms of training, the IDF "could make do for the time being on such a basis if the government were to decide to stay in Lebanon."[45] Viewing the conflict in a more positive light, Major General Einan suggested in 1985 that "There were some gains from the war for the Army... New weapon systems were tested under combat conditions, and large numbers of troops received indispensable operational experience."[46]

Individual IDF officers were likely driven by a range of interests and issues, but concerns closely aligned with the legitimacy motive seemed to galvanize military leadership as a collective. When discussing the prospect of abandoning the war in Lebanon, military leaders looked back to the fallout of the Yom Kippur War. They spoke in terms of the IDF's prestige and reputation. They worried the ongoing war was having a negative impact on society's view of the IDF and could "tarnish the army's image." At a minimum, such concerns affected military leadership's interpretation of the uncertain strategic situation and balanced more traditional bureaucratic incentives. Whatever the basis, it was clear by early 1984 that military leadership had "resolved its own internal controversy over whether to retreat and had become committed to a withdrawal as soon as possible."[47]

Initial versus New Political Leadership

Perlmutter aptly describes Prime Minister Menachem Begin's Likud government that started the war as "without a doubt the most hawkish government in Israeli history."[48] In 1977, Likud defeated Labor and effectively ended 29 years of uninterrupted Labor rule. The first Likud government under Begin was more hawkish than its Labor predecessor, but still, the cabinet retained a moderate element that served to restrain Begin's "most intransigent inclinations."[49] A more fundamental change came with the 1981 elections. Likud was once again victorious and subsequently formed a government even further to the right. This government, often described as "Neo-Revisionist," adopted an aggressive security stance emphasizing the proactive use of military force to defeat terrorism and affect geopolitical changes in the region. The government's policy toward Lebanon was a natural extension of this broader policy. Where Labor and even the first Likud government had exercised a cautious and limited approach toward Lebanon, political leadership after 1981 "was now *eager* to intervene in internal Lebanese affairs, believing that through force and coercion, it would be able not only to influence events but actually to control the country (original emphasis)."[50]

After launching Operation Peace for Galilee, Begin remained staunchly committed to achieving Israel's war aims despite the numerous setbacks. Like other cases of political leadership responsible for starting an unsuccessful war, "Likud could not afford to admit—by ordering a retreat—that the entire edifice was coming apart."[51] Primarily due to declining health, Begin retired from political life in September 1983, fifteen months into the conflict. He was succeeded as prime minister by fellow Likud hard-liner Yitzhak Shamir, with the governing coalition and bulk of the cabinet remaining the same. Although not in power at the start of the war, Shamir is best categorized as part of "initial" political leadership:

> Being a government of continuity based largely on Begin's cabinet, the Shamir ministry could not dissociate itself abruptly from the policy of the previous cabinet which had led the IDF into the Lebanese quicksands. Most of Shamir's colleagues had been members of Begin's cabinet, felt a strong personal loyalty to their retired leader, had been strongly in support of the war, and were concerned not to lose ground in their own party and in the country as might happen if they were suddenly to affect a complete policy shift.[52]

Shamir had little desire to remain in Lebanon long term but remained wedded to the war's objectives, or at least to salvaging the most possible. Shortly before the 1984 elections, his government publicized an "optimistic" assessment that Israel could be out of Lebanon in two years.[53]

Conversely, Labor leader Shimon Peres came to power as prime minister in 1984 having long criticized the war as the leader of the opposition. As part of the election campaign, he promised an end to the war in three to six months.[54] And as head of the new government, Peres put forth as his most immediate policy goal "to extricate Israel from the Lebanese quagmire."[55]

Labor achieved some gains in the 1984 elections and came out ahead of Likud, but these gains were not as large as party leadership had hoped. The result was not a clear Labor win but instead an outcome of political stalemate. Peres attempted to form a Labor government but without success. After seven weeks of intense negotiations and political wrangling, Labor and Likud finally agreed to form the coalition National Unity Government (NUG) with Peres as the head. Thus, while the new prime minister was strongly in favor of withdrawal, and had promised such prior to the elections, he was not necessarily in a dominant position to affect a rapid change to existing policy.

Initial Political Leadership and Facilitative Military Leadership

As noted previously, a number of military officers questioned the Lebanese campaign at the outset, but once the war was underway, the IDF as a collective exhibited strong support for the Likud government's war policy. The government took advantage of this position while it lasted, keeping senior military leaders in the public eye in a conscious effort to add credibility to war-related policies and arguments. The value of civil-military consensus was especially evident with the August 1983 redeployment of the IDF to the Awali River line. By June 1983, both political and military leadership agreed on the move. Neither viewed it as a retreat. The purpose was to establish a position that could be better defended and sustained for the long term while Israel continued to pursue its political objectives in Lebanon. However, political leadership feared that the opposition would try to depict the move as a sign of policy failure.[56] Consequently, when Begin presented the plan to the Knesset Foreign Relations and Security Committee, he explicitly referenced the IDF recommendation, making clear that military leadership viewed the move as advantageous. Two weeks later, he called upon General Levi to appear on a prime-time television program to announce and explain the change in policy. Levi was careful to frame the move in terms of tactical redeployment as opposed to strategic withdrawal and went to "pains to explain that the move was not unilateral."[57]

The Squanderer Narrative

In a media interview the first week of January 1984, however, General Levi proposed the need to de-link the question of IDF departure from the demand that Syria also remove its troops. He went on to argue that the continued presence of Syrian forces in Lebanon might even be to Israel's advantage.[58] This opinion, expressed in public by Israel's top military leader, was in sharp contradiction to the government's position. Part of the government's justification for refusing to leave Lebanon was Syria's refusal to reciprocate. A week after Levi gave his interview, the cabinet secretary vigorously "denied that Israel was willing to withdraw its troops from Lebanon without a reciprocal pullout by Syrian forces," and declared, "We insist on this policy."[59] Pressed on the matter, political leadership for the first time had to confront publicly the gap with military leadership. In a subsequent interview, a cabinet spokesperson stated that, on the question of an Israeli pullout, the cabinet "had not shifted its position" but then acknowledged, "The military might have other ideas."[60]

About this same time, the classified IDF Planning Division report recommending unilateral withdrawal was "somehow made available" to members of the opposition. The opposition seized upon the opportunity to attack Likud, publicizing the report "as a means of arguing that the government refused to affect a withdrawal for reasons of prestige and internal power struggles despite, or even against, the best professional advice of the IDF."[61] The report was initially brought to the public's attention by Shulamit Aloni, a Knesset member aligned with the Labor party. Although unclear how Aloni gained access to the secret document, the Likud government blasted her for its public release. Drawing upon the *squanderer* narrative, Aloni claimed that she "considered it an obligation to use her parliamentary immunity to stop what she termed unnecessary bloodshed."[62] Once the opposition released the document, General Levi made his announcement that the IDF as a whole was in favor of withdrawal. The tables had turned, and the public took notice, with the gap between political and military leadership quickly emerging as a focal point of domestic discourse.[63] As result, political leadership found it more difficult to justify increasing costs, the opposition became more aggressive in its critique, and for the first time since the outset, public support for the ongoing war significantly declined.

This put Shamir and his Likud colleagues in a difficult position. Political leadership had been able to keep the growing gap with military leadership under wraps for some time, but once the gap became publicized, there was little that could be done to fix it. There is evidence the Likud government at least considered pursuing a more rapid exit from Lebanon in response to the strategic setbacks and military leadership's position. At a minimum, the issue became a source of intense internal government debate.[64] But in the end, initial political leadership proved unwilling or unable to commit to a meaningful policy shift, and any reappraisal of the existing policy was interrupted by the July 1984 elections.

New Political Leadership and Facilitative Military Leadership

As public backing for the war faded, the Likud government's public approval ratings also suffered. In the July 1984 elections, Likud lost control of the government for the first time since 1977. Leading up to the elections, Peres had promised to end the war in three to six months. Once in office, however, Peres found achieving this objective more difficult and fraught with political pitfalls than anticipated.[65] To start, the nascent National Unity Government under Labor leadership still contained a sizable Likud contingent. This proved a hurdle for Peres and the other Labor ministers, as the Likud faction continued to oppose any immediate move toward withdrawal. And both Labor and Likud leadership recognized that if Israel pulled out of Lebanon and the security of the northern settlements was subsequently threatened, Likud could pin this outcome on Peres and the rest of Labor leadership. Labor did not initiate the conflict and was thus largely free from the same "emotional and political entanglements" as Likud. Still, Peres had limited room to maneuver. As Evron articulates, "Labor had to act under two sets of constraints: it had to consider the position of its partner in government, the Likud, and it had to take into consideration the possible domestic political effects of renewed terrorist attacks following the withdrawal."[66]

The Sellout Narrative

By the time Peres became prime minister, few believed Israel could still achieve its original military and political objectives at an acceptable cost. This was generally true across the political spectrum, largely a product of the Shi'ite takeover of West Beirut and the collapse of the Maronite Lebanese government. But the terms and timing of withdrawal were still up for debate. Even if victory was unattainable based on original war objectives, the impact of failure in terms of Israeli security and influence in the region could still be managed. Again, there was genuine fear that with a withdrawal, Shi'ite terrorism might follow the IDF into Israel. The Likud faction claimed it necessary to keep the IDF deployed for at least two more years to adequately mitigate this threat, lambasting Peres' more rapid push as a foolhardy notion that threatened to wipe out even the modest gains hard-earned from three years of fighting and thousands of IDF troops killed or wounded. For Peres, this was a very real concern, both from a regional security and domestic political perspective. Yaniv explains, "If Shi'ite attacks were to follow the IDF to the Galilee, how would Peres face those in the cabinet, the Knesset, and the country who had warned all along that Israel should stay?"[67] In essence, Peres was at risk of culpability as a *sellout*, or of being accused of failing to achieve an acceptable settlement despite inheriting a failed war. Israeli political analysts predicted this scenario even before the elections, questioning "if either party would have the courage to pull the Israel Defense Forces from advanced bases in areas dominated by Shiite militant . . . Wouldn't a Likud government fear the charge of failure, a Labor government the charge of treachery?"[68]

The Cabinet Debate and Decision to Withdraw

Faced with this dilemma, Peres made two calculated moves. First, he completely divorced himself from the liberal antiwar movement as is discussed later in this chapter. Second, he sought an explicit alliance with IDF leadership in order to "gain support for a unilateral withdrawal from the Israeli military establishment."[69] Achieving the latter was not overly difficult, and having secured military leadership's backing, Peres made clear his push to exit Lebanon was based on IDF recommendation.[70] When the question came to the cabinet for formal debate and vote in January 1985, Peres and his Labor colleagues framed their proposal as the "Rabin/IDF plan." This was despite the fact the proposal was very similar to what Peres had advocated since his time as leader of the opposition. Peres recognized that even the semblance of military leadership endorsement provided an insurance policy not only for himself but also for the other ministers he convinced to vote for the plan.

On January 14, 1985, the cabinet voted 16 to 6 in favor of complete and unilateral withdrawal of Israeli forces back to the prewar international boundary.[71] This result was by no means a foregone conclusion and came as somewhat of a surprise to many observers. Pundits praised the outcome as "illustration of the political skills of Peres" and, in particular, noted the prime minister's deftness in both securing and capitalizing upon military leadership backing.[72] Peres continued to exploit this backing after the cabinet vote. In his first public statement announcing the decision, the prime minister made clear that, while open to many different options and opinions, the government had ultimately opted to pursue the course of action military leadership thought best.[73] His message was that this course of action, endorsed by military leadership, represented the best possible settlement given the less-than-favorable situation. By most indications, the approach worked. Subsequent public opinion polls revealed that a majority of Israelis viewed the outcome of the war as a failure. Nonetheless, nearly 94 percent approved of the new government's withdrawal policy.[74]

Further, throughout the five-month and three-phased process of bringing the IDF home, Peres faced little domestic pushback, even from the government's remaining pro-war faction. This lack of pushback over the course of the withdrawal process is particularly telling given the surge of violence directed against the IDF in southern Lebanon. Once Israel announced its decision to depart, militant groups did not just sit back and let it happen. Instead, attacks intensified against what the militants perceived a retreating and broken army. In response, Israel launched a series of "Iron Fist" raids in order to deter further attacks as well as weaken terrorist cells in southern Lebanon; but the withdrawal process continued unabated and largely unchallenged in the domestic domain.[75]

Explaining Withdrawal: Liberal Elites versus Civil-Military Bargaining

The foregoing discussion emphasizes the effects of both leadership change and civil-military bargaining, and I argue that the case suggests an important role for each. In comparison, proponents of what is arguably the leading domestic politics-type theory of "why democracies lose small wars" cite the case of Israel in Lebanon as evidence that the activity of liberal, intellectual elites has a dominant causal effect on political leadership behavior.

Influence of Liberal Antiwar Elites

As espoused by Gil Merom, this competing theory privileges intellectuals and activists of the political left, particularly of the "soft left."

The basic argument is that in a democracy, a minority group of liberal, intellectual elites, particularly sensitive to the costs and moral concerns associated with military intervention, can take control of the national debate, generate overwhelming societal opposition, and thus force the government to disengage from the armed conflict. Through their critiques and various protest activities, these liberal antiwar elites "shift the war's center of gravity from the battlefield to the marketplace of ideas, where the state's capacity to pursue its objectives is checked."[76] Although a minority, this group is able to dominate the domestic debate based on the fact that, being largely made up of intellectuals, it is among society's "most articulate." From this, Merom offers the "radical conclusion" that "the opinion of a *minority* among the public can defeat state policy in the toughest circumstances of national security: during war" (original emphasis).[77]

Applied to democracies, this argument is compelling. And it certainly resonates with popular conceptions of America's experience in Vietnam. In the case of Israel in Lebanon, Merom highlights the role of Israel's Peace Now activist group as well as the unprecedented level of domestic antiwar activity associated with the conflict. There is no question Israel experienced a level of liberal critique and antiwar activity unprecedented in its history and at times sensational. This factor cannot, and should not, be ignored, as it certainly had an impact on the domestic debate. And the liberal antiwar activity certainly caught the attention and spurred the imagination of the Western media. Nonetheless, one must be careful not to overstate the influence of this activity or conflate the sensational with the causal.

There are at least three reasons to question the explanatory power of the Liberal Elite model in the case of Israel in Lebanon. First, the protest movement associated with liberal antiwar elites peaked early in the war and then quickly lost steam, becoming marginalized long before there was any meaningful shift toward withdrawal. Next, there is little evidence the protest movement shaped broader public opinion. Further, liberal antiwar elites exercised little influence over political leadership or the political decision-making process. The Peace Now movement, in particular, was shunned not only by political leadership under the Likud government but also by Peres and his Labor colleagues once assuming power as part of the National Unity Government.

On June 26, 1982, approximately three weeks after the start of the conflict, the radical Committee Against War in Lebanon staged its first mass protest. Surpassing original expectations of 3,000–5,000, the number of participants swelled to 10,000–20,000. A week later, the more moderate Peace Now rallied 100,000 protesters. After this, Peace Now emerged as the dominant antiwar group in Israel. The protest movement peaked in late September 1982, three months into the conflict, with a rally in Tel Aviv numbering around 200,000 participants.[78] In June 1983, the first anniversary of the war's start, another Peace Now rally generated what its leaders considered to be a disappointing crowd of 100,000. A year later, on the second anniversary, similar efforts resulted in a gathering in the mere hundreds. Yaniv explains that after an early surge, protest activities were "reduced to colorful street theater featuring antiwar themes, a weekly demonstration opposite the prime minister's office, and a number of conventional rallies which failed abysmally to draw any public interest."[79] Thus after the first year of the three-year war, the liberal antiwar movement dried to a trickle, unable to generate much public attention or support.

Even at its highest point, the protest movement appears to have had little effect on domestic public opinion. Again, the antiwar movement peaked in September 1982, but, according to various polls, public support for the war did not began to decline until January 1984, well after the protest movement had faded.[80] Interestingly, it was precisely during the peak period of liberal antiwar activity that overall *support* for the war also peaked. A PORI survey from December 1982 indicates a small, temporary shift in public approval from "justify all actions" in Lebanon to "justify 40km," with the latter representing more limited war aims; so it is possible to argue some influence on the margins. But overall support for the war peaks here as well, and within a month, public approval for "all actions" jumps back up. A series of additional polls taken by the *Jerusalem Post* between October 1982 and August 1983 similarly asked, "Are you for an IDF withdrawal from Lebanon?" The results likewise reveal that, over this period of peak protest activity, public support for continuing the war remained consistently high. In particular, these polls indicate that from October 1982 to August 1983, the percentage of Israelis in favor of withdrawal from Lebanon *prior* to achieving stated political objectives increased only slightly from 13 to 15.5 percent.[81] Public support for political leadership responsible for starting the war also remained consistent over the period when the liberal antiwar movement was in full swing.[82]

There is also little evidence the activities of the liberal antiwar elite caused the government to alter its war policy. Early on, the movement may have had an opposite effect, leading the Likud government to dig in its heels. Prime Minister Begin and his associates viewed the liberal antiwar elite as being motivated primarily by partisan politics and perceived even the largest of the antiwar demonstrations as being organized and manipulated by the opposition Labor Party. Political leadership argued that "neither the war nor its objectives were the cause of the controversy... The opposition parties were simply using the prolonged duration of the war to promote their own particular interests, injure the Likud, and engineer a change of government."[83] In particular, Begin dismissed the mass gathering following the Sabra and Shatilla massacre "as strictly a Labor opposition ploy."[84] Demonstration participants were similarly viewed as "typical Labor supporters" unlikely to back Begin and the Likud Party in any event.[85]

While the liberal antiwar movement did little to diminish the government's commitment to the war, public protest did spur the Kahan Commission. Prime Minister Begin initially refused to establish an independent inquiry after the Sabra and Shatilla incident but eventually ceded to public pressure. But this pressure affected Begin's decision indirectly. Some of Begin's allies in the Knesset grew nervous after the mass demonstration and pushed for a formal investigation. Elazar notes, "Sophisticated observers of Israeli politics knew that what brought Begin to accept a full scale investigatory commission was not that gathering."[86] Instead, "What ultimately made Begin change his mind was not a reconsideration of the moral and public aspects of the issue but the pressure from some of his coalition partners."[87] And even here, the outcome of the Kahan Commission had little immediate bearing on the course of the conflict. Sharon stepped down as defense minister but stayed in the government as a minister without portfolio and also remained on the cabinet's Defense Committee where he continued to exert a great deal of influence.[88] Sharon's replacement, Moshe Arens, was no less of a hawk and proved to be one of the most obdurate opponents of withdrawal for the remainder of the war. Despite having little apparent impact on political leadership, the Kahan Commission did, as discussed earlier, spark a shift in military leadership's view of the war, a development that would have significant implications down the road.

That liberal antiwar activists were effectively ignored by political leadership under the Likud government is not necessarily surprising. It is more telling that Peres and his Labor colleagues of the National Unity Government explicitly sought to distance themselves from the movement as well. As the opposition party, Labor initially tied its critique of the government's war policy to the Peace Now movement and helped stage some of the early rallies. But by mid-1983, Labor had largely severed these ties. This was due in part to concerns that the activities of the liberal antiwar elite were not supported by or deemed acceptable by the bulk of Israeli populace, and that further association could have a negative impact on the party. In particular, Labor's role in creating a spectacle of the Sabra and Shatilla incident backfired. As Bavly and Salpeter note, "Opposition hopes that the events following the commission's report would actually undermine the government's standing were dashed by the public opinion polls and by the growing hostility of the marketplace toward the inquiry commission and its recommendations."[89]

Further, it became clear after the 1984 elections that the Labor faction of the National Unity Government, although seeking a rapid end to the war, wanted nothing to do with Peace Now and other activist groups. As prime minister, Peres blatantly refused Peace Now requests for collaboration and support. Leaders of the liberal antiwar movement justifiably perceived themselves as being tossed aside and marginalized during what became the most critical phase of the domestic political debate. One prominent Peace Now activist complained to an Israeli journalist, "We've stopped being an acceptable party fit for cooperation."[90]

Effects of Civil-Military Bargaining

By late 1983, it was clear that military leadership was collectively in favor of a rapid withdrawal from Lebanon. This became known to the public in early January 1984, and the opposition moved immediately to exploit the gap between political and military leadership. It was not until shortly after this series of events that public support for the war began to observably decline. Unfortunately, available polling data does not provide enough specificity to determine the cause of this decline, but the timing is compelling. Like Merom, Gabriel cites the Sabra and Shatilla incident, with its subsequent mass demonstration, as the primary event that "shook to the core Israel's civilian support for the war."[91] But again, public support actually peaked a few months after the incident and remained high until well after the liberal antiwar movement had faded. In contrast, public support dropped suddenly and precipitously after military leadership's divergent views became known. And one is hard-pressed to locate any other significant event up through January 1984 that can account for the sudden decline in public opinion after 18 months of consistent support.[92]

It is also interesting to consider the role of the Israeli media. Prior to the 1982 Lebanon War, Israel's professional media corps had a reputation for being supportive of the government and its policies during times of armed conflict.[93] The Lebanon War started out this way as well but, over time, saw a meaningful shift, with the media becoming an important source of domestic critique of the war. As the gap with military leadership became evident, the Likud government argued that negative press was undermining the war effort by demoralizing and feeding dissent among the troops. In truth, though, media critique of the war did not serve to feed military dissent as much as this critique was a reaction to military dissent. As one prominent Israeli journalist explains, "We did not create the atmosphere against the war. We only conveyed it from the front to the rear . . . what soldiers, commanders, senior commanders, and generals told us. We expressed accurately the thinking of generals, who literally begged us to create this outcry."[94] Accordingly, Feldman describes civilian war correspondents during the war as "the prime intervening factor, reporting the dissent within the IDF to the other strata of Israeli politics."[95] In other words, media critique of the war, like the decline of public support, came after and was largely a reflection of the emergence of a civil-military gap.

In terms of political leadership behavior, the Likud government was flat out dismissive of the liberal antiwar movement. At the same time, the Likud government was unable or unwilling to alter its policy in response to military leadership's shift in preferences. Still, the government was very much aware of and concerned with the difficulties of continuing the war despite the fact "the military might have other ideas." Defense Minister Arens, in particular, took steps to prevent, and then contain, the emerging gap with military leadership over the latter half of 1983. Then, after this gap became evident, Likud leadership at least considered altering its war policy in response to military leadership's stance. But as expected, political leadership responsible for starting the war proved unwilling or unable to affect significant policy reversal.

The change in political leadership mattered, as the new prime minister did not have the same emotional and political entanglements as his Likud predecessor. But Peres was not given a free pass to abandon Israeli war aims and bring the conflict to a rapid close. When taking office, Peres faced powerful domestic rivals seeking to undermine his withdrawal plan, and he remained susceptible to blame as a *sellout*. These rivals attacked the planned withdrawal as being too soon and too fast, claiming that the outcome would not only generate greater security risks but would also undo what the IDF had sacrificed so much to achieve. The escalation of violence that occurred once the withdrawal process was underway provided ample underpinning for the opposition's critique. Still, while Peres did not quite meet his campaign pledge to have Israeli troops out in three to six months, he did achieve a relatively quick end to the protracted war. There is no way to determine the extent to which Peres was actually at risk of domestic punishment for an unfavorable outcome, because he was not punished for the unfavorable outcome. But it is clear that Peres explicitly sought and then exploited military leadership's collaboration in his dealings with the opposition and Israeli public, and he leveraged military leadership's backing of the withdrawal plan to secure the necessary votes in the cabinet.

CHAPTER 5

The Netherlands in Indonesia (1946–1949)

Although generally overlooked in the war termination literature, the Dutch-Indonesian conflict represents a significant and interesting case. Not only was it the largest overseas military operation in Dutch history, but it was also one of the nation's most politically divisive events. Writing in 1968, Dutch political scientist Arend Lijphart observes, "All major political problems facing the Dutch during the past century have been resolved peacefully and constitutionally," making Dutch politics appear "to be not just healthy and stable, but decidedly dull and unexciting." The only exception, or "the only big blot on their record," he notes, was the Indonesian conflict from 1946 to 1949, which "produced serious strains in Dutch domestic politics, similar in nature but to an even greater extent than the internal political tensions in the United States over the Vietnam issue."[1]

The case also presents a relevant puzzle. Following the general elections of early 1948, over two years into the conflict, the Dutch formed a new coalition government under Prime Minister Willem Drees of the left-wing Labor Party (PvdA), replacing Catholic Peoples Party (KVP) leader Louis Beel. Drees and his PvdA associates held little responsibility for initiating the war and took office hoping to rapidly bring it to a close via settlement. Fighting continued nonetheless, and in late 1948, the Dutch armed forces launched the Second Police Action, a move that markedly escalated the conflict and violated a number of Security Council resolutions. American and British officials, already confounded by what they regarded as Dutch intransigence, were shocked by the renewed military action.[2] Just a few months prior, these same officials had confidently predicted the Netherlands was ready to call it quits, and any hints of pending escalation had been dismissed as little more than "nostalgic mutterings of Dutch military officers."[3]

One American diplomat attributed the unexpected move to the Dutch being "stupid and arrogant."[4] Another blasted the Dutch government for its "unilateral defiance" of world opinion.[5] But from intraparty communications, it is clear that Drees, Foreign Minister Dirk Stikker, and the bulk of PvdA leadership privately opposed the Second Police Action and remained committed to a negotiated settlement in accordance with UN dictates. These leaders believed escalation would likely result in a longer and costlier war with yet little hope of victory; further, they were well aware severe international sanctions would likely follow. Still, these "non-culpable" leaders not only granted approval for the Second Police Action but also backed it with unfettered public endorsement.

The case is of further interest, and was in part selected for further study, because it represents a "failure" of the proposed logic within the framework of the cross-case analysis. New political leadership endorsed the Second Police Action, thus escalating the conflict, but eventually ended the war under less-than-favorable terms despite obstructive military leadership. Drees achieved this outcome less than two years after taking office, which was relatively quick compared to De Gaulle in Algeria and Nixon in Vietnam among others. And further, he came out unscathed from a domestic political standpoint. On the surface, then, the case not only fails but fails in a big way. With this in mind, I ask three primary questions of the case. First, did political leadership fear repercussions for losing a war it did not start, and, if so, did this influence political leadership's behavior? Second, did political leadership's interaction with obstructive military leadership contribute to or exacerbate this concern? Third, how did political leadership deal with these constraints and eventually succeed in bringing the protracted war to a close?

Background and Case Overview

Over 200 years of Dutch colonial rule in the East Indies came to an abrupt end with the Japanese invasion of early 1942. Although a sizeable force, the Dutch East Indies Army (KNIL) proved little match for the Japanese. There were pockets of stiff resistance, but a good portion of the Dutch army gave in without much fight. The Dutch commander formally surrendered to the Japanese on March 9, 1942, the rapid capitulation duly noted by the indigenous population. According to a British intelligence report, in the eyes of the locals, "The catastrophe of 1942 had ruined Dutch prestige . . . for an army of 100,000 had surrendered without fighting a battle."[6]

The subsequent period of Japanese occupation proved instrumental to the emergence and consolidation of a robust and militant Indonesian nationalist movement. The Japanese dismantled the Dutch colonial edifice and sought to erase any reminder of Dutch influence and authority. Further, they encouraged the involvement of Indonesians in local politics and granted meaningful authority to prewar nationalist leaders; and by providing military training to a large number of native residents in anticipation of an Allied invasion (which never came), the Japanese also created the nucleus of what would eventually be the Indonesian nationalist army. By April 1945, Japanese leaders in Indonesia realized an end to the war was likely near, and, "desiring to leave as embarrassing a situation as possible for the victors," they set up an Independence Preparatory Committee.[7] On August 17, 1945, two days after the Japanese surrendered to the Allies in Tokyo Bay, nationalist leaders in Java declared the formation of the independent Republic of Indonesia.[8]

The sudden end of the war in the Pacific caught the Allies somewhat by surprise, and they were not prepared to immediately take over many Japanese-held territories to include the Indonesian archipelago. Accordingly, the surrender agreement with the Allies obligated Japan to retain control in Indonesia until relieved by Allied forces. In practice, however, the Japanese relinquished "the whole of Java to the Republic" to include all government facilities, public utilities, and modes of mass communication, and thus "the new Republic had the whole machinery of administration and economy in its hands"[9] Also in violation of the surrender agreement, the Japanese handed over vast amounts of weapons and supplies to a newly formed Republican army.

For the Dutch, the declaration of Indonesian independence came as a shock. Still, they were not overly concerned by the development, at least not at the start. Most Dutch viewed the Indonesian Republic as nothing more than a Japanese creation with little indigenous support. Once the Japanese left, the Republic would crumble and the Dutch could simply move back in and fill the power vacuum. At this early stage, the Dutch were largely oblivious to the fundamental changes that had taken place over the preceding three-and-a-half years. They "expected to resume in Indonesia where they had left off, confident that the excellence of their colonial system was such that the Indonesians would welcome their return."[10]

It is important to recognize the Dutch had little intent or desire to reassert direct colonial rule. There were certain Dutch elements that preferred this, but it was never government policy. Instead, Dutch leadership envisioned a loose federation of semiautonomous Indonesian states formally linked to the Netherlands as part of a Commonwealth.[11] The development of this new structure would take place gradually and only after the Dutch had reestablished order, and had reasserted their authority, across the archipelago. Even this was anathema to Indonesian Republic leaders who sought to establish at once a fully independent, centralized state with at most a loose, voluntary tie to the former colonial power.[12]

British forces were the first to arrive in the former Dutch colony, assigned the job of disarming and evacuating the Japanese army. In the meantime, the Dutch government "did everything in its power to replace British forces as early as possible."[13] The first Dutch military units landed in October 1945 and began arriving in mass by January 1946. Although hesitant to assume the role of mediator, the British worked to encourage negotiations between the Indonesian Republicans and the Dutch. The resultant talks went nowhere and violence between the Dutch and Indonesian forces erupted in the spring of 1946 with the British unable to exercise adequate influence over either party. British troops finally departed in November 1946; with this development came a sense of foreboding, as the British believed "their presence had been the chief factor in preventing open war between the Dutch and Republicans."[14]

The two sides agreed to a truce in mid-November 1946, but this had little effect in practice, with the violence continuing unabated. In further violation of the agreement, the Netherlands continued to build up its armed forces in Indonesia and imposed a blockade of Republican-held territories. Among British diplomats as well as the Indonesians, there were doubts regarding the sincerity of Dutch overtures, the general impression being that "the Dutch are merely playing for time with a view to being able to force the issue by military means rather than negotiations."[15]

By mid-1947, the Netherlands had over 100,000 troops in country; and after issuing an unrealistic ultimatum, the army launched a major attack against the Republic on July 20, 1947. The campaign, known as Operation Product or the First Police Action, initially appeared a great success. Within two weeks, Dutch military forces had seized approximately two-thirds of Java and a third of Sumatra, the seized territory encompassing some of the most vital economic and agricultural areas previously held by the Republic. Overall, resistance was minimal, and casualties were light. As one witness stated, "The Dutch advanced more in the nature of a parade than a military operation."[16]

But success soon proved illusory. The action consisted of a number of spearhead attacks along major lines of communication. For the most part, Republican forces did not stand and fight but instead receded into the mountainous countryside. From there, these forces initiated guerrilla-type operations, effectively denying Dutch control outside the initial avenues of advance. In an August 2, 1947 report, the British Consul at Batavia noted,

> In spite of general jubilation over their rapid advance, a feeling of uneasiness can be detected in Dutch military circles at the vanishing tactics adopted by the Republicans... They are only beginning to realize that their problem, far from being solved, is only postponed, and that failure to destroy opposition can only result in intensified guerrilla warfare at a later date.[17]

And, a week later,

> From the point of view of territorial expansion, the Dutch gains appear impressive on the map, but in reality, their troops can only operate in strength along the main highways, and then only as long as they are in convoy and covered by their superior firepower and armored strength. In the few cases where they have attempted to leave the beaten path for mopping-up purposes, they have met stiff opposition and suffered considerable casualties. At this late date, it's only now the Dutch are beginning to realize the war is far from won, and the real struggle for supremacy is yet to come.[18]

By this point, it was clear the war would be longer, more difficult, and more costly than expected at the outset.

Beyond provoking widespread guerrilla warfare, the First Police Action also served to internationalize the conflict by bringing in the nascent United Nations Security Council (UNSC) as a central actor. In August 1947, the UNSC issued a resolution calling for a ceasefire between the warring parties and in October dispatched a Committee of Good Offices to facilitate negotiations. Under pressure from the UNSC, the Dutch and Republicans signed the Renville Agreement on January 17, 1948. This agreement did not represent a political settlement but instead merely consisted of a military ceasefire and a framework for future political negotiations.[19] The subsequent talks collapsed and armed conflict persisted, primarily in the form of Republican hit and run attacks and Dutch "pacification" efforts.[20] Consequently, the Dutch continued to suffer casualties at a higher rate than before the ceasefire.

In the meantime, the Dutch military presence continued to grow, peaking at approximately 170,000 troops toward the end of 1948.

Frustrated by the inability to stabilize the situation and bring guerrilla activity under control, the Dutch army launched the Second Police Action (Operation Kraii) on December 19, 1948.[21] Similar to the first major campaign in 1947, the Second Police Action resulted in some conventional military gains. The Dutch seized much of the remaining Republican-held territory. Further, they bombed and then captured the Republican capital at Djokjakarta, taking most of the Republican political leaders as prisoner. But once again, Republican forces did not offer much direct resistance. They instead withdrew in order to bolster existing guerrilla networks, plans for which had been worked out long in advance; and the stalemate continued.

The Second Police Action was in blatant defiance of previous UNSC resolutions and caught the United States and the rest of the UNSC by surprise.[22] The UNSC convened an emergency session on December 22, 1948 and demanded a complete ceasefire, Dutch release of all political prisoners, and the timely transfer of all territory, as well as territorial sovereignty, to the Indonesians.[23] Of greatest concern to the Dutch was the accompanying threat of economic and military sanctions by the United States. In response to the Second Police Action, the United States immediately cut off the portion of Marshall Aid designated for Dutch development efforts in Indonesia. This was followed by threats to cut off US economic assistance to the Netherlands completely.[24] In addition, American diplomats issued veiled warnings that Dutch membership in the soon to be formed NATO, or at least the US military assistance to be provided NATO members, was in jeopardy.[25]

Largely in response to this pressure, Dutch resolve began to crack, and there emerged a clear shift in Dutch government policy by May 1949. By that point, the Dutch "changed their priority from one of defeating the Republic, to saving as much face as they could while pulling out of Indonesia."[26] Reporting in June 1949, the US Ambassador to the Netherlands observed, "With respect to Indonesia, the Dutch have seen a steady drain on their resources, guerrilla warfare, and no real progress made... They have now resigned themselves to the inevitable and want the Indonesian question cleared up quickly."[27] A final truce went into effect on August 1, 1949, and the Round Table Conference commenced at The Hague three weeks later. In November, the Dutch government formally agreed to remove its armed forces from Indonesian territory and transfer sovereignty completely and unconditionally by the end of the year.

Military Leadership Preferences

Dutch military leadership in this case can best be categorized as obstructive over the duration of the war. For military leadership, the use of force to eliminate the Republic was not only preferred, but was also "the only adequate answer in the circumstances."[28] After it became clear by the spring of 1949 that political leadership was determined to withdraw, military leadership refrained from taking strong measures, of the type seen later with the French in Algeria, to block the process; but this was not necessarily a given. Kroes observes, "It will always remain a matter of speculation why no upsurge of praetorianism occurred at the height of antiguerrilla warfare when the military seemed in full sway but attempts at solving the problem with political means began to prevail."[29] Still, military leadership remained opposed to any negotiated settlement with the Republic and, once the settlement was finalized, complained that Dutch armed forces in Indonesia had been "sold down the river."[30]

In assessing military leadership's position, there is need to account for the distinction between the Dutch East Indies Army (KNIL) and the regular Dutch army, or Royal Netherlands Army. Prior to World War II, the former represented a completely separate branch of the armed forces with very little career crossover, particularly within the officer corps.[31] Further, many KNIL officers had spent their entire careers in Indonesia. Thus, they could be expected to have different views on preserving Dutch influence. Officers of the Royal Netherlands Navy were similar to those of the KNIL in this regard. Many naval officers had also spent the bulk of their careers in the colonies and effectively considered the Dutch East Indies as "their land."[32] Most key military leaders serving in Indonesia during the conflict, to include the senior Dutch commander General Hendrik Spoor, came from a KNIL or naval background.

After World War II, however, the line between the KNIL and regular army became far less pronounced. The prewar KNIL was effectively dismantled by the Japanese. Out of necessity, Dutch forces sent to Indonesia beginning in 1945 were cobbled together from units across the organizational divide. Further, the Dutch relied extensively on conscripts from the metropole. This was unheard of in the previous colonial army. At its peak strength in late 1948, the Dutch army in Indonesia consisted of 65 percent regular Dutch troops and 35 percent colonial forces, with approximately half of these colonial forces consisting of indigenous Indonesian recruits.[33] Perhaps of more significance, there was little evidence throughout the war of a difference in preferences between military leaders in Indonesia and those back in the

Netherlands. The Chief of the Army, General H. J. Kruls, had no colonial experience. Nonetheless, he was particularly outspoken in favor of staying the course. At one point, Kruls went so far as to threaten that "the loyalty of the army could no longer be counted on" if political leadership gave in to Republican demands.[34]

The Basis of Military Leadership Preferences

As to the basis of military leadership preferences, there is little in the case to suggest that bureaucratic incentives played a dominant role. Such incentives would probably have been better served by ignoring Indonesia altogether and focusing on the Netherlands' growing commitment to Western security cooperation in Europe. The demands of the war in Indonesia significantly reduced the Netherlands' contribution to Western security structures, but this did not seem to affect military leadership's views toward the protracted war in Indonesia. General Kruls was among the strongest advocates of a large Dutch contribution to the emergent NATO, and again, he had no colonial experience. His staunch support for military operations in Indonesia is thus telling.

Bureaucratic incentives may have been present but were at least balanced by factors closely linked to legitimacy. A relevant factor that particularly stands out is the collective memory of failure. Schoeman describes Dutch military leadership as being consumed by the need to "save face" for the armed forces' poor showing in World War II.[35] The rapid capitulation to the Japanese in Indonesia was a particularly acute and lingering source of humiliation. According to Van Doorn, "The army had many good reasons to feel angry and even desperate . . . In 1942 it had been defeated in a way that could hardly be considered to be honorable."[36] Dutch historian Petra Groen similarly describes military leadership as driven by a desire to "make up for the dishonorable defeat of the colonial army against Japan in 1942."[37] The perceived connection between Indonesian nationalists and the Japanese only made this desire more poignant. By crushing the "Japanese-contaminated Republic," the Dutch army was by proxy redeeming itself and avenging the earlier defeat.[38]

New Political Leadership

On the surface, political leadership appeared committed to the war up through the spring of 1949, the observable change in policy taking place gradually. In mid-January 1949, after a discussion with the Dutch

Ambassador to the United Nations, a US diplomat reported, "So as far as this conversation went, there was no indication that the Dutch were prepared to accommodate themselves to any Security Council Resolution whatever."[39] A subsequent British analysis noted that, by the end of March, the Dutch Government was at "a curious midway position between their obstinate military on the one hand, and the Security Council on the other." And by the end of April, the Dutch government was clearly in "the phase of cooperation" with the UNSC.[40]

Domestic Constraints

Behind the scenes, though, the Dutch government had been deeply split for at least two years. When forming a new cabinet in early 1948, Prime Minister Drees and his PvdA associates had long since given up hope the Dutch could succeed militarily, at least at an acceptable cost. In their view, the only responsible course was to end the fighting, comply with UNSC demands, and settle with the Indonesian nationalists. Conversely, the prime minister's rivals in the Catholic Peoples Party (KVP) remained set on eliminating the Indonesian Republic by force or at least marginalizing it within a loose federal system.[41]

Because of the nature of the Dutch multiparty system, the cabinet is almost invariably made up of diverse coalitions, often bringing rivals with divergent policy agendas together in "the politics of accommodation."[42] This held true over the course of the Netherlands' war in Indonesia. For the period of interest to this case, the governing coalition consisted of a close balance between the PvdA and KVP. Even though Drees was named prime minister in 1948 and his close political ally Stikker took over as Foreign Minister, KVP rivals successfully lobbied to retain the Ministry of Overseas Territories and the High Commissionership in Indonesia. According to Stikker, this was a signal that despite losing the top post in the government, "the Catholic Party wanted to be in full control of Indonesian matters."[43]

Even with the balance in the government and the PvdA's leadership role, the KVP continued to dominate Dutch policy toward Indonesia. The politics of accommodation looked for the most part like the PvdA accommodating the KVP. The new prime minister and other PvdA leaders wanted to negotiate a quick end to the war but kept this relatively hidden from the public at least until early 1949, with the coalition government presenting a unified pro-war, anti-Republican front.[44] This image of unity culminated with the government's unfettered endorsement of the Second Police Action.

Again, Drees opposed the action, as it would only prolong the stalemated war and increase associated costs. Plus he foresaw the international backlash. Nonetheless, the prime minister publicly supported the action and made little attempt to constrain military leadership.[45] Along with other PvdA leaders, Drees stood before the country and declared, "The government has left military strategy and tactics to the army leaders with every confidence."[46] For those with insider knowledge, however, it was clear the outward appearance was a façade. A few weeks prior to the Second Police Action, an Australian diplomat reported that contrary to the unity and optimism "publicly displayed by the Dutch government . . . the actual atmosphere in the Dutch cabinet at this time is one of dissension and pessimism."[47] In the same period, Stikker ostensibly confided to a US official that despite appearances to the contrary, PvdA leadership believed it "vitally necessary to get a quick peaceful settlement."[48]

Threat of Domestic Repercussions

There are indications the hesitancy to push more aggressively for withdrawal stemmed from fear of domestic repercussions. PvdA leadership anticipated that a sharp reversal of policy would result in a collapse of the Dutch government and spur a new round of elections. Even more troubling was the likelihood of the PvdA being excluded from any subsequent government. Responding to PvdA rank and file frustrated by party leadership's unwillingness to take positive steps toward ending the war, Drees and party leadership claimed they "also felt uneasy about overall government policies" toward Indonesia but then argued the need to back the ongoing military effort. The given rationale was that remaining part of the executive served the party's interests better than the "more passive role of the opposition."[49] When pressed by Western diplomats, PvdA leadership similarly hinted at a fear of domestic backlash, threatening, "the succeeding Government would in no circumstances be more accommodating than the administration they would replace."[50] According to a senior British official at The Hague, key government leaders raised this concern repeatedly in private conversations.[51]

It is important to recognize there was little linking Prime Minister Drees and the PvdA to the start of the conflict. Drees was a career politician and was serving in the government at the start of the war. However, the impetus for initiating and then escalating the war came primarily from Prime Minister Beel and other more conservative elements of the government.[52] Even though Drees served in the earlier Beel cabinet, it would be a stretch to label Drees a member of Beel's faction. The two were political rivals. And prior to being named prime minister, Drees was criticized by the conservative media for failing to wholeheartedly support the war at the outset. In sum, the new prime minister was in no meaningful sense culpable for starting the war.

Bargaining with Obstructive Military Leadership

Describing the Dutch armed forces during this period, Kroes observes, "From the point of view of rules of the game and institutionalized ways of access to centers of decision-making, it would appear that the military by and large worked in a framework of civilian political primacy."[53] Still, when Drees became head of the government in 1948, he was not in a particularly strong position to bargain with military leadership. His views on the war and its termination diverged significantly from those of top military leaders, and the prime minister lacked leverage, a shortcoming that stemmed primarily from the makeup of the coalition government combined with the explicit collusion between military leadership and the KVP.

Collusion with the Opposition

Military leaders worked hand in hand with the KVP to promote the view that the war in Indonesia was both worthwhile and winnable. Despite numerous setbacks and the unanticipated stalemate, military leaders held fast to the claim victory was well within reach. As Groen notes, "Right up to the last stage of the conflict... military leaders remained convinced that the Netherlands could settle the conflict satisfactorily through military force."[54] Prior to the First Police Action in 1947, General Spoor argued the insurgent problem could be solved in as little as two weeks, quickly paving the way for a favorable political settlement.[55] This did not quite pan out, but military leadership remained optimistic and continued to claim the Dutch army, if given adequate resources and leeway, could rapidly crush Republican forces. After meeting with military commanders in November 1948, roughly a month before the start of the Second Police Action, Foreign Minister Stikker recounted,

> All with whom I met spoke of the absolute necessity for military action, the forecasts of which were uniformly optimistic. Once the decision was taken, it was said, action could start in six days, and would not last

> longer than three weeks. After three months the new administrative reconstruction could begin, and Dutch soldiers might be repatriated by August of 1949.[56]

Further, military leadership pushed the view that most Indonesians still favored the Dutch, and once enough guerrillas had been killed and extremist leadership had been taken out, moderate Indonesians would flock willingly back to the Dutch fold.[57] Thus, the war was still worthwhile because, if given a chance, most Indonesians would still welcome Dutch influence.

To promote its views, military leadership waged a near-incessant information campaign aimed at political elites and the Dutch populace at large. Senior officers propagated a pro-war message in both government and public forums. Along these lines, a British diplomat reported on the activities of military officers "busy preaching this gospel at Dutch hustings."[58] In one of the more dramatic episodes, Admiral Helfrich, the well-respected chief of the Dutch navy, resigned in October 1948 (roughly two months prior to the Second Police Action) to protest that the government was not being aggressive enough. A week after his resignation, Helfrich held a press conference in which he declared that the only way to restore law and order in Indonesia was to "march on Djocja and clean up the Republic."[59]

Beyond this overt advocacy, military leadership took advantage of its ability to control and shape information related to the war. Back in the Netherlands, there was a great deal of ambiguity as to the political and military situation in Indonesia stemming from the limited flow of information to the metropole. There is substantial evidence Dutch military leadership purposely crafted reports and presented facts in a manner that signalled progress and supported a continuation of the war effort. According to one US diplomat, military reports coming out of Indonesia were often "impressive," but it was not clear "how much is straight propaganda and whether the facts and figures are accurate."[60]

The military also controlled access of Dutch and foreign journalists to the war zone. Military leadership used this control to help discourage what they considered "prejudicial reporting," with "prejudicial" being the code word for anything that undermined a pro-war stance.[61] There was also a steady stream of Dutch political delegations visiting Indonesia on various fact-finding missions. But these visitors rarely ventured outside of the Dutch-Indonesian capital of Batavia and were instead provided briefings by military commanders whose strategic judgment was largely accepted without question. According to a British official who witnessed this first hand, military leaders in Indonesia were quite apt at "convincing Dutch Parliamentary missions of their fundamental objections to sincere compromise with the Indonesians."[62]

Military leadership was also successful in its combined efforts with the KVP to enlist the support of the Dutch populace. There was some public critique, but the large majority of Dutch citizens were in favor of military action against the Republic at the start, and there was little erosion of this backing over the course of the conflict. Public opinion polls taken over the duration showed "the hawkish approach to the problem never failed to find widespread support among the voters."[63] Of particular note, only 19 percent of the Dutch public disapproved of the Second Police Action, with support expressed across the political spectrum.[64] Mirroring broader public approval, the Dutch media also demonstrated little in terms of antiwar sentiment or negative critique. Conservative media outlets offered clear endorsement of the war effort. The left-wing media was more hedged in its assessment but refrained from maligning the Dutch military or its prosecution of the war.[65] This high degree of cost tolerance and support for the war was not a given. Dutch troop losses in Indonesia were not excessive by some standards. But still, as Foreign Minister Stikker notes, "the daily casualty reports were appalling."[66] To fight the war, the Dutch relied heavily on conscription, which could easily have become a point of domestic contention. Even more problematic were the economic costs. Coming out of World War II and several years of German occupation, the Dutch economy was in ruins. For some, this made a hard-line stance in Indonesia appealing, but it also made a costly, protracted war even more unattractive than usual. The war was an economic burden the Dutch could ill-afford.

Undermining Negotiations

Beyond promoting an optimistic view of Dutch operations, military leadership collaborated with the KVP to undermine any compromise settlement. This dynamic was very much at play with the collapse of the Renville Agreement, which in turn provided the context for the debate over the Second Police Action. Again, the Renville Agreement incorporated both a military truce and a framework for further political negotiations, with the former largely a requisite for the latter. Actions by the Dutch military in the field were highly detrimental to the associated negotiating process. General Spoor conveniently interpreted the ceasefire to mean no further military advancement beyond territory taken during the First Police Action. He argued the ceasefire did not prevent the army from further establishing control within the boundaries of the occupied areas. Aggressive pacification, or what Spoor termed "mopping up" operations, continued unabated. Unsurprisingly, Indonesian Republican leadership decried these operations as being in violation of the ceasefire agreement. The agreement also called for the establishment of a demilitarized zone between areas held by the Republic and those occupied by Dutch forces. Spoor acknowledged this zone but claimed the authority to exercise "policing" as opposed to military operations within its boundaries. The fact that Dutch soldiers accomplished this policing did not seem to matter. A US diplomat noted the absurdity that "if troops drew back one day, they would return the next as police."[67]

The upshot was intensified fighting despite the truce, and the political negotiations called for by the Renville Agreement had little chance from the start. This was not by accident. Spoor received multiple warnings of the potential impact of Dutch military activities on the negotiating process. Plus there was widespread belief Spoor was intentionally trying to provoke Republican forces into truce violations.[68] When resultant violations did occur, military leadership would publicize the incidents and offer them as evidence "one could not take the word of Indos" and that anyone "was wrong in thinking an agreement could work."[69]

In November 1948, US envoy Merle Cochran reported on this situation to the US Secretary of State. He observed, "It was to be expected of course that any agreement with the Republic . . . would meet with violent opposition on the part of such local figures as General Spoor and Vice Admiral Pinke." Cochran highlighted Spoor as being "responsible largely for publicity campaign on infiltrations, incidents, etc," the implication being that this publicity campaign was consciously aimed at undermining a potential peace agreement.[70] In a later memorandum recounting a discussion with Foreign Minister Stikker, Cochran notes, "I let Stikker know that a bad atmosphere for renewed conversations was already being created by Spoor and his information service."[71]

Drees, Stikker, and other proponents of withdrawal recognized that this "bad atmosphere for continued conversations" extended beyond Indonesia. By stoking the opinion that "one could not take the word of Indos," military leadership was also poisoning any settlement back in the Netherlands. Even if a settlement seemed favorable from the Dutch perspective, the "Indos" could not be trusted to honor the settlement. In late January 1949, the US Secretary of State identified Spoor's influence as the "principal factor in our judgment militating against the chance of success of a settlement along the lines of the Security Council resolution."[72] Cochran became so frustrated by military leadership's obstructionism that he asked to be removed from his post as lead US negotiator if Spoor was to remain in place. Cochran felt that there was little chance of reconciling the warring parties and little possibility he could "contribute constructively toward salvaging something from the situation" absent Spoor's departure.[73]

The Politics of Withdrawal

Given the widespread belief in the viability of a military solution and popular view the Indonesians would renege on any settlement favorable to the Dutch, elements of the *backstabber* narrative were likely in play, and Drees was in a difficult position as he sought a way out of the protracted conflict. The risk of domestic repercussions factored into his calculus and contributed to the decision to approve of and endorse the Second Police Action. Groen characterizes this endorsement as a simple matter of ceding to the formidable alliance of military leadership and the KVP. Reflecting on the decision-making process leading up to the action, she notes,

> The army leaders again joined the debate, and once more sided with the hawks. The influence of the army leaders on the decision-making process was greater in the autumn of 1948 than it had been previously... The right wing of the cabinet welcomed arguments from the army commander. These served to strengthen their conviction that a new offensive was requisite and enabled them to exert pressure on the cabinet's left wing... The left wing was again averse to renewed military action. In mid-December 1948, however, they succumbed to pressure from the right wing.[74]

Military leadership's stance clearly bolstered the position of the prime minister's more hawkish political rivals. But Drees' actions were not necessarily a matter of passively succumbing to right wing pressure, and he was certainly not being "stupid and arrogant" as suggested by some outside observers. Instead, from the perspective of a strategic blame minimizer, the new prime minister deftly played the hand he was dealt.

Drees recognized an Indonesian settlement inconsistent with Dutch war aims was likely just a matter of time. The United States was rapidly growing impatient with Dutch defiance of the UNSC. For the United States, any specific concerns related to the situation in Indonesia were overshadowed by worry that the credibility of the nascent UNSC was at risk.[75] Further, the United States perceived Dutch intransigence as bolstering the efforts of Communists across the broader region.[76] In private meetings, US officials made clear to Dutch political leadership the "absolute necessity of compliance" with UNSC demands and also that the United States would take whatever steps necessary to ensure such compliance.[77] While the Dutch could stand up to the Indonesian Republic indefinitely, facing the United States was a different matter. The Netherlands was "running a losing race in the international arena," and Drees knew it.[78]

Supporting the Second Police Action

Recognizing the near-inevitability of a compromise settlement, Drees postured the PvdA the best he could to avoid being blamed for the outcome. Drees did not believe the Second Police Action would have the decisive and rapid effects the army claimed. But Drees was operating under a logic similar to that offered by Bundy concerning the 1965 bombing of North Vietnam. If the offensive did actually succeed, the Dutch would be in a stronger negotiating position once settlement talks commenced. On the other hand, going back to Bundy, "What we can say is that even if it fails, the policy will be worth it . . . At a minimum it will damp down the charge that we did not do all that we could have done."[79]

When endorsing the Second Police Action, Drees chose his words carefully and made clear he was giving military leadership a free hand. Again, the cabinet's message to the Dutch public was that, "The government has left military strategy and tactics to the army leaders with every confidence."[80] Military leadership welcomed the compliment and freedom of action. For Drees, the move served as an insurance policy. Looking back to the First Police Action of mid-1947, military leadership had also promised decisive results. Wary of an escalating military commitment and international backlash even back then, Drees and other PvdA leaders serving in the KVP-dominated cabinet of Louis Beel took steps to constrain the military and limit the operation. In the aftermath, it was clear that military leadership had not delivered on its promise to solve the Indonesian problem in two weeks. But military leadership was adamant in its argument that domestic political interference was to blame. This interference had "cheated them of a solution to their Indonesian problem," a message that resonated with the domestic audience.[81] With the Second Police Action, Drees did not provide military leadership the same excuse and opportunity to deflect blame.

International Sanctions and the Fracturing of the Opposition

The resultant sanctions played into Drees' hand as well, whether he thought through all the implications or not. By endorsing the escalation and giving military leadership a free hand, the prime minister could "damp down" charges the government had not supported the military and had not done everything it could to win the war. By provoking a withering international response, the Second Police Action also provided the government a potential out by shifting the locus of blame from the domestic to the international arena. As such, the UNSC presented itself as a potential third-party scapegoat. Political leadership could maintain the narrative it had stayed committed to Indonesia and supportive of the armed forces to the very end, withdrawing begrudgingly and only after being forced to do so by the international community and UNSC.

As expected, the Second Police Action achieved some conventional gains but did little to quash the insurgency, and guerrilla-style attacks continued unabated. Since military leadership had been given complete freedom in the campaign, the "winnability" argument lost credibility. Also, as Drees anticipated, international pressure came "thick and fast."[82] In light of imposed and pending sanctions, even the KVP could no longer reasonably argue the fight in Indonesia was worthwhile, and its stance against a settlement began to crack. In February, KVP stalwart Louis Beel proposed a plan which, although not fully in accordance with the UNSC demands, would end the conflict and impose a sharp loss of Dutch influence in Indonesia.[83] Fellow KVP leader and Minister of Overseas Territories E. M. Sassen adamantly opposed the plan; according to official Dutch sources in Batavia, "Whereas three months previously these two men had seen eye to eye with respect to policy in Indonesia, they were now far apart."[84] With some KVP backing, the Dutch government endorsed Beel's proposal—a move which led to Sassen's resignation—but the concessions did not go far enough to be acceptable to the United States or to Indonesian nationalists.[85] Nonetheless, the proposed settlement plan reflected a significant shift in the KVP position and overall government policy.

The Elimination of General Spoor

This fracturing of the KVP signalled the beginning of the end. However, military leadership, General Spoor in particular, still presented a potential hurdle. Following Sassen's resignation in mid-February, US Ambassador

Lewis Douglas met with Robert Scott, chief of the Southeast Asia division of the British Foreign Office. After the meeting, Douglas reported to the US Secretary of State, "With (Minister for Overseas Territories) Sassen out of the Dutch government, the Foreign Office hopes that General Spoor will also be eliminated, thus opening the door to more conciliatory policy re Indonesia."[86] A number of other US and British officials similarly expressed the need to fire or otherwise "eliminate" Spoor as a requisite for bringing the conflict quickly to a close in compliance with UNSC demands.[87] Looking ahead to the proposed Round Table Conference at The Hague, Cochran wrote to the US Secretary of State, "Scarcely need to warn the Department that once at The Hague, real trouble will begin... While the conference is in session, Spoor and others will undoubtedly be doing everything possible to sabotage negotiations."[88] Such fear was justified, as Cochran had witnessed first-hand Spoor's role in undermining the earlier Renville Agreement.

In one of those unexpected twists of history, Spoor was, in effect, "eliminated." On May 23, 1949, the general suffered a heart attack. He died two days later.[89] Within four months of Spoor's passing, the Dutch agreed to a final ceasefire and entered into peace talks with the Indonesian nationalists at The Hague. Of course there is no way to determine whether or not Spoor's death mattered. Still, the timing is intriguing. As noted earlier, the key players viewed Spoor as a serious impediment to a negotiated settlement right up to the point of the prestigious and well-known general's passing. With Spoor's unexpected and untimely death, Drees effectively got rid of his MacArthur without having to fire his MacArthur.

The Outcome of Withdrawal

In November 1949, the Dutch government formally granted full independence to Indonesia and agreed to unconditionally remove Dutch forces by the end of the year. The independent United States of Indonesia was established on December 27, 1949 with the Republic as one of many states in the union. However, this loose federal structure was a temporary veil, and most Dutch and international observers knew it. Within eight months, the Republic had incorporated the other federal states into the centralized, unitary polity that nationalists had sought from the beginning. This was precisely what the Dutch had fought for three years to prevent, and the settlement accordingly garnered a great deal of resentment back in the Netherlands. Overall, the Round Table Agreement dictating Dutch withdrawal received the approval of only 21 percent of the Dutch population.[90] Despite the public's dissatisfaction with the settlement, Drees and other PvdA leaders effectively avoided blame and domestic repercussions for how the war ended. Drees actually gained in popularity and stature, continuing to serve as prime minister for another decade while leading four successive cabinets.

It is clear in this case that Prime Minister Drees was not given a free pass to end the protracted war under less-than-favorable terms. He faced significant domestic constraints and remained very much concerned about domestic repercussions resulting from a policy shift. It is also fairly clear that obstructive military leadership exacerbated Drees' position by colluding with the prime minister's political rivals and bolstering the view that the war remained winnable and worthwhile. Further, there is solid evidence this affected political leadership's war termination calculus. Drees and other proponents of withdrawal viewed military leadership as a hurdle, and this factor influenced relevant decision-making in a manner that altered the course of the conflict and the timing of efforts to bring the conflict to a close. In the end, though, a unique confluence of circumstances related to the Second Police Action, international sanctions, and even General Spoor's death helped mitigate political leadership's risk of blame despite the lack of an effective civil-military bargain. Even though the case represents a "failure" within the rudimentary framework of the cross-case analysis, a closer look suggests the theorized mechanisms were still in play and shows these mechanisms interacting with factors outside the scope of the theory in an unexpected and interesting way.

CHAPTER 6

South Africa in Namibia (1966–1989)

In a September 1986 interview concerning South Africa's ongoing war in Namibia, South African Defense Force (SADF) General Georg Meiring observed, "In this long war there are two statements which were accepted in the past but which we have proved to be false. Firstly, that time is always on the side of the terrorists. Wrong. We have been fighting for 20 years, and they (the terrorists) are deteriorating. Secondly, that you can't win a counterinsurgency war. You can. They are losing here and at the same time we are winning."[1] Three aspects of this statement stand out. The first is simply that the war was already two decades old. Even by the standards of protracted war in this day and age, South Africa's counterinsurgency campaign in Namibia was protracted. Next, Meiring points to this duration as a sign South Africa was doing something right, that South Africa had proven time could favor the powerful state. And finally, even after 20 years of fighting, he remains confident South Africa is on the path to victory.

Less than three years later, South Africa withdrew all of its forces from Namibia, effectively ceding control to the South West Africa People's Organization (SWAPO), the insurgent group South Africa had fought since 1966 to eliminate. For South Africa, this was not a clear-cut loss but neither was it an obvious win; and just a year prior to the settlement agreement, US envoy and regional expert Chester Crocker claimed that an end to the war still "seemed like a distant dream."[2] How the war ended is thus interesting. But also of note is how long the war lasted. This study examines both aspects of the case and explores how civil-military bargaining mattered for each.

As with the previous two cases, political leadership responsible for starting the war did not end the war. But this case is different from the previous two in that new political leadership took office fully committed to the ongoing war effort and even sought to expand this effort. In this sense, P. W. Botha very much came to "own" the war. Like the second case (the Netherlands in Indonesia) but unlike the first (Israel in Lebanon), new political leadership inherited military leadership best categorized as obstructive. For most of the war, political and military leadership exhibited strong consensus in favor of persistence. But this perspective eventually softened, and ten years into his tenure as executive, Botha agreed to a war-ending settlement. Such a shift was highly contentious within South African political circles, and powerful right-wing elements did everything they could to undermine negotiations. But instead of siding with the hawkish right wing as seen in the Dutch case, military leadership backed, even encouraged, political leadership's moves to terminate the protracted war.

The following analysis asks three primary questions of the case. To start, to what extent did military leadership's backing of the government's war policy hedge against domestic critique, bolster domestic support, and enable prosecution of the war effort over the long term? Also, to what extent did political leadership fear domestic repercussions for an unsuccessful outcome, and how did this influence behavior? Lastly, how did civil-military bargaining affect the move to withdraw after over two decades of fighting?

An aspect of this case that is at the same time interesting and challenging to the analysis is the coincident domestic unrest linked to the National Party (NP) government's apartheid-era polices and the growing internal threat to the white regime associated with the African National Congress (ANC) and other Black Nationalist groups. From the mid-1980s on, these internal problems escalated and unavoidably bled over into how the government viewed and dealt with the war in Namibia. The ANC allied itself with SWAPO and also with the Soviet-backed Popular Movement for the Liberation of Angola (MPLA) in Angola, relying on both for support and protection. This linkage increased the potential domestic costs of failure in Namibia. As is discussed later in this chapter, the centrist NP government became increasingly vulnerable to attacks from the right-wing opposition for its limited domestic reforms and inability to effectively quell the internal violence. Whether justified or not, the opposition associated the growing domestic threat with the government's inability to eliminate SWAPO in Namibia. And any settlement that left SWAPO in place could be used as ammunition against the government if the situation south of the Orange River continued to deteriorate.[3] In this sense, domestic unrest in South Africa provided incentive to persist in Namibia. At the same time, this growing domestic turmoil prompted critics of the war to argue South Africa should cut its losses at the Orange River and focus exclusively on matters at home.[4]

As a final note, the case of South Africa is different in terms of where it falls on the regime-type spectrum. Whereas both Israel and the Netherlands are both considered strong democracies, South Africa during the period of interest is classified a weak democracy based primarily on its discriminatory, apartheid-era policies and central role of the state bureaucracy and internal security structures. While not nearly as extreme as the Portuguese case in terms of lack of effective democratic institutions, the case of South Africa in Namibia adds some variation and helps demonstrate how a common set of causal mechanisms operates with similar effect across a wide range of political and institutional settings. Throughout the 1980s, critics glibly cast Botha as an autocrat who "conducts foreign policy with little need to be accountable to its constituents, to Parliament or the public at large."[5] In reality, Botha was very much aware of domestic opinion and attuned to the need to garner public support, specifically the support of the white electorate, for the ongoing war as well as any attempt to end the war. He recognized this support could not be taken for granted and was also aware of potential domestic pitfalls, often speaking candidly of not wanting a repeat of the experience of the United States in Vietnam.[6]

Background and Case Overview

During World War I, South African forces seized the German colony of South West Africa, later known as Namibia, at the behest of Great Britain; and postwar, the League of Nations granted the territory to South Africa as a mandate. After World War II, the United Nations denied South Africa's request to annex Namibia and determined the mandate would be transferred to UN trusteeship in preparation for independence. South Africa, however, refused to acknowledge the authority of the UN, arguing that "with the death of the League the mandate system was also at an end and therefore its (South Africa's) sovereignty over Namibia was now unrestricted."[7] The International Court of Justice ruled in favor of South Africa in terms of not being required to cede the mandate. However, the court also determined South Africa could not annex or unilaterally change the status of the territory. Namibia thus remained a ward of South Africa under nebulous UN supervision. In the meantime, South Africa's NP government installed a white regime in the Namibian capital of Windhoek and proceeded to exploit the territory as a *de facto* province.

Throughout the 1950s, a number of indigenous political organizations emerged in Namibia, to include a labor movement that would serve as the foundation for SWAPO. Shedding its modest goals, by 1962 SWAPO had become the dominant nationalist group. By 1963, SWAPO activists had begun military training outside of the country. Utilizing its military branch known as the People's Liberation Army of Namibia (PLAN), SWAPO launched an armed struggle for independence in September 1966. This outbreak of violence coincided with the passage of UN Resolution 2145. In October 1966, the UN General Assembly finally voted to terminate South Africa's mandate and declared Southwest Africa a direct responsibility of the United Nations, citing that South Africa had "failed to fulfill its obligations in respect of the administration of the Mandated Territory." Further, the resolution affirmed the right of the inhabitants to self-determination and called upon South Africa to "refrain and desist from any action, constitutional, administrative, or otherwise, which will in any manner whatsoever alter or tend to alter the present international status of Southwest Africa."[8]

South Africa effectively ignored the UN resolution and moved to quell the armed uprising by force. From the South African perspective, the conflict remained little more than a policing campaign until the early 1970s. Around 1971, however, SWAPO formalized ties with and began to receive substantial military assistance from the Soviet bloc. The insurgency concomitantly grew in both scope and intensity. In 1972, the South African government declared a state of emergency in Namibia and, in early 1974, transferred responsibility for the operational area from South African Police (SAP) internal security forces to the SADF. This move was based on the realization that the conflict had grown well beyond the scope of police action and required a larger commitment of South Africa's regular military forces.

Another key turning point came in 1974–75 with the overthrow of the Caetano regime in Portugal and subsequent Portuguese withdrawal from Angola. This allowed the MPLA to seize power in Angola and also paved the way for the introduction of Cuban troops to the region. Once in power, the MPLA provided SWAPO with bases in southern Angola, these bases serving as sanctuaries for organizing, training, and reconstituting the PLAN as well as staging areas for cross-border attacks into Namibia. SWAPO was thus in a much stronger position, and its military operations escalated significantly. In response, the SADF continued with its counterinsurgency operations in Namibia but also initiated a series of large-scale raids into Angola to target SWAPO and its MPLA host. Although the first such raid, Operation Savannah, was relatively unsuccessful, subsequent cross-border attacks over the next 13 years proved more effective in disrupting and diminishing the capability of the insurgents. These SADF attacks also supported National Union for the Total Independence of Angola (UNITA) rebels against the MPLA, but SADF operations in Angola were always linked to the war in Namibia.[9]

As the conflict escalated in the 1970s, South Africa's political aims clarified. South African leadership was not, in principle, opposed to Namibian independence. But the government also wanted to insure that, prior to any such change, South African economic interests were secure and that Namibia's white population (approximately 70,000) was protected. Further, Pretoria hoped to marginalize extremist elements in any future Namibian polity. SWAPO, in particular, needed to be ousted.[10] While the possibility of an early exit became a major topic of domestic debate, the government firmly rejected any settlement that would result in SWAPO victory. Violent takeover in Namibia by a Cuban- and Soviet-backed SWAPO was a worse-case scenario. But even a peaceful transition accompanied by free elections was problematic as long as SWAPO served as a Soviet surrogate, Cuban forces remained in the region, and PLAN operated freely from bases in Angola.[11]

The question of South African withdrawal from Namibia ultimately came to hinge upon the situation in Angola. As early as March 1986, South African leadership indicated to US officials a willingness, at least in theory, to withdraw militarily from Namibia and agree to Namibian independence if Cuba removed all of its forces from Angola and the Soviet Union ceased its activities in the region. Nonetheless, this "linkage" proved problematic for all parties involved, and negotiations failed to get off the ground. From mid-1987 to mid-1988, a number of factors served to at least open the door to a settlement, not the least of which was the broader thawing of US-USSR relations. A more proximate trigger was the sharp escalation of hostilities between the Cuban-backed MPLA and South African-backed UNITA that threatened to draw the two sponsors into a direct, large-scale confrontation neither wanted. US-brokered negotiations accordingly accelerated over the first half of 1988. The key players agreed in principle to a settlement in July 1988 and then announced a formal ceasefire in August. South Africa signed the final treaty in December 1988, essentially agreeing to the terms of UNSCR 435 from a decade earlier.[12]

The settlement required the removal of South African forces from Angola, a transition between South African forces and a UN peacekeeping mission in Namibia, and acquiescence to full independence and UN-sponsored elections for Namibia. SWAPO would be allowed to participate freely in the elections as one of several political parties. By November 1989, the last of the SADF had left Namibia, and Namibia formally became an independent state four months later. The South African NP government held out hope that the Namibian political party it had built, developed over years, and continued to back, would take control of the new government in Namibia. But this was not to be, as SWAPO emerged the winner in Namibia's first independent elections.

The Contours of Civil-Military Bargaining

At the height of South Africa's war in Namibia, political and military leadership maintained a robust and mutually supportive partnership, exhibiting consensus on strategy as well as a shared commitment to continuing the war effort. But this partnership did not exist at the outset. Botha's predecessor John Vorster came from a police background. Upon becoming prime minister in 1966, Vorster accordingly turned to his long-time associate Chief of Police Hendrik van den Bergh to form and head a new security department, the Bureau for State Security. The mandate was to coordinate and oversee all government intelligence operations. In practice, however, Vorster and Van den Bergh used the bureau to consolidate personal control over all state organs, to include the SADF. Consequently, the SADF found itself on the losing end of bureaucratic battles for resources and influence, marginalized in favor of the South African Police (SAP) and other internal security organizations.[13]

Military leadership was especially troubled by the decision to give primary responsibility for external counterinsurgency operations, including those in Namibia, to the SAP. Not surprisingly, this move was instituted under the recommendation and direction of Van den Bergh. General Viljoen explains, "We resented it when Vorster, under pressure from Van den Bergh, used the police in Rhodesia. We felt it was a military task. Then the situation arose in South West Africa (Namibia) and we knew the police would not have the capacity to do the job. We wanted to do it... We thought they were trespassing on our terrain."[14] This situation changed, however, in 1973 when it became clear the police did not, in fact, have the capacity to do the job. SADF troops began deploying to Namibia in large numbers in 1973, and the SADF was given formal responsibility for the operational area in early 1974.

Although the move pleased SADF leadership, civil-military relations did not improve, and military leadership increasingly criticized the Vorster administration for its overly cautious approach to Namibia.[15] Civil-military conflict came to a head in 1975 over the decision to launch the initial cross-border operation into Angola. Military leadership had long recommended raids into Angola, but Van den Bergh opposed and had effectively blocked any such action. Vorster finally gave in and authorized Operation Savannah in late 1975, although it was scaled-down from what the SADF recommended. And when the operation stalled, military leadership was quick to point the finger at Vorster for the debacle, suggesting the prime minister had imposed too many restrictions on the SADF while failing to provide adequate resources. Behind the scenes, Vorster's political rival P. W. Botha, then serving as Minister of Defense, joined military leadership in critiquing Vorster's approach to the war. Steenkamp recalls, "On the one hand there was Vorster, strongly influenced by his henchman Van den Bergh's open contempt for the military viewpoint. On the other hand there was the more pugnacious Botha, totally supportive of his generals' argument that it was necessary to reach beyond the borders in order to contain the insurgency."[16]

The Civil-Military Partnership under Botha

In 1978, Vorster stepped down amidst the "Muldergate" domestic intelligence scandal, clearing the way for Botha's election as prime minister. Serving as minister of defense since 1966, Botha had developed close ties with, and was highly respected by, military leadership even before taking over as executive. For the SADF, his election was a welcome development. General Malan explains, "For the first time we had the advantage in having a prime minister who came through the military and not the police... He was fairly involved in the military because, remember, he had the experience of Savannah and he learned the lessons that we did in Savannah and he applied them. He gave us the money."[17]

Malan's latter point on money is well put. From his time as minister of defense, Botha had pushed to expand, modernize, and better fund the SADF. As prime minister, he continued this trend. From the perspective of military leadership, "the prime minister's demonstrated concern with the institutional interests of the SADF" stood in "sharp contrast to previous experiences with lackluster civil leadership."[18] Further, Botha gained the trust and loyalty of the SADF as a whole by eschewing political manipulation and "divide and conquer" tactics. According to a mid-1980s assessment, "Botha is held is held in very high regard by the military chiefs because he has consistently advanced Defence Force interests largely without injecting political strife into relations between the various power blocs internal to the military... In the South African situation, the executive has sought to curry favor among the soldiers by addressing itself to the interests of the military as a whole institution."[19]

Beyond the boost in resources, Botha also provided military leadership a more prominent role in the state apparatus. One of Botha's first actions as prime minister was to demand the resignation of Van den Bergh and strip the Bureau for State Security of much of its resources, autonomy, and responsibilities, most of this to the advantage of the SADF. The reorganization was formalized with the creation of the National Security Management System (NSMS) centered on the State Security Council (SSC) in 1979. Granted key positions throughout this system, senior SADF leaders became entrenched within the core of South African policy-making processes, particularly as related to the Namibia conflict.[20] Given the increased prominence of the SADF under Botha, there was chatter in left-wing circles of a silent military coup; but this was only talk, as Botha remained jealous of his authority and independence of action. Military leaders never dictated policy but instead were "extremely well positioned to make their views heard."[21]

In terms of preferences associated with the war, the new prime minister quickly made clear a hardline stance toward Namibia, stating shortly after his election, "I am not going to allow foreign people to foist a minority government with guns on the majority of the people of South West Africa (Namibia)... as long as these conditions exist, there will be no withdrawal of South African troops."[22] In 1979, the new government produced its first Defense White Paper, which explicitly outlined South Africa's increasing military responsibility in Namibia and also implicitly warned surrounding states of the costs for harboring and supporting the insurgents.[23] Up until 1988, Botha remained defiant of the United Nations and showed little sign of wavering in his commitment to the war and associated objectives. Military leadership similarly exhibited a strong preference of staying the course. Having nearly unfettered access to SADF leadership of the period, South African journalist Hilton Hamann concludes, "In all my interviews with the generals, not once did they give an inkling of anything other than unfaltering support for P. W. (Botha), and they were fully behind the war effort."[24] Senior military leaders made clear they could, and were quite willing to, fight as long as necessary to achieve a favorable outcome. And when needed, they signaled to the politicians "that they (the politicians) had better not do anything impetuous or irresolute."[25]

The Basis of Military Leadership Preferences

For the SADF, there were clearly bureaucratic incentives associated with the ongoing war in Namibia. The war brought with it increased resources, greater influence within the state apparatus, and, after 1974, advantages vis-à-vis bureaucratic rivals. But the war was also relevant to perceptions of legitimacy. Trying to explain the SADF's level of commitment, US envoy Chester Crocker described the war as not only "a means of assuring plentiful military budgets" but also "a source of prestige and status."[26] In the mid-1980s, Frankel similarly characterized the war as enhancing the "symbolic values of the military establishment" and providing a "measure of their social status and their professional self-esteem."[27] Military leaders basked in the knowledge that, among the relevant political community, "Troopies were affectionately regarded as sons and protectors of white South Africa . . . the revered warriors defending the Republic's borders against Communist takeover."[28] Failure in Namibia could hurt this image at home and also diminish the SADF's status in the region. Neither was acceptable to the generals.

Another relevant aspect of this case is the lack of blame directed at the SADF. Botha generally heeded military advice and gave the military a great deal of leeway in its conduct of operations. At the same time, Botha made clear he would accept responsibility for an unfavorable outcome and also took pains to shield the military from backlash associated with the conduct of these operations. Similar to other counterinsurgency campaigns, there were periodic reports of atrocities, civilian killings, and other human rights abuses committed by the armed forces. As seen with the case of Israel in Lebanon, the insurgents exaggerated and exploited such incidents to generate media attention.[29] In contrast to his counterpart in Israel, however, Botha refused to publically censure the SADF and instead worked with his generals, who recognized the potential harm to both the counterinsurgency campaign and domestic support, behind closed doors to curb further incidents. The upshot was a greater degree of trust and collaboration, as military leadership remained confident Botha would not try to protect himself by throwing the SADF under the proverbial bus.

Why Persistence was Difficult

Persistence in this case, especially for 20 plus years, was not a given. The government had to deal with an active and well-organized anti-war movement, intense international pressure, internal turmoil associated with apartheid-era policies, a heavy reliance on conscription, and a domestic coalition of religious leaders, academic elites, and liberal politicians critical of the war and advocating withdrawal. Further, the Namibian insurgency enjoyed widespread international support, substantial financial and military backing, and, after 1975, a safe haven in Angola. By the early 1980s, contemporary observers were likening South Africa's experience in Namibia to that of the United States in Vietnam and questioning the government's resolve to continue the war effort much longer.[30] On top of this, the white electorate remained highly sensitive to casualties, and Botha recognized that domestic support for the war could easily be lost.

As leader of the centrist NP, Botha found himself and the government's war policy under attack by the opposition of both the left and the right. His ability to prosecute the war over the long run, and keep his job in the process, hinged upon defending against each. Maintaining the necessary domestic support was problematic for a number of reasons. In absolute terms, South African casualties were not that high. But the bulk of the SADF consisted of white soldiers, and at the peak of the war, the minority white population of South Africa only numbered around five million. By percentage of the white population, SADF casualty rates at the height of the war were on par with those seen with the United States in Vietnam and France in Algeria.

Military conscription also took a heavy toll. Merom points to a reliance on conscripts and civilian reserve forces as highly detrimental to the state's capacity to prosecute small war over the long run.[31] As evidence, he looks primarily at Israel's reliance on these types of forces in Lebanon (1982–85). The Israeli case is relevant because the SADF was modeled after the IDF, and for the period of interest, South Africa's reliance on conscripts and citizen-soldiers was at least on par with that seen in Israel. At the outset of the Namibian conflict, the Permanent Force amounted to only 9 percent of total SADF strength. South Africa instituted universal conscription for white males in 1967, and in 1977 the period of compulsory national service was extended from one to two years. After completing this period of full-time national service, every conscript was required to remain in the civilian reserves for 12 years; and throughout the war, reserve call ups became more frequent and of greater duration. By the early 1980s, SADF manpower had increased from approximately 150,000 to 500,000, but the size of the Permanent Force remained relatively constant at around 10 percent of the total force. As result, South Africa had one of the highest rates of compulsory military service in the world.[32]

Opposition to compulsory service became the central theme of the domestic antiwar movement. Significant domestic antiwar activity first emerged in the mid-1970s, centered on the issue of conscientious objection and facilitated by English (as opposed to Afrikaner) religious organizations.[33] By the early 1980s, the locus had shifted to university campuses, with the movement consolidated around the theme of putting a stop to conscription. This shift was reflected in the formation of the End Conscription Campaign (ECC), an umbrella organization for over 50 different protest groups.[34] The ECC would eventually adopt a wide range of social issues and become a key player in the internal antiapartheid struggle. But its primary focus at the start was ending South African involvement in Namibia, establishing the "No War in Namibia" platform as its first order of business.[35] At its peak in the mid-1980s, the ECC was active, well-organized, and received a great deal of media attention. Further, as ECC leader Laurie Nathan observes, the ECC's efforts aimed at ending the Namibian war were "characterized by a level of creativity unknown in white politics."[36] Beyond the more radical elements involved directly with this protest movement, the NP government also faced a coalition of religious leaders, academic elites, and liberal politicians—precisely the type of group Merom claims is able to "take control over the agenda" and check a government's war policy—at least skeptical of, if not openly opposed to, ongoing military actions in Namibia and Angola.[37]

The international community's condemnation of South Africa's operations in Namibia fueled these domestic critics. From day one of the war, South Africa was subjected to harsh external criticism and international pressure to end the war.[38] The United States initially provided behind-the-scenes encouragement and assistance to South Africa's military efforts in the region. But this came to an end with the passage of the Clark Amendment in January 1976, which effectively disavowed South Africa military action and fostered a sense of outrage and abandonment among South African leadership.[39] External pressure intensified in 1977 with sanctions in the form of an arms embargo and the issuance of UN Security Council Resolution 435 demanding an immediate ceasefire with SWAPO and withdrawal of South African forces.[40] In 1983, the Security Council adopted Resolution 539, which "condemns South

Africa for its continued illegal occupation of Namibia in flagrant defiance of the General Assembly and decisions of the Security Council."[41] Altogether, from 1966 to 1989, there were over a thousand statements and initiatives put forth by different UN bodies in opposition to South Africa's actions in Namibia.[42]

External critique did not come only from foreign governments and international institutions, but also from the foreign, primarily Western, press. Throughout the conflict, the Western press was highly critical of South African military activities and often facilitated the spread of SWAPO propaganda. The Western press was particularly sensitive to stories of atrocities and civilian deaths, and South Africa's adversaries were happy to exploit this sensitivity. The Cassinga raid of 1978 stands out in this regard. As part of an incursion into Angola known as Operation Reindeer, the SADF launched an air and ground attack against a suspected SWAPO training base located near a number of Namibian refugee camps. The SADF reported the deaths of nearly 1,000 terrorists in the action, but SWAPO and MPLA spokespersons claimed that most of those killed were civilian refugees to include women and children. Five days after the incident, MPLA leadership transported a group of Western correspondents to visit Cassinga and made sure the visitors "could make out the brightly colored dresses of a large number of women among the dead."[43]

On top of all of these other challenges was simply the war's duration and the high potential for war weariness. As noted up front, 20 years into the war, there were no clear signs of success and no clear indications the war could soon be won, only vague descriptions of the terrorists "deteriorating." Yet the NP government under Botha showed little sign of wavering in its commitment, and the bulk of the white electorate continued to exhibit support for the war and how it was being conducted.

Why Persistence was Possible (and probable)

Despite the factors discussed above, for Botha, the potential domestic costs of ending the war under less-than-favorable terms were probably greater than the domestic costs of continuing the war. In the early 1980s, prominent South African journalist Willem Steenkamp reported, "Domestic opinion within the White electorate had to be taken into account. Generally speaking, the electorate accepted the necessity for the war, but on the other hand, a failure – particularly one which involved heavy casualties—would be a political disaster for the South

African government."[44] With a loss in Namibia, Botha risked the fall of the NP government or at least his own ouster as NP chief and head of the government.

But again, to keep the war going and keep his job in the process, Botha had to defend the government's war policies against attacks coming from the left and the right. The active collaboration of military leadership enabled this effort in two broad respects. First, this collaboration bolstered Botha's justification of the ongoing war and its associated costs, thus hedging against critique and blame emanating from the left. This included political and military leadership working hand in hand to undermine the antiwar movement and also limit the extent to which the political opposition could benefit from this movement. Second, civil-military collaboration curbed the ability of the right-wing opposition to target the NP government for not doing enough to win the war.

Civil-Military Collaboration (in favor of continuing the war)

From early on, the NP government conducted an aggressive domestic information campaign tied to the war in Namibia. This became more pronounced in 1975, roughly the point at which the conflict was proving to be much longer and far more costly than expected at the outset. From then on, "Maintaining the credibility of South Africa's presence in Namibia and the prosecution of the Border War was an important political project for the National Party government."[45] The associated information campaign had two broad aims. The first was fostering public confidence in the eventual success of the military campaign. The second was a widespread acceptance of the "total onslaught" narrative linking war in Namibia to the broader threat of Communism and Black Nationalism. The combined message was that the protracted war in Namibia was both winnable and worthwhile. And this message seemed to stick. According to polls taken at the peak of the war, a large majority of South Africans remained convinced that the Communist threat to South Africa was real, South Africa *could* win the military struggle against SWAPO in the long run, and South Africa should *not* negotiate with SWAPO to reach a settlement in Namibia.[46]

Military leadership was a full partner in this project. In 1977, the SADF established its own Public Relations Directorate as a full-time office staffed by professional journalists. This office, serving as a press liaison and locus of the military's public relations efforts, continued to grow and become more professionalized over the subsequent decade. By 1980 the SADF was putting out at least 20 different publications for both internal military and broader domestic consumption, with a number of these publications aimed at generating and maintaining support for the SADF's role in Namibia. The SADF even used its helicopters to drop pamphlets encouraging public support for the war and denouncing the peace crowd.[47]

Beyond developing and utilizing its own internal capabilities, the SADF took advantage of external sources and media outlets to articulate its views on the war and support for the government's war policy. Toward this end, the SADF worked to establish close ties with journalists and capitalized on its access to the operational area. Baines describes,

> The SADF attempted to win over the local media by inviting carefully vetted journalists and military correspondents to accompany units in the field... These public relations exercises clearly convinced the correspondents who duly reported that the SADF's prowess and superior training ensured victory. Thus the mainstream media that monopolized radio and television broadcasts lent their support to the "boys on the border."[48]

By controlling access in this manner, military leadership not only developed useful links with the media but was also able to dictate the flow of information. On this point, Pottinger depicts the SADF as the "purveyors" and "guardians" of information related to the ongoing war and further suggests that SADF public relations sections exploited this power sparingly but "suavely."[49] Military leadership also exhibited bias in terms of which politicians were permitted to see the war zone first hand. While the SADF regularly assisted NP "fact-finding" missions in this regard, right-wing Conservative Party (CP) and left-wing Progressive Federal Party (PFP) politicians were often left in the lurch. The lack of equal access handicapped the opposition in policy debates, and it is not surprising that both CP and PFP leadership registered complaints against the SADF for exhibiting partisan favoritism in the selection of war zone visitors.[50]

Undermining the Left-Wing Opposition

Political and military leaders also collaborated in undermining the antiwar movement as well as the opposition's ability to capitalize upon this movement. The primary target here was the ECC. SADF leadership joined the NP government in denigrating the ECC and everyone involved with the movement as unpatriotic, Communist sympathizers. According to a report put out by the ECC in the final year of the war, "The cumulative effect of the smears was very damaging... They successfully created in many people's minds the perception of ECC as treasonous."[51] The result was that, despite high levels of activity, the antiwar movement never expanded significantly beyond its natural, limited support base and was never able to mobilize significant segments of the white community.[52] Further, it had negligible sway on the government's war policy. ECC leader Laurie Nathan concedes that the ECC remained a "marginal pressure group on the fringes of white politics," confined to radical sectors while "the broader white community regarded it as irrelevant and subversive."[53]

The left-wing opposition, represented by the PFP, was generally opposed to the government's war policy and sought a more conciliatory approach to dealing with the Namibian problem. Still the PFP remained hesitant to align itself with the ECC or related organizations despite the fact the ECC and PFP drew from the same core support base.[54] Just as the Israeli Labor Party feared domestic backlash from an association with the Peace Now movement, the PFP recognized that ties to the ECC could have serious political consequences. The ECC sought to undermine the government's war policy by protesting conscription and exorbitant defense spending. Such arguments played well in certain religious and academic circles but carried serious risks for political actors. In 1984, a South African political analyst observed that given the "visibility and prestige of the military today... it is difficult for any white politician intent on survival to denigrate the value of military service, to deny military expenditure or claims."[55] The NP government took advantage of this constraint. After criticizing the antiwar movement and naming the ECC as "a direct enemy of the SADF" at a preelection public forum, General (retired) Malan called out the political opposition in stating, "The Progressive Federal Party does nothing about it. I wish to ask the PFP: Where do you stand in regard to the ECC? Where is your patriotism?"[56] During the lead-up to the 1987 elections, the NP likewise branded the PFP as being "in league with" the ECC. While not entirely accurate, this alleged linkage still hurt the PFP at the polls.[57]

The Threat from the Right-Wing Opposition

Overall, the left-wing opposition remained relatively hedged in its critique of the government's war policy and refrained from taking meaningful steps to curtail the war effort. Botha had more trouble with the hawkish right wing. Critique emanating from the right-wing Conservative Party and similar opposition groups was broadly of the nature that the government was not doing enough to defeat SWAPO and protect South African interests in Namibia. As seen with General Westmoreland and President Johnson in Vietnam, SADF leadership checked such claims by endorsing Botha's policy and the level of support provided to the military. This endorsement proved highly effective up until the mid-1980s when the white regime came under increasing internal threat from the ANC, and the NP government responded by implementing limited domestic reforms.

Playing upon the fears of the white population, the right-wing opposition attacked these reforms and tied Botha's lack of resolve in the domestic arena to his inability to secure victory over SWAPO in Namibia. The opposition also pointed to the government's lack of success in Namibia as a cause of the ANC's rise. As result, Botha felt pressured to step up military activity, and the increasing forays into Angola ostensibly had both military and political rationales. According to Van Rooyen, these cross-border strikes "became a common method... of demonstrating to the white electorate that the NP, in spite of its reforms, had not lost its capacity for strong-arm tactics."[58] Still the NP lost significant ground to the CP in the 1987 general and 1988 municipal elections, largely as backlash for the domestic reforms and an inability to quell growing internal violence. The NP maintained control of the government, but its hold on power was becoming more tenuous.

For Botha, then, the domestic unrest associated with failing apartheid-era policies increased the potential political costs of failure in Namibia. There were numerous indicators the increasingly influential right-wing opposition would exploit any settlement that left SWAPO in place to target the NP government, especially in the event the ANC continued to gain ground and the domestic situation in South Africa continued to deteriorate. Observing this dynamic, a South African political analyst noted the NP government had become more constrained by "a resurgent right... which is bound to derive considerable capital from any situation which even remotely appears as a 'sell-out' of white interests" in Namibia.[59]

The Politics of Withdrawal

Up until 1987, there were few signs the war was nearing an end. According to Crocker, however, "The second half of 1987 was the great turning point in the long history of the Namibia and Angola conflicts.

This was the moment when the situation 'ripened.'"[60] There has been a great deal written on the various external factors that made the situation "ripe" for a settlement. The thawing of the Cold War provided the broader context, with the Soviet Union exhibiting a waning interest in propping up its surrogates in Angola and Namibia. The relevance of South Africa's "total onslaught" justification concomitantly began to wane. Likewise, Cuba was sending credible, albeit mixed, signals that it was prepared to leave Angola in exchange for a South African withdrawal from Namibia in accordance with UN directives. In the meantime, the situation in Angola was getting out of hand. When SADF and UNITA troops threatened the MPLA stronghold of Cuito Cuanavale in late 1987, Castro introduced another 15,000 Cuban troops along with heavy weaponry into Angola, positioning most of these troops in the southwestern Cunene Province, provokingly close to the Namibian border. In response, the South African government activated another 140,000 soldiers from the Citizen Force and threatened to turn northern Namibia into a killing field. Neither side wanted an escalation to the conflict, yet, as Crocker recalls,

> The risks of hairtrigger reactions and miscalculations were substantial. No matter what Castro's true objectives were, his bold moves risked being misperceived, triggering a major confrontation . . . It was a scenario fraught with dangers. A small spark—caused, for example by a SWAPO contact in Cunene Province—could have ignited a cycle of bigger clashes engaging the honor and pride of P. W. Botha and Fidel Castro, two high-strung gentlemen.[61]

In Namibia, SWAPO was not beaten and still remained a powerful political actor, but the South Africans had spent at least a decade building up local political and legal institutions aimed at protecting white interests and containing extremist political elements within a future Namibian government. South African pundits assessed that "by 1988 these preconditions had been prepared for as far as was politically possible."[62] Further, South Africa was very much concerned about its economic position, and as part of its overall strategy, the government enacted measures to ensure South African capital would continue to dominate the Namibian economy despite a lack of political control. By the late 1980s, there was progress in this arena as well; and "as details of Namibian financial dependency unfolded" after the war ended, "it became evident just how manipulative the South African government had been."[63]

The Sellout Narrative and Policy Stalemate

For all of these reasons, by early-1988, a withdrawal from Namibia linked to Cuban departure from Angola made strategic sense despite the failure to defeat SWAPO. But this did not make things easy for Botha or unify the NP government around a given course of action. Domestic factors were still at play. Again, the NP government was taking a beating from the right-wing opposition based on domestic policies, and a loss in Namibia could make this even worse. Botha did not start the war but had very much come to own the war. Years of pro-war propaganda and scare tactics aimed at the left were coming back to haunt the NP government, with the right-wing opposition applying the same rhetoric to discredit the government, undermine any move toward a settlement, and raise the specter of a *sellout* narrative. On the latter, Crocker elaborates, "The negative political imagery of a UN-led transition that would favor SWAPO . . . and the prospect of a chaotic exodus from Namibia of its white minority, leading to charges at home of a sellout . . . played directly into the most neuralgic points of white South African politics.[64]

The result was indecision and policy stalemate at the top. After ten days of observing the South African government in early 1988, a US official reported he had "seldom seen a government so utterly confused and at cross-purposes over basic questions of policy."[65] In March 1988, South Africa agreed to talks but at first tried to take Namibia out of the equation, with NP government officials "pushing the line that perhaps it would be better if everyone just forgot Namibia for a while and concentrated on Angola . . . Today, it would be very difficult to persuade anyone at the top to contemplate leaving Namibia."[66] But this attempt to separate the matters and maintain the status quo in Namibia was a nonstarter with the other parties to negotiations and led Crocker to observe, "To say that the South Africans were behind the curve in March 1988 would be an understatement."[67]

Civil-Military Collaboration (in favor of ending the war)

The South Africans eventually came around, though, and, after eight months of frustrating negotiations, agreed to a final settlement dictating the complete removal of South African forces from Angola, a transition between South African forces and a UN peacekeeping mission in Namibia, and acquiescence to full independence and UN-sponsored elections for Namibia. The progress from March to December toward this final outcome was gradual, with no clear trigger or dramatic turn of events. What stands out about the end game, though, is that instead of siding with pro-war factions, as seen with the Dutch army in Indonesia, SADF leadership backed negotiations and worked to create a unified front in favor of the settlement.

SADF leadership remained committed to, and supportive of, Botha's war policy throughout. However, starting around the mid-1980s, there was a subtle softening of the SADF's stance. At a minimum, senior military leaders became increasingly "attentive to the 'dove' argument that further military investment in Namibia represents wasted resources" and that South Africa's total strategy and security interests might best be served by consolidation behind national borders.[68] Further, SADF leaders had long conceived the role of military operations as setting the conditions for a political solution in Namibia. In this sense, military leadership often exhibited a more "political" perspective than did political leadership.[69] General Viljoen's recollection is illustrative:

> I think the politicians in South Africa had a very unrealistic dependence on the military. They didn't realize that in this type of clash the military only represents about 20 percent of the clash and 80 percent is the political, psychological and economic situation. I recall in the days when I was Chief of the Army and later Chief of the SADF at least four occasions where the Command Council of the Defence Force briefed the Cabinet on the kind of war that was going on. I remember being very frank with the Cabinet, telling them we could carry on militarily for a very long period but eventually they would have to make some political moves to solve the problem.[70]

By the late 1980s, the need for a political solution was becoming even more apparent. SADF leadership also feared that an escalation in Angola would fail to garner the same level of public support enjoyed when operations were clearly centered on Namibia.[71]

Conway goes so far to suggest that in this final stage, SADF leadership "pressed NP leaders for a swift end to the Border War" via a settlement.[72] This may have been true, but any such effort was kept well hidden and was much subtler than seen in other cases. The high level of civil-military collaboration seen with efforts to justify and maintain the war effort continued once the government began to look for a way out. According to Crocker, who has first-hand knowledge of the dealings, SADF leadership, Chief of Staff Jannie Geldenhuys in particular, in the end determined that victory was "not in the works" and that "continued war would not lead anywhere."[73] But Geldenhuys and other senior officers remained loyal to Botha, disciplined not to say or do anything to undermine or pressure the government, suggest a civil-military gap, or cast political leadership in a negative light. Geldenhuys accordingly refrained from making the types of public gestures seen with General Spinola in Portugal and General Levi in Israel. Still, Crocker observes, "I knew in my gut he (Geldenhuys) wanted this (the settlement) to work."[74] The SADF as a whole remained divided over the best course of action in Namibia and Angola, with some officers less amenable to a negotiations; but once the negotiations were underway, the SADF chief of staff worked to ride herd on the more hawkish elements, quietly but effectively curbing the remaining "ideological enthusiasm" among the officer corps.[75]

Further, Geldenhuys was assigned as a lead, and highly visible, member of South Africa's negotiating team. By itself, this was significant in that any resultant peace agreement would automatically have the imprimatur of the SADF. The SADF chief also recognized that in pursuing a settlement, the NP government would be "walking down a hazardous trail" and saw it as his job to "blaze the trail" and then "escort political leadership down it."[76] He worked at the edge of his mandate in trying to achieve an agreement acceptable to all parties but also remained sensitive to Botha's domestic constraints and the need to be able to present the exit as an honorable and voluntary one. At one point, for example, Geldenhuys chastised his counterpart from Cuba for Cuban rhetoric, making clear he could not "sell a final pull-out at home if it were being described by the other side as some sort of retreat at gunpoint."[77] At the same time, Geldenhuys did what was necessary to "gently steer P. W. Botha and his faithful sidekick Magnus Malan (Minister of Defense) away from positions that would have killed negotiations."[78]

Once the key delegates to negotiations had tentatively agreed to a deal, the SADF chief worked to sell Botha on the merits of the settlement but kept these discussions behind closed doors. According to Crocker, these efforts were successful, and, overall, Geldenhuys was instrumental in unifying the civil-military team behind the settlement.[79] In this manner, military leadership played an important facilitative role but did not feed into or bolster the opposition's critique. This proved critical to breaking the government out of its indecision and stalemate. And it made Botha's difficult choice at least somewhat easier. In the end, as Marcum observes, "The National Party government of P. W. Botha concluded that it could weather allegations of a Namibian 'sell out.'"[80]

Postwar Legitimation

For South Africa, the outcome of the war was neither a clear-cut victory nor an obvious defeat. Regardless, once the matter was decided, Geldenhuys and other military leaders proceeded to promote the settlement as a military and political success. Geldenhuys claimed South Africa's campaign in Namibia "must be rated among the most successful wars of its kind since World War II." Countering the claim South Africa had achieved nothing, he responded, "It was not our strategy to gain a quick overall military victory; it certainly was to fight over a period in order to create a situation conducive to the favorable settling of political disputes. And that we did."[81] General Viljoen echoed, "There is absolutely no doubt we won the military war... We never lost a battle. Our victory had a direct bearing on the collapse of the Soviet Union."[82] Such sentiments were at least in part self-serving. SADF leadership was anxious to defend its own performance against critics, and there was likely some symbolic legitimation at play. For military leadership to defend its performance in this way is the norm. But it is still significant that SADF leadership refrained from directing blame at the NP government for any shortcomings to include the failure after over 20 years of fighting to bring SWAPO to its knees. This is not the norm.

In reference to the war in Namibia, Liebenberg does not credit SADF leadership with the same facilitative role that characterized its counterpart in the Portuguese case. Critiquing the SADF, she writes, "One may conclude that if only South Africa had generals of the caliber of Anotnio de Spinola, who rejected the impulses of an authoritarian state and its frontier army and questioned the hawkish politicians... would things not have turned out far differently earlier?"[83] The "caliber" of military leaders aside, Liebenberg fails to mention that Spinola backed Portugal's protracted wars in Africa for 13 years before deciding it was time to get out. The SADF took over responsibility for the counterinsurgency effort in Namibia in 1974. Fourteen years later, Geldenhuys similarly determined "continued war would not lead anywhere." But instead of going to the media and stirring up domestic trouble as seen in Portugal, or in Israel for that matter, Geldenhuys worked quietly yet effectively to steer political leadership toward a negotiated settlement. The end state in terms of bringing protracted war to a close was essentially the same. The real difference between the South African and Portuguese cases was not the caliber of military leadership but instead the caliber of the civil-military bargain.

CHAPTER 7

Conclusion

This book addresses political leadership behavior after the state is embroiled in war that has proven longer, costlier, and more difficult than expected at the outset. But it says nothing about why states have repeatedly found themselves in such circumstances. The simplest answer may be, as Walt articulates, "Getting out of a quagmire is a whole lot harder than getting into one."[1] But to some extent, the phenomenon also stems from an arrogance of power and faith in technology that is often disabused only to be reborn at another time and in another form. After the rapid collapse of the Afghani Taliban in 2002, leading defense analysts were quick to proclaim the "Afghan Model" as a revolutionary new form of warfare that would allow the external power to rapidly achieve extensive military and political objectives on the cheap, thus mitigating the pitfalls of protracted armed conflict.[2] Reflecting a hint of irony, the war in Afghanistan (2001-??) would become the longest in US history. Whatever the reason, states will likely continue to engage in the types of costly, protracted, and stalemated wars discussed throughout this book. And to the extent this occurs, political leaders will continue to struggle with the dilemma of "how to bring an end to the war without being blamed for how it ended."[3]

Considering the Evidence

The preceding chapters advanced the argument that the interplay between political and military leadership affects the domestic politics of war termination by altering blame attribution. The associated risk of culpability factors into a political leader's wartime calculus, influencing whether he or she will remain committed to fighting a protracted armed conflict or else prove willing to cede all or some of the state's objectives and withdraw short of victory. While relevant to all political leaders, the effects of civil-military bargaining are most pronounced with those who come to power after the start of the war.

The empirical analysis provides at least moderate support for this argument. A key observation from the cross-case analysis is that leadership change, by itself, is a poor predictor of political leadership behavior. While the leadership change model can effectively account for the behavior of initial political leaders, it does not do as well with new political leaders. The analysis also suggests a combined framework linking the effects of leadership change and civil-military bargaining may be useful for understanding the behavior of political leaders of both types. Although rudimentary, this framework succeeds with 86 percent of the 81 cross-case observations.[4]

Further, the cross-case findings are consistent with the claim that given an obstructive bargaining scenario, the behaviors of initial and new political leaders should, in aggregate, converge; and given a facilitative scenario, these behaviors should diverge, with new political leaders being more likely to withdraw. These findings suggest an answer to the original empirical puzzle of variation in behavior among new leaders and the question of why so many new leaders, despite being non-culpable in the conventional sense, still struggle to extricate the state from costly, protracted war. At a minimum, the cross-case analysis yields an empirical pattern consistent with the proposed logic and thus provides a basis for assessing the underlying causal mechanisms through more detailed within-case analysis.

The case of Israel in Lebanon is useful in that it provides observations of both initial and new political leaders bargaining with facilitative military leadership. The Likud government responsible for starting the war found itself in a difficult position once military leadership made clear it was collectively committed to withdrawal. Following this shift, the opposition became more brazen in its attacks, criticizing the government for unnecessary bloodshed and for refusing to withdraw despite the best professional advice of the IDF, in effect exploiting the civil-military gap to cast the incumbent as a *squanderer*. Public support for the war, which had remained strong even at the peak of the liberal antiwar movement, began to wane. This mattered, but not enough to make Prime Minister Shamir and the rest of the Likud government back down and affect a meaningful policy shift. The case thus shows how initial political leadership remains prone to persistence even with facilitative military leadership.

In contrast, after taking control of the government following the 1984 elections, Prime Minister Peres of the Labor Party proved both willing and able to extricate Israeli forces relatively quickly. On the surface, the case aligns well with the basic leadership change logic. But the case also illustrates why ending a war can still be difficult for new leaders and why securing the collaboration of military leadership matters. There is no way to determine how this case would have played out if military leadership had taken the opposite stance and actively opposed Peres' efforts to withdraw from Lebanon. What is clear, though, is that Peres viewed military leadership's endorsement as vital. Peres faced powerful pro-war rivals seeking to undermine his efforts, and there is evidence he feared being blamed if terrorist attacks followed the IDF as it retreated back to Israel. Pundits with intimate knowledge of the domestic setting openly questioned whether the new prime minister would have the courage to extricate the IDF from Lebanon given the potential of being branded a traitor, a charge closely connected to the *sellout* narrative. Under these circumstances, Peres aggressively pursued military leadership's backing and then capitalized on this support in his dealings with the opposition as well as the Israeli public. At a minimum, civil-military collaboration mattered because Peres believed and behaved as if it mattered. And even if withdrawal was not surprising, the fact that the majority of Israelis approved of an outcome generally perceived as the state's first military defeat is fairly remarkable.

The Netherlands in Indonesia is a more difficult case in that new political leadership elected to withdraw despite military leadership playing an obstructive role. Further, political leadership accomplished this withdrawal relatively quickly and avoided domestic repercussions in the process. Such an outcome counts as a definitive "failure" within the framework of the cross-case analysis. Nonetheless, the challenge of bargaining with obstructive military leadership still affected domestic politics and altered new political leadership's behavior in a manner that hindered or delayed war termination. In this sense, the case highlights the limitations of the cross-case analysis. The case also highlights the difficulty of isolating domestic political factors even in the small war context. The threat of international sanctions played an important part, which is something the book's argument, focused on domestic factors, fails to take into account. Prior to international sanctions emerging as a dominant factor, though, political leadership behavior was very much in line with the proposed logic. And instead of subsuming the proposed logic in this case, the intervening factor of international sanctions provides an interesting twist to both civil-military bargaining and the dynamics of blame attribution.

One of the most intriguing aspects of the Dutch case is Prime Minister Drees' decision to not only approve but also openly endorse the Second Police Action. We know Drees favored a negotiated settlement in accordance with UNSC demands. He privately opposed the military escalation, doubted it would have the decisive outcome military leadership claimed, and recognized that severe international sanctions would likely follow. But from the perspective of a strategic blame minimizer, his behavior makes perfect sense. Whether calculated or not, Drees deftly played the hand he was dealt and thus succeeded where many political leaders in the same position have failed. Although less extreme, the Second Police Action served a similar function as the Battle of Buzenval during the Franco-Prussian War. Drees gave military leadership a free hand and made sure the public knew he had given military leadership a free hand. When the action failed to bring the Republic to its knees, the assertion victory was readily within reach lost credibility. And once the sanctions came "thick and fast" as Drees anticipated, even the KVP had little choice but to reconsider its position. It is telling that KVP stalwart Louis Beel introduced the plan that would eventually serve as the basis for a settlement. Further, the sanctions presented the Dutch government the opportunity to shift blame from the domestic to the international arena. Drees could credibly argue he had done everything he could to support the military and win the war, but the UNSC had forced a negotiated settlement. The unexpected and untimely death of General Spoor, in some respects the Dutch equivalent of General MacArthur, also probably helped. Again, the outcome of the Israeli case is interesting in that the bulk of the population approved of the withdrawal. The Dutch case is equally interesting in that the bulk of the population opposed the final settlement yet political leadership came away unscathed.

South Africa in Namibia represents an extreme case in terms of both the duration of the conflict and the closeness of ties between political and military leadership. The case thus proves useful for assessing how such ties can aid a political leader in efforts to maintain domestic support and keep the opposition at bay even as a costly war drags on for decades with no clear end in sight. Perhaps a more interesting aspect of this case, though, is how the high level of civil-military collaboration, initially geared toward efforts to keep the war going, stayed intact during efforts to bring the war to a close. As seen in cases ranging from the United States in Vietnam to France in Algeria, this is not the norm.

The Namibian war did not have to end in 1989. It could have easily continued, without really surprising anyone, until 1994 when the NP ceded control of the government to the African National Congress. Further, Botha did not start the war, but he very much came to own the war and exhibited some of the same "emotional and political entanglements" seen with initial leaders. For better or worse, though, Botha had developed such a strong, mutually supportive relationship with military leadership that when withdrawal from Namibia began to make more sense from a strategic perspective, he was in a better position to affect policy change and bring the war to a close despite significant domestic risks. This aligns with the claim made in chapter 3 that a high degree of leverage has the somewhat paradoxical effect of increasing the likelihood political leadership will abandon its original preference of persistence and align itself with facilitative military leadership. Again, this is because political leadership with greater leverage can make the move with less risk.

Theoretical Implications

The book's arguments and findings suggest a number of implications relevant to the study of both civil-military relations and war termination. The first is simply that political leadership change does not matter as much for war termination as is generally thought. At the same time, political leadership change matters more than some critics of the conventional wisdom suggest. The leadership change model, employing the concept of leader culpability, remains one of the most deeply entrenched domestic politics-type theories of war termination. Over the past seven decades, scholars have repeatedly shown, whether through anecdotal evidence or statistical studies, that political leaders responsible for starting a war have a hard time ending the war short of outright victory or outright defeat. But this does not imply all or even most new leaders are more apt to end protracted war. The data are relatively clear on the point that a significant number of new leaders behave in a manner similar to initial leaders. This is true even when one takes a fairly liberal view of who is responsible for the decision to go to war.

Some critics have proposed that we discard the leadership change argument altogether. This is too severe a reaction and misses some of the complex causality at play. The ouster of political leadership responsible for starting the war has a powerful effect in every case where such change occurs. But such effects are not always reflected immediately, if ever, in an observable outcome. This is because leadership change removes an important basis for blame but does not obviate the risks of blame altogether. For some, particularly those of a positivist bent, this may not be a satisfying answer. Even if one does not buy my answer, though, I believe it is still important one recognizes the puzzle, as the formulation of the right question is often more important than the solution. Recent work expanding what it means to be culpable for starting a war has done much to promote our understanding of the domestic politics of war termination. To progress further, though, we would do well to move past this focus on initial culpability and look more at variation in the behavior of new leaders. The politics of war termination often has very little to do with how the war started, or with who started the war.

In addressing unexplained variation in the behavior of new political leaders, this book helps fill an empirical gap in the literature. By applying a civil-military lens to the problem, the book also addresses an important theoretical gap. There has been a recent upturn in studies focused on the domestic politics of war termination. One can also observe growing scholarly interest in civil-military relations, and in the effects of the "civil-military variable" on a range of social and political phenomena.[5] But there is a marked lack of scholarship effectively bringing the war termination and civil-military relations literatures together. This book cuts across the two literatures, hopefully adding to and challenging each.

As noted earlier, the book purposefully avoids any form of regime-type argument. Civil-military bargaining may look different across various regimes, but it has similar effects on war termination decision-making. In this sense, the book challenges a number of competing works claiming the domestic politics of war termination looks fundamentally different based on the presence or lack of democratic institutions. Merom dismisses the role of domestic politics in nondemocracies altogether, arguing that autocratic states "are not prone to lose small wars, and when they do fail in such wars, it is mostly for realist reasons."[6] The case of Portugal in the African Territories, which I draw upon for theory building, is important in that Portugal for the relevant period represents the least democratic state in the entire population of cases. Although the Portuguese case contains an anomalous military coup, a number of other domestic political aspects of the case look similar to what is seen in cases involving liberal democracies with dysfunctional civil-military relationships. While at opposite ends of the regime-type spectrum, Caetano's dilemma looked a lot like what Prime Minister Shamir faced in Israel. Of course Caetano did not encounter the liberal antiwar movement seen in Israel or even South Africa for that matter, but there is little evidence to suggest these movements made much difference in either of the more democratic states. Regime type may matter, but civil-military bargaining also matters and can have similar effects across cases regardless of regime type.

In developing the claim that new leaders remain at risk of blame for a failed war, the book offers a novel conceptual framework of political leadership culpability, delineating the *pretender, bungler, backstabber, squanderer,* and *sellout* narratives as ideal types. Other works emphasizing political leadership culpability make no such distinction and treat blame amorphously. But all blame does not look the same, and a more refined theoretical classification is needed whether one accepts this book's classification scheme or not. By highlighting the need for and demonstrating the potential utility of such classification, the book at a minimum suggests an avenue of further theorizing and research.

Looking specifically at the "civil-military variable," the book also problematizes the prevailing conception of military leadership as rigidly obstructive. Such a view is misguided, or at least too simplistic, but has gone largely unchallenged for over four decades. Military leadership is, perhaps, strongly biased toward staying the course. This is not necessarily a bad thing. Most polities would probably prefer military leaders who want to win and are not overly quick to throw in the towel. But such bias does not mean military leadership preferences are rigid or that the pressure to end protracted war will almost always come from civilian leadership. The interplay between political and military leadership is far more complex and interesting.

The associated emphasis on the legitimacy motive not only helps explain variation in military leadership preferences but also hints at why these preferences can become so intense and why the problem of war termination can lead to extreme and unprecedented levels of civil-military conflict. Institutional legitimacy is hard enough to describe let alone observe, measure, or predict. It is for such reasons that in most studies of institutional legitimacy unrelated to the military or the problem of war termination, "legitimacy motives for organizational actions have tended to be imputed after the fact."[7] But this does not mean the concept lacks utility. Across regime type, military leaders faced with the prospect of costly, protracted, and potentially unsuccessful war consistently use terms like honor, prestige, social esteem, public trust, and the "professional good name" of the armed forces. Viewed in isolation, these sentiments could potentially be dismissed as rhetoric, a cover for more mundane bureaucratic concerns. But when combined with the extreme and unprecedented behaviors often tied to war termination, such sentiments suggest something more is going on, that something beyond what "all bureaucracies seek" is at stake.[8]

Despite the potential contributions, this book at best puts a mere dent in what Maoz and Siverson identify as an "unexplained lacuna of the politics of war." The book leaves a number of questions unanswered, and there are unresolved tensions internal to its argument. On one hand, the book claims military leadership is in a unique position—given its access to the war zone, informational advantages, epistemic authority, and moral competence—to influence how a wartime narrative resonates with the domestic audience. On the other hand, the book suggests the experience of protracted war can pose a threat to the military's institutional legitimacy, undermining the "public confidence and esteem" and "public support and political trust" shown toward the armed forces. There is an inherent tension between these two ideas.

The problem is that one can observe both dynamics at play simultaneously. In Korea, senior US military officers spoke of a "forgotten war," yet at the same time, the Truman-MacArthur dispute mesmerized the American public and shook the domestic debate; and the fired general returned home to a hero's welcome. IDF leaders complained the war in Lebanon was having a negative impact on the army's image in Israeli society, yet IDF leadership's push for an end to the war had a profound impact on the domestic political debate, arguably more so than an unprecedented level of liberal antiwar activity. Commiserating on the stalemated wars in Africa, Portuguese officers claimed the armed forces had been "humiliated, discredited, and presented to the country as if they were those mainly responsible for the disaster."[9] Yet, "desperate for a prestigious figure who could point the way out of the colonial labyrinth," the country rallied behind General Spinola.[10] This apparent dichotomy repeats itself time and again. While I sense that understanding this dichotomy is critical to understanding how the interplay between political and military leaders affects the conduct of war and its termination, this is something the book leaves unsolved.

Epilogue (April 2015): US Exit from Afghanistan

As I complete this book, the US war in Afghanistan is also slowly and fitfully coming to a close. How and when the war ends remains to be seen, but certain aspects of the case are still interesting in light of the book's claims. One thing that stands out is the steady flow of news articles, editorials, and blog posts over the past few years debating whether President Obama and other Democratic leaders should be blamed if the

United States fails in Afghanistan, and elaborating efforts by these leaders to avoid such blame.[11] While on the surface this may all just appear to be politics as usual, the implications fly in the face of one of the most deeply entrenched domestic politics-type theories of war termination. If, as the conventional wisdom suggests, those with little to no responsibility for starting a war are immune to culpability for losing a war, it makes little sense for President Obama and other Democratic leaders to worry about being blamed for Afghanistan. But these political leaders are and probably should be worried.

The war in Afghanistan may be winding down, but the endgame process is halting and erratic. In May 2014, President Obama announced a termination of US combat operations against the Taliban by the end of the year, the removal of all but 9,800 US troops by the end of 2015, and a complete exit by the end of 2016. This schedule is not coincidental. Obama's second term will end at the beginning of 2017, and according to one administration official, "The president wants his legacy to be ending overly long, overly costly and inadequately effective wars."[12] But the president and other Democratic leaders also want this legacy to be a positive one. Prior to the announcement, Obama was already under fire from Republicans for the emergence and spread of Islamic State extremists in Syria and Iraq. Critics claim Obama's pullout from Iraq in 2011 was premature, creating a vacuum, leaving Iraqi troops ill-prepared for the new threat, and placing in jeopardy what the US armed forces had worked for so many years, and had sacrificed so much, to achieve. Following the May 2014 announcement, Republicans immediately attacked the proposed Afghanistan withdrawal on grounds that the outcome would be a repeat of the collapse in Iraq. Congressman Howard McKeon, the Republican chairman of the House Armed Services Committee, pointedly asked, "Does the president seek to replicate his mistakes in Iraq, where he abandoned the region to chaos and failed to forge a real security partnership?"[13]

US military leadership also pushed back against the president's plan, with generals at the Pentagon as well as in Afghanistan echoing the perspective that the proposed withdrawal was too soon and too fast. It is no secret that civil-military interactions tied to the war have exhibited at least some tension since Obama's 2009 firing of General Stanley McChrystal, the top US commander in Afghanistan, an incident which, according to one US officer cited in the *New York Times,* "embarrassed the entire military as an institution."[14] And by some accounts, military leadership's negative view of the withdrawal policy is exacerbated by a lingering wariness toward the administration and its motives, to include an underlying perception that past decisions associated with the war have been "made with an eye to domestic politics."[15]

In a sense, though, any such eye to domestic politics might serve in military leadership's favor. In November 2014, the administration surprised many within Washington by reversing its earlier decision and laying out plans to continue combat operations at least for an additional year. According to Mark Mazzetti and Eric Schmitt of *The New York Times*, this shift "was the result of a lengthy and heated debate that laid bare the tension inside the Obama administration between two often-competing imperatives: the promise Mr. Obama made to end the war in Afghanistan, versus the demands of the Pentagon that American troops be able to successfully fulfill their remaining missions in the country."[16] Frustrated with the move, which went against the counsel of top civilian advisers, one administration official complained, "The military pretty much got what it wanted." Other Democratic lawmakers have similarly argued that in seeking to hedge domestic criticism, Obama is effectively allowing military leadership "to dictate the terms of the endgame in Afghanistan."[17] Such an assessment is not entirely accurate. There may be a gap between political and military leadership, but the opposition, taking advantage of this gap, is also playing a central role. According to David Sedney, Deputy Assistant Secretary of Defense for Afghanistan, "It's not just the generals against the civilians. It's the generals and the civilians against the White House."[18]

In March 2015, the administration hinted at the possibility of slowing the pace of troop withdrawals even further.[19] How this all plays out remains to be seen, and it would be unfair to make any assessments or draw conclusions until after the smoke finally settles, literally and figuratively. What we do know is that "every war must end," and the US war in Afghanistan is no exception. That being said, the process will likely continue to be a difficult and contentious one. Reflecting on these challenges, President Obama recently opined, "I think Americans have learned that it's harder to end wars than it is to begin them."[20] This is certainly a valuable and well-founded lesson, and it applies whether or not political leadership trying to end the war is also responsible for starting the war. Perhaps the current administration has also been reminded of the timeless lesson that when preparing for a war, "military leaders and civilian officials can effectively work together . . . by contrast, planning to end a war where victory seems out of reach is not a task on which men can easily collaborate."[21]

Appendix

Table A.1 Protracted war observations

Case	*Dates*	*Regime Type*[a]	*Casualties (KIA)*	*Outcome (End State)*	*Total Ldrs*	*New Ldrs*	*Mil Obs*[c]	*Mil Fac*[d]
China in Tibet	1956–59	-8	40000	Success	1	0	1	0
Egypt in Yemen	1962–67	-7	1000	Withdrawal	1	0	0	1
Ethiopia in Somalia	2006–09	-2	2700	Withdrawal	1	0	0	1
France in Algeria	1954–62	5[b]	17456	Withdrawal	7	5	7	0
France in Cameroon	1957–62	5[b]	600	Success	4	2	4	0
France in Indochina	1946–54	10	20685	Withdrawal	11	10	9	2
France in Madagascar	1947–48	10	350	Success	2	1	2	0
France in Tunisia	1952–55	10	2141	Withdrawal	5	4	5	0
Great Britain in Cyprus	1955–59	10	358	Withdrawal	3	1	3	0
Great Britain in Indonesia	1945–46	10	622	Withdrawal	1	0	0	1
Great Britain in Kenya	1952–60	10	300*	Success	3	2	3	0
Great Britain in Malaya	1948–60	10	1443	Success	4	3	4	0
Great Britain in Palestine	1945–48	10	754	Withdrawal	1	0	1	0
India in Sri Lanka	1987–90	8	1200	Withdrawal	2	1	0	2
Israel in Lebanon	1982–85	9	664	Withdrawal	3	1	1	2
Netherlands in Indonesia	1946–49	10	3000	Withdrawal	2	1	2	0

Continued

Table A.1 Continued

Case	*Dates*	*Regime Type*[a]	*Casualties (KIA)*	*Outcome (End State)*	*Total Ldrs*	*New Ldrs*	*Mil Obs*[c]	*Mil Fac*[d]
Portugal in Angola	1961–75	-9	2991	Withdrawal	3	1	1	2
Portugal in Guinea-Bissau	1963–75	-9	2070	Withdrawal	3	1	1	2
Portugal in Mozambique	1964–75	-9	3229	Withdrawal	3	1	1	2
Russia in Chechnya I	1994–96	3	6000	Withdrawal	1	0	0	1
Russia in Chechnya II	1999–09	6	6300	Success	3	1	3	0
South Africa in Namibia	1966–89	4	2200	Withdrawal	2	1	1	1
US in Korea	1950–53	10	33651	Withdrawal (armistice)	2	1	1	1
US in Vietnam	1962–73	10	58220	Withdrawal	3	1	3	0
USSR in Afghanistan	1979–89	-7	14453	Withdrawal	4	3	3	1
USSR in Baltic States	1945–52	-7	20000	Success	1	0	1	0
USSR in Hungary	1956–58	-7	2260	Success	1	0	1	0
Vietnam in Cambodia	1979–89	-7	15000	Withdrawal	4	3	3	1
					81	44	61	20

[a] Polity IV score.
[b] Polity IV score drops from 10 to 5 in 1958 (corresponds to establishment of 5th Republic).
[c] Number of political leaders with obstructive military leadership.
[d] Number of political leaders with facilitative military leadership.
* Different sources cite British casualties ranging from 63 to 519 KIA. The discrepancy seems to come from the extent to which indegenous security forces are included in the count.

Notes

1 An Unexplained Lacuna of the Politics of War

1. William R. Corson, *Consequences of Failure* (New York: Norton, 1973), 44.
2. Fred Charles Iklé, *Every War Must End*, Columbia Paperback (New York: Columbia University Press, 1971), 85.
3. Morton H. Halperin, "War Termination as a Problem in Civil-Military Relations," *The Annals of the American Academy of Political and Social Sciences* 392(1970): 86–95.
4. Zeev Maoz and Randolph M. Siverson, "Bargaining, Domestic Politics, and International Context in the Management of War: A Review Essay," *Conflict Management and Peace Science* 25(2008): 178.
5. Ibid., 173, 85. In contrast, there is substantial work focused on civil-military relations and decisions to initiate armed conflict. See Richard K. Betts, *Soldiers, Statesmen, and Cold War Crises*, Morningside ed. (New York: Columbia University Press, 1991); Peter Feaver and Christopher Gelpi, *Choosing Your Battles: American Civil-Military Relations and the Use of Force* (Princeton: Princeton University Press, 2004).
6. Previous applications of the bargaining construct to war termination focus on the interaction between belligerents. See Paul R. Pillar, *Negotiating Peace: War Termination as a Bargaining Process* (Princeton: Princeton University Press, 1983). Also, Robert Powell, "Bargaining Theory and International Conflict," *Annual Review of Political Science* 5 (2002): 1–30.
7. Taken from "Letter from the Chief of the M.A.A.G. In Vietnam (McGarr) to the Chairman of the Joint Chiefs of Staff (Lemnitzer), Saigon, 12 October 1961," in *F.R.U.S., 1961–1963, Volume 1.*
8. Iklé, *Every War Must End*, 16.
9. Sarah Croco, "The Decider's Dilemma: Leader Culpability, War Outcomes, and Domestic Punishment," *American Political Science Review* 105, no. 3 (2011): 460.
10. Ibid., 457. Also see George W. Downs, "The Lessons of Disengagement," in *The Dynamics of Foreign Military Intervention*, ed. Ariel Levite, Bruce W. Jentleson, and Ilan Berman (New York: Columbia University Press, 1992), 294–96.
11. H. A. Calahan, *What Makes a War End?* (New York: Vanguard Press, 1944), 209; Michael I. Handel, *War Termination, a Critical Survey*, Jerusalem Papers

on Peace Problems (Jerusalem Hebrew University, Leonard Davis Institute for International Relations, 1978).

12. Stanley Karnow, *Vietnam, a History*, rev. and updated ed. (New York: Viking, 1991), 220.
13. A number of works on war termination focus on the distinction between hawkish and dovish political leaders, or between hawkish and dovish political coalitions. The basic logic is that hawkish leaders are more likely to keep fighting while dovish leaders are more apt to sue for peace. See Michael T. Koch and Patricia L. Sullivan, "Should I Stay or Should I Go Now? Partisan Approval and the Duration of Major Power Democratic Military Interventions," *Journal of Politics* 72, no. 3 (2010): 617. Stanley adds the factor of political leadership change, or coalition shift, and argues that a hawkish shift is likely to prolong a war while a dovish shift will greatly enhance the probability of the war ending. See Elizabeth A. Stanley, *Paths to Peace: Domestic Coalition Shifts, War Termination and the Korean War* (Stanford, CA: Stanford University Press, 2009). Such arguments may be valid but are also somewhat tautological. A leader or coalition is "hawkish" if it acts like a hawk. A leader or coalition is "dovish" if it acts like a dove.
14. Croco, "The Decider's Dilemma," 457.
15. This is based on the author's own analysis of Croco's data. The point made here is not immediately evident given how Croco presents the data. Croco shows a statistically significant relationship, but this is skewed by the fact that the bulk of her dataset (87 percent) consists of initial (culpable for starting the war) leaders; even with the statistical relationship, there is still a large qualitative gap in explanatory power.
16. Croco, "The Decider's Dilemma," 458–60.
17. The lack of clear-cut distinction between initial and new leaders in many cases has led a handful of critics to question the causal effects of leadership change altogether. Flores, for one, argues, "Leader changes may have no effect on the probability of war termination" across the board, while specifically in large coalition systems, "Under no circumstance does leader change... increase the probability of war termination." See A. Quiroz Flores, "A Competing Risks Model of War Termination and Leader Change," *International Studies Quarterly* 56, no. 4 (2012): 816.
18. Croco, "The Decider's Dilemma," 461.
19. See Christopher Hood, *The Blame Game: Spin, Bureaucracy, and Self-Preservation in Government* (Princeton: Princeton University Press, 2011); Debra Javeline, *Protest and the Politics of Blame: The Russian Response to Unpaid Wages*, Interests, Identities, and Institutions in Comparative Politics (Ann Arbor: University of Michigan Press, 2003); Richard Ellis, *Presidential Lightning Rods: The Politics of Blame Avoidance*, Studies in Government and Public Policy (Lawrence, KS: University Press of Kansas, 1994); Kathleen M. McGraw, "Managing Blame: An Experimental Test of the Effects of Political Accounts," *The American Political Science Review* 85, no. 4 (1991); Mark D. Alicke, "Culpable Control and the Psychology of Blame," *Psychological Bulletin* 126, no. 4 (2000);

Raanan Sulitzeanu-Kenan and Lior Sheffer, "A Formal Model of Social Blame in Political Context," Paper Presented at the 69th Annual Midwest Political Science Association Conference, March 31-April 3, 2011 (Chicago, IL).

20. R. Kent Weaver, "The Politics of Blame Avoidance," *Journal of Public Policy* 6, no. 4 (1986): 381.
21. Mark Bovens et al., "The Politics of Blame Avoidance," in *When Things Go Wrong: Organizational Failures and Breakdowns,* ed. Helmut K. Anheier (Thousand Oaks, CA: Sage Publications, 1999), 123.
22. See Alister Miskimmon, Ben O'Loughlin, and Laura Roselle, *Strategic Narratives: Communications and the New World Order* (London: Routledge, 2013), 2; Robert D. Benford and David A. Snow, "Framing Processes and Social Movements: An Overview and Assessment," *Annual Review of Sociology* 26(2000): 615–16.
23. Barry R. Schlenker et al., "The Triangle Model of Responsibility," *Psychological Review* 101, no. 4 (1994).
24. Adopted from Soviet diplomat Anatoly Adamishin's claim, "Victory has many pretenders, defeat only one." See J. E. Davies, *Constructive Engagement? Chester Crocker & American Policy in South Africa, Namibia & Angola, 1981–8* (Athens, OH: Ohio University Press, 2007), 173.
25. Wolfgang Schivelbusch, *The Culture of Defeat: On National Trauma, Mourning, and Recovery,* 1st American ed. (New York: Metropolitan Books, 2003), 205–8; Jeffrey Kimball, "The Stab-in-the-Back-Legend and the Vietnam War," *Armed Forces and Society* 14, Spring (1988); Jenny Macleod, *Defeat and Memory: Cultural Histories of Military Defeat in the Modern Era* (New York: Palgrave Macmillan, 2008), 233–50.
26. Peter Feaver, *Armed Servants: Agency, Oversight, and Civil-Military Relations* (Cambridge, MA: Harvard University Press, 2003), 57. 296
27. Graham T. Allison and Philip Zelikow, *Essence of Decision: Explaining the Cuban Missile Crisis,* 2nd ed. (New York: Longman, 1999), 255–8.
28. See Deborah D. Avant, *Political Institutions and Military Change: Lessons from Peripheral Wars,* Cornell Studies in Security Affairs (Ithaca: Cornell University Press, 1994); Feaver, *Armed Servant*; Thomas Sowers, "Beyond the Soldier and the State: Contemporary Operations and Variance in Principal-Agent Relationships," *Armed Forces and Society* 31, no. 2 (2005).
29. See for example John O. Brehm and Scott Gates, *Working, Shirking, and Sabotage: Bureaucratic Response to a Democratic Public* (Ann Arbor: University of Michigan Press, 1997).
30. James G. March, *A Primer on Decision Making: How Decisions Happen* (New York: The Free Press, 1994), 214.
31. Feaver, *Armed Servants,* 88.
32. The terms obstructive and facilitative relate to military leadership's stance on the question of withdrawal from a given war and do not necessarily imply support, or lack thereof, for a given political leader's policy.
33. Stephen Walt, "Top Ten Reasons Why Wars Last Too Long," http://walt.foreignpolicy.com/posts/2010/09/01/ (accessed March 29, 2015).

34. George Armstrong Kelly, *Lost Soldiers: The French Army and Empire in Crisis, 1947–1962* (Cambridge, MA: M.I.T. Press, 1965), 145.
35. Few leaders, whether civilian or military, will want a protracted war to last indefinitely. There will almost always be talk about the need to bring the war to a close and bring the troops home as soon as possible. However, such sentiments do not necessarily indicate a preference of withdrawal or willingness to settle short of victory. These sentiments may instead reflect a push to take whatever steps necessary to end the war more quickly, but also in a manner consistent with the state's primary war aims. The critical turning point comes when either political or military leadership de-links war termination from the state's primary war aims, or when ending the war becomes an objective itself more important than these aims.
36. H. E. Goemans, *War and Punishment: The Causes of War Termination and the First World War*, Princeton Studies in International History and Politics (Princeton, NJ: Princeton University Press, 2000); Bruce Bueno de Mesquita and Randolph M. Siverson, "War and the Survival of Political Leaders: A Comparative Study of Regime Types and Political Accountability," *American Political Science Review* 89, no. 4 (1995); Michael J. Englehardt, "Democracies, Dictatorships and Counterinsurgency: Does Regime Type Really Matter?" *Conflict Quarterly* Spring (1992).
37. See Max Boot, *The Savage Wars of Peace: Small Wars and the Rise of American Power*, 1st paperback ed. (New York: Basic Books, 2003); A. Hamish Ion and Elizabeth Jane Errington, *Great Powers and Little Wars: The Limits of Power* (Westport, CT: Praeger, 1993); T. V. Paul, *Asymmetric Conflicts: War Initiation by Weaker Powers*, Cambridge Studies in International Relations 33 (Cambridge; New York, NY: Cambridge University Press, 1994); C. E. Callwell, *Small Wars: Their Principles and Practice* (Lincoln, NE: University of Nebraska Press, 1996); Eliot A. Cohen, "Constraints on America's Conduct of Small Wars," *International Security* 9, no. 2 (1984). Ivan Arreguin-Toft, "How the Weak Win Wars: A Theory of Asymmetric Conflict," *International Security* 26, no. 1 (2001).
38. Andrew Mack, "Why Big Nations Lose Small Wars: The Politics of Asymmetric Conflict," *World Politics* 27, no. 2 (1975): 177.
39. John E. Mueller, "War Has Almost Ceased to Exist: An Assessment," *Political Science Quarterly* 124, no. 2 (2009).
40. For a discussion of causal mechanisms as applied here, see Tulia G. Falleti and Julia F. Lynch, "Context and Causal Mechanisms in Political Analysis," *Comparative Political Studies* 42, no. 9 (2009); Jon Elster, "A Plea for Mechanisms," in *Social Mechanisms: An Analytical Approach to Social Theory*, ed. Peter Hedström and Richard Swedberg (New York: Cambridge University Press, 1998).
41. Harry Eckstein, "Case Studies in Political Science," in *Strategies of Inquiry*, ed. Fred I. Greenstein and Nelson W. Polsby, Handbook of Political Science V. 7 (Reading, MA: Addison-Wesley Pub. Co., 1975). Also, see Alexander L. George and Andrew Bennett, *Case Studies and Theory Development in the*

Social Sciences, B.C.S.I.A. Studies in International Security (Cambridge, MA: MIT Press, 2005), 121.

42. See Jason Seawright and John Gerring, "Case Selection Techniques in Case Study Research," *Political Research Quarterly* 61, no. 2 (2008): 294–308.

2 The Civil-Military Variable and How It Varies

1. Portions of this chapter draw upon Shawn T. Cochran, "The Civil-Military Divide in Protracted Small War: An Alternative View of Military Leadership Preferences and War Termination," *Armed Forces & Society* 40, no. 1 (2014). See SAGE Journal Author Reuse Policy, dated March 20, 2013.
2. Borrowed from Edward Feit, *The Armed Bureaucrats: Military-Administrative Regimes and Political Development* (Boston: Houghton Mifflin, 1972).
3. Samuel P. Huntington, *The Soldier and the State: The Theory and Politics of Civil-Military Relations* (Cambridge: Belknap Press of Harvard University Press, 1957), 84.
4. S. E. Finer, *The Man on Horseback: The Role of the Military in Politics*, 2nd enlarged ed., Peregrine Books (Baltimore: Penguin, 1976), 21–4. See also Bengt Abrahamsson, *Military Professionalism and Political Power* (London: Sage Publications, 1972), 13, 17.
5. Amos Perlmutter and Harvard University. Center for International Affairs, *The Military and Politics in Modern Times: On Professionals, Praetorians, and Revolutionary Soldiers* (New Haven: Yale University Press, 1977), 6; Eric A. Nordlinger, *Soldiers in Politics: Military Coups and Governments*, Prentice-Hall Contemporary Comparative Politics Series. (Englewood Cliffs, NJ: Prentice-Hall, 1977), 63–4.
6. Morton H. Halperin, Priscilla Clapp, and Arnold Kanter, *Bureaucratic Politics and Foreign Policy* (Washington: The Brookings Institution, 1974); Graham T. Allison and Morton H. Halperin, "Bureacratic Politcs: A Paradigm and Some Policy Implications," *World Politics* 24(1972); Francis E. Rourke, *Bureaucracy and Foreign Policy*, Studies in International Affairs, (Baltimore: Johns Hopkins University Press, 1972).
7. Barry Posen, *The Sources of Military Doctrine: France, Britain, and Germany between the World Wars*, Cornell Studies in Security Affairs (Ithaca: Cornell University Press, 1984), 38. Stephen Van Evera, "Causes of War" (PhD dissertation, Unversity of California, Berkeley, 1984), 206–7.
8. Morton H. Halperin, "War Termination as a Problem in Civil-Military Relations," *The Annals of the American Academy of Political and Social Sciences* 392(1970): 89.
9. Ibid., 86–95.
10. As a notable exception, see Iklé, *Every War Must End*, 13.
11. Halperin, "War Termination as a Problem in Civil-Military Relations," 90–1.
12. See Dan Reiter, *How Wars End* (Princeton: Princeton University Press, 2009), 7.

13. Philippe Devillers and Jean Lacouture, *End of a War: Indochina, 1954* (New York: Praeger, 1969), 41; Van Evera, "Causes of War," 380. Alistair Horne, *The French Army and Politics, 1870–1970*, 1st American ed. (New York: Peter Bedrick Books: Distributed in the United States by Harper & Row, 1984), 74.
14. Devillers and Lacouture, *End of a War: Indochina, 1954*, 64.
15. Ibid., 66.
16. Bruce D. Porter, "The Military Abroad: Internal Consequences of External Expansion," in *Soldiers and the Soviet State: Civil-Military Relations from Brezhnev to Gorbachev*, ed. Timothy J. Colton and Thane Gustafson (Princeton: Princeton University Press, 1990), 317–18.
17. Scott R. McMichael, *Stumbling Bear: Soviet Military Performance in Afghanistan* (London; Washington: Brassey's, 1991), 61.
18. Anthony Arnold, *The Fateful Pebble: Afghanistan's Role in the Fall of the Soviet Empire* (Novato, CA: Presidio, 1993), 137. Also see Milan Hauner, *The Soviet War in Afghanistan: Patterns of Russian Imperialism* (Philadelphia, PA: University Press of America, 1991), 118.
19. "C.P.S.U. C.C. Politburo Meeting Minutes, 13 November 1986," in *Cold War International History Project.*
20. See "Memorandum from the President's Assistant for National Security Affairs (Kissinger) to President Nixon, Coup in Portugal, April 29, 1974," in *F.R.U.S., 1969–1976, Volume 28*, 237; António de Spínola, *Portugal and the Future* (Johannesburg: Perskor Publishers, 1974).
21. See Posen, *The Sources of Military Doctrine*, 239–40.
22. Walter W. Powell and Paul DiMaggio, *The New Institutionalism in Organizational Analysis* (Chicago: University of Chicago Press, 1991); John W. Meyer and Brian Rowan, "Institutionalized Organizations: Formal Structures as Myth and Ceremony," *American Journal of Sociology* 83, no. 2 (1977); Lynne G. Zucker, "Institutional Theories of Organization," *Annual Review of Sociology* 13(1987).
23. Mark C. Suchman, "Managing Legitimacy: Strategic and Institutional Approaches," *Academy of Management Review* 20, no. 3 (1995): 574. Also, Allen Weiss and Erin Anderson, "Perceptions of Legitimacy as a Motive to Change Inter-Organizational Relations," (Research Paper #1175, Graduate School of Business, Stanford University, November 1991), 1; John Dowling and Jeffrey Pfeffer, "Organizational Legitimacy: Social Values and Organizational Behavior," *Pacific Sociological Review* 18, no. 1 (1975): 133.
24. Suchman, "Managing Legitimacy," 571.
25. J. A. A. Van Doorn, "The Officer Corps: A Fusion of Profession and Organization," *Journal of European Sociology* 6, no. 2 (1965). There are similarities here with Moskos' distinction between institutional and occupational models of the military. See Charles C. Moskos, "From Institution to Occupation: Trends in Military Organization," *Armed Forces and Society* 41, no. 1 (1977).

26. J. A. A. Van Doorn, *The Soldier and Social Change: Comparative Studies in the History and Sociology of the Military*, Sage Series on Armed Forces and Society V. 7 (Beverly Hills, CA: Sage Publications, 1975), 29–39.
27. ———, "Continuity and Discontinuity in Civil-Military Relations," in *The Military, Militarism, and the Polity: Essays in Honor of Morris Janowitz*, ed. Michel L. Martin and Ellen Stern McCrate (New York: Free Press, 1984), 44.
28. The concepts of effectiveness and appropriateness closely align with Suchman's categories of "pragmatic" legitimacy and "normative" legitimacy. See Suchman, "Managing Legitimacy: Strategic and Institutional Approaches," 577.
29. J. A. A. Van Doorn, "The Military and the Crisis of Legitimacy," in *The Military and the Problem of Legitimacy*, ed. J. A. A. Van Doorn and Gwyn Harries-Jenkins (London: Sage Publications, 1976), 19, 30; Rob Kroes, *Soldiers and Students: A Study of Right- and Left-Wing Radicals*, International Library of Sociology (London; Boston: Routledge & K. Paul, 1975), 32. Anthony Forster, "The Military Covenant and British Civil-Military Relations: Letting the Genie out of the Bottle," *Armed Forces and Society* 38, no. 2 (2012): 280.
30. W. Richard Scott, *Institutions and Organizations*, Foundations for Organizational Science (Thousand Oaks: SAGE, 1995), 46. Van Doorn, *The Soldier and Social Change*, 95.
31. Burk suggests that when a state is clearly threatened, the "social distance" between the military and society is inherently marginalized. The military's legitimacy accordingly becomes more secure. See James Burk, "The Public and the Military," *Javnost—The Public* 1, no. 4 (1994): 14.
32. Orrin Schwab, *A Clash of Cultures: Civil-Military Relations during the Vietnam War*, In War and in Peace (Westport, CT: Praeger Security International, 2006), 64, 88.
33. Porter, "The Military Abroad," 332.
34. Orville D. Menard, *The Army and the Fifth Republic* (Lincoln: University of Nebraska Press, 1967), 89; Michael C. Desch, *Civilian Control of the Military: The Changing Security Environment* (Baltimore: Johns Hopkins University Press, 1999).
35. Wilfried von Bredow, "The Order of Violence: Norms, Rules, and Taboos of Organized Violence and the De-Legitimization of the Military," in *Handbook of the Sociology of the Military*, ed. Giuseppe Caforio (New York: Kluwer Academic/Plenum Publishers, 2003). Reuven Gal, "Limits of Military Legitimacy and Its Relation to Military Commitment," in *Legitimacy and Commitment in the Military*, ed. Thomas C. Wyatt and Reuven Gal (New York: Greenwood Press, 1990).
36. See John E. Mueller, *War, Presidents, and Public Opinion* (New York: Wiley, 1973), 150. Also, Robert Mason, *Richard Nixon and the Quest for a New Majority* (Chapel Hill: University of North Carolina Press, 2004), 63. Charles Benedetti and Charles Chatfield, *An American Ordeal: The Antiwar Movement of the Vietnam War* (Syracuse: Syracuse University Press, 1990), 238–40.

37. Stuart A. Cohen, "Why Do They Quarrel? Civil-Military Tensions in LIC Situations," in *Democracies and Small Wars*, ed. Efraim Inbar (London: Frank Cass, 2003), 32.
38. T. R. Fehrenbach, *This Kind of War: The Classic Korean War History* (London: Brassey's, 1994), 438.
39. Kevin Doyle, "Vietnam's Forgotten Cambodian War," http://www.bbc.com /news/world-asia-29106034 (accessed March 31, 2015).
40. Kuldip S. Ludra, *Operation 'Pawan'* (Chandigarh: Strategic Research Centre, 1999), 48.
41. Blake E. Ashforth and Barrie W. Gibbs, "The Double-Edge of Organizational Legitimation," *Organization Science* 1, no. 2 (1990): 178.
42. Ibid., 181.
43. "Letter from the Chief of the M.A.A.G. In Vietnam (McGarr) to the Chairman of the Joint Chiefs of Staff (Lemnitzer), Saigon, 12 October 1961," in *F.R.U.S., 1961–1963, Volume 1.* Also see Robert Buzzanco, *Masters of War: Military Dissent and Politics in the Vietnam Era* (New York: Cambridge University Press, 1996), 150.
44. In Richard K. Betts, *Soldiers, Statesmen, and Cold War Crises* (Cambridge: Harvard University Press, 1977), 11.
45. Douglas Porch, *The Portuguese Armed Forces and the Revolution*, Hoover Institution Publication 188 (London: Croom Helm; Hoover Institution Press, 1977), 58.
46. Robert Buzzanco, "Hawks as Doves: Military Dissent in Vietnam and Iraq," (Colonel John B. Mckinney Lecture, unpublished manuscript, University of Tennessee, 2006), 20.
47. Ibid., 25.
48. Jan R. Schoeman, "Netherlands," in *The Political Role of the Military: An International Handbook*, ed. Constantine P. Danopoulos and Cynthia Watson (London: Greenwood Press, 1996), 285.
49. Mark Bovens et al., "The Politics of Blame Avoidance," in *When Things Go Wrong: Organizational Failures and Breakdowns,* ed. Helmut K. Anheier (Thousand Oaks, CA: Sage Publications, 1999), 123–4.
50. Philip H. Frankel, *Pretoria's Praetorians: Civil-Military Relations in South Africa* (New York: Cambridge University Press, 1984), 34. Also see James Michael Roherty, *State Security in South Africa: Civil-Military Relations under P.W. Botha* (Armonk, NY: M. E. Sharpe, 1992), 27. "Intelligence Note from the Director of the Bureau of Intelligence and Research (Hughes) to Secretary of State Rogers, South Africa: The Indivisible Government, June 24, 1969," in *F.R.U.S., 1969–1976, Volume 28.*
51. For a broader discussion of leverage in civil-military bargaining, see Abrahamsson, *Military Professionalism and Political Power*; Risa Brooks, *Shaping Strategy: The Civil-Military Politics of Strategic Assessment* (Princeton, NJ: Princeton University Press, 2008); Peter Feaver, *Armed Servants: Agency, Oversight, and Civil-Military Relations* (Cambridge, MA: Harvard University Press, 2003).

52. "Military Contests and Settlement," http://www.fsmitha.com/h2/ch24kor8.htm (accessed April 11, 2015).
53. Carl Gustaf von Mannerheim, *The Memoirs of Marshal Mannerheim* (London: E. P. Dutton & Company Ltd., 1953), 471.
54. Iklé, *Every War Must End*, 65.
55. Ibid., 66. Also see, Mannerheim, *The Memoirs of Marshal Mannerheim*, 491–513.
56. I employ the concept of side payments liberally, combining the narrow conception found in bargaining theory with the related factor of issue linkage. See Frederick W. Mayer, "Managing Domestic Differences in International Negotiations: The Strategic Use of Internal Side-Payments," *International Organization* 46, no. 4 (1992).
57. Damon Coletta and Peter Feaver, "Civilian Monitoring of U.S. Military Operations in the Information Age," *Armed Forces & Society* 33, no. 1 (2006).
58. Rowland Evans and Robert D. Novak, *Nixon in the White House: The Frustration of Power* (New York: Random House, 1971), 80.
59. Dale R. Herspring, *The Pentagon and the Presidency: Civil-Military Relations from FDR to George W. Bush*, Modern War Studies (Lawrence: University Press of Kansas, 2005), 192. Also Mark Perry, *Four Stars* (Boston: Houghton Mifflin, 1989), 219; Charles A. Stevenson, *Warriors and Politicians: US Civil-Military Relations under Stress*, Cass Military Studies (London; New York: Routledge, 2006), 65.
60. Henry Kissinger and Clare Boothe Luce, *White House Years* (Boston: Little, Brown, 1979), 476.
61. Anthony Clayton, *The Wars of French Decolonization*, Modern Wars in Perspective (London; New York: Longman, 1994), 7.
62. See "France: The Juin Affair," *Time* April 12, 1954. Also, Martin Thomas, *The French North African Crisis: Colonial Breakdown and Anglo-French Relations, 1945–62*, Studies in Military and Strategic History (New York: St. Martin's Press, 2000), 44.
63. Frank Giles, *The Locust Years: The Story of the Fourth French Republic, 1946–1958* (London: Secker & Warburg, 1991), 216.
64. See Ibid., 187.
65. John S. Ambler, *The French Army in Politics, 1945–1962* (Columbus: Ohio State University Press, 1966), 230.
66. Brian Crozier, *De Gaulle* (New York: Scribner, 1973), 506; Michael Kettle, *De Gaulle and Algeria 1940–60: From Mers El-Kebir to the Algiers Barricades* (London: Quartet Books, 1993), 568. See also Edmond Pognon, *De Gaulle et l'Armée*, Collection Espoir (Paris: Plon, 1976), 300; William George Andrews, *French Politics and Algeria: The Process of Policy Formation, 1954–1962*, Current Political Problems (New York: Appleton-Century-Crofts, 1962), 117.
67. Charles De Gaulle, *Memoirs of Hope: Renewal and Endeavor* (New York: Simon and Schuster, 1971), 86.
68. Referenced in Edgar Stephenson Furniss, *De Gaulle and the French Army: A Crisis in Civil-Military Relations* (New York: Twentieth Century Fund, 1964), 221.

69. Referenced in Crozier, *De Gaulle*, 506. See also C. L. Sulzberger, *The Test: De Gaulle and Algeria* (New York: Harcourt, 1962), 143; Alexander Harrison, *Challenging De Gaulle: The O.A.S. and the Counterrevolution in Algeria, 1954–1962* (New York: Praeger, 1989), 40.
70. P. R. Chari, "The I.P.K.F. Experience in Sri Lanka," *ACDIS Occasional Paper* (February 1994): 13.
71. See Shelton U. Kodikara, W. B. Dorakumbure, and Bandaranaike Centre for International Studies, *Domestic Politics and Diplomacy: A Study of Linkage Politics in Indo-Sri Lanka Relations* (Colombo: Bandaranaike Centre for International Studies, 2008), 153.
72. Porter, "The Military Abroad," 308. See also Mark Galeotti, *Afghanistan, the Soviet Union's Last War* (London, England; Portland, OR: Frank Cass, 1995), 171.
73. Anatol Lieven, *Chechnya: Tombstone of Russian Power* (New Haven: Yale University Press, 1998), 103. See also Dale R. Herspring, *The Kremlin & the High Command: Presidential Impact on the Russian Military from Gorbachev to Putin*, Modern War Studies (Lawrence: University Press of Kansas, 2006), 97; Carlotta Gall and Thomas De Waal, *Chechnya: Calamity in the Caucasus* (New York: New York University Press, 1998), 177.
74. Quoted in Lieven, *Chechnya: Tombstone of Russian Power*, 103–4.
75. Thomas C. Bruneau, *Politics and Nationhood: Post-Revolutionary Portugal* (New York, NY: Praeger, 1984), 37.
76. John P. Cann, *Counterinsurgency in Africa: The Portuguese Way of War, 1961–1974*, Contributions in Military Studies, (Westport, CT: Greenwood Press, 1997), 31.
77. From António de Spínola, *País Sem Rumo: Contributo Para a História De Uma Revolução* (Lisboa: SCIRE, 1978), 251.
78. Quoted in Antonio R. Bandeira, *Military Interventions in Portuguese Politics: Antecedents of the Armed Forces Movement* (Toronto: Brazilian Studies, 1975), 29. Also Douglas Porch, *Correspondence with Author, February 2012.*
79. Halperin, "War Termination as a Problem in Civil-Military Relations," 94.
80. Michael D. Pearlman, *Truman & Macarthur: Policy, Politics, and the Hunger for Honor and Renown* (Bloomington: Indiana University Press, 2008).
81. Mueller, *War, Presidents, and Public Opinion*, 229. Also see Richard E. Neustadt, *Presidential Power, the Politics of Leadership* (New York: Wiley, 1960); John W. Spanier, *The Truman-Macarthur Controversy and the Korean War* (Cambridge, MA: Belknap Press, 1959).
82. "Yalu Could've Been Taken in 1951: Ridgway Doubts Its Worth in Yank Lives," *Chicago Tribune* (February 21, 1956), http://archives.chicagotribune.com/1956/02/21/page/37/article/yalu-couldve-been-taken-in-1951-ridgway (accessed April 11, 2015). Halperin, "War Termination as a Problem in Civil-Military Relations," 93; "Memorandum, Gen. M. B. Ridgway for General and Flag-Officer Members of the U.N. Delegation, 7 July 1951," (GHQ, UNC SGS files).

83. Although probably a source of debate, with the case of the United States in Korea, I assess US military leadership by early 1953 to be best categorized as weakly facilitative. Military leadership was not defeatist but was instead firmly behind a negotiated settlement in line with political leadership's intent to end the war, and well short of MacArthur's more aggressive aims. By the time Eisenhower was elected president in late 1952, Ridgway had been replaced by General Mark Clark as commander of UN forces in Korea. When the president-elect visited Korea in December 1952, Clark had planned to present Eisenhower with an operations plan aimed at achieving decisive victory in the stalemated war. However, Clark soon realized the new president was seeking nothing more than an "honorable truce". After this point, Clark refrained from talk about victory and focused the army's efforts, even harsh escalatory measures, on pressuring the Chinese to accept a settlement in lines with the president's limited objectives. In the end game, Clark firmly backed Eisenhower in debates with the allied South Korean (ROK) government over the terms of a settlement and was instrumental in pushing the ROK to acquiesce to the final armistice. More broadly, "JCS recommendations were keeping with the desire of the new administration to extricate the United States from the Korean conflict." See James F. Schnabel and Robert J. Watson, "The Korean War Part Two," in *The Joint Chiefs of Staff and National Policy, Vol 3, 1951–1953* (Washington DC: Office of the Chairman of the Joint Chiefs of Staff, 1998), 194–9, 221–8. Along these lines, Jeffrey Record argues that, once MacArthur was gone, the civil-military dynamic in Korea looked fundamentally different from what was seen later in Vietnam. Specifically, "Unlike their Vietnam War successors, the Chiefs during the Korean War supported the White House's determination to cap U.S. investment in the war... This fundamental consensus on the conflict's proper scope accounts in no small measure for the Korean War's lack of an attendant stab-in-the-back myth." See Jeffrey Record, "The Wrong War: Why We Lost in Vietnam." (Naval Institute Press, 1998), https://www.nytimes.com/books/first/r/record-war.html (accessed April 11, 2015).
84. Robert Buzzanco, "The American Military's Rationale against the Vietnam War," *Political Science Quarterly* 101, no. 4 (1986): 561.
85. Referenced in Gall and De Waal, *Chechnya: Calamity in the Caucasus*, 181. On the nature and extent of military dissent, also see Pavel Felgenhauer, "Russian Military Reform: Ten Years of Failure," in *Russian Defense Policy towards the Year 2000*, ed. Elizabeth Skinner and Mikhail Tsypkin (Naval Postgraduate School, Monterey, CA, 1997); Herspring, *The Kremlin & the High Command: Presidential Impact on the Russian Military from Gorbachev to Putin*, 95–7; Robert V. Barylski, *The Soldier in Russian Politics: Duty, Dictatorship and Democracy under Gorbachev and Yeltsin* (New Brunswick, NJ: Transaction Publishers, 1998), 299–300.
86. Robert Brannon, *Russian Civil-Military Relations*, Military Strategy and Operational Art (Farnham, England; Burlington, VT: Ashgate Publishing, 2009), 58; Sebastian Smith, *Allah's Mountains: The Battle for Chechnya* (London; New York: TPP, 2006), 256.

87. Gall and De Waal, *Chechnya: Calamity in the Caucasus*, 346–53.
88. Timothy J. Colton, "Perspectives on Civil-Military Relations in the Soviet Union," in *Soldiers and the Soviet State: Civil-Military Relations from Brezhnev to Gorbachev*, ed. Timothy J. Colton and Thane Gustafson (Princeton: Princeton University Press, 1990), 35–6. See also Steven Lukes, *Power: A Radical View*, 2nd ed. (New York: Palgrave Macmillan, 2004), 23.
89. James N. Druckman and Arthur Lupia, "Preference Formation," *Annual Review of Political Science* 3(2000): 2–4; Jon Elster, *Explaining Social Behavior: More Nuts and Bolts for the Social Sciences* (Cambridge; New York: Cambridge University Press, 2007), 193.

3 Civil-Military Bargaining and the Politics of Blame

1. On the role of a "moderating variable," see R. M. Baron and D. A. Kenny, "The Moderator-Mediator Variable Distinction in Social Psychology Research: Conceptual, Strategic, and Statisitical Considerations," *Journal of Personality and Social Psychology* 51, no. 6 (1986).
2. Bruce Bueno de Mesquita, *The Logic of Political Survival* (Cambridge, MA: MIT Press, 2003), 8.
3. Ibid., 28–9. Also see Jessica L. Weeks, "Autocratic Audience Costs: Regime Type and Signaling Resolve," *International Organization* 62, no. 1 (2008): 36.
4. Bruce Bueno de Mesquita and Randolph M. Siverson, "War and the Survival of Political Leaders: A Comparative Study of Regime Types and Political Accountability," *American Political Science Review* 89, no. 4 (1995): 842–3.
5. Charles Tilly, *Credit and Blame* (Princeton: Princeton University Press, 2008), 127.
6. See Bruce Bueno de Mesquita, Randolph M. Siverson, and Gary Woller, "War and the Fate of Regimes: A Comparative Analysis," *American Political Science Review* 86, no. 3 (1992): 640.
7. Henry Kissinger and Clare Boothe Luce, *White House Years* (Boston: Little, Brown, 1979), 476–7.
8. R. Kent Weaver, "The Politics of Blame Avoidance," *Journal of Public Policy* 6, no. 4 (1986): 377. Christopher Hood, *The Blame Game: Spin, Bureaucracy, and Self-Preservation in Government* (Princeton: Princeton University Press, 2011), 10–14; Matthew A. Baum, "Going Private: Public Opinion, Presidential Rhetoric, and the Domestic Politics of Audience Costs in U.S. Foreign Policy Crises," *Journal of Conflict Resolution* 48, no. 5 (2004): 609–10.
9. Fred Charles Iklé, *Every War Must End*, Columbia Paperback (New York: Columbia University Press, 1971), 60–61.
10. Weaver, "The Politics of Blame Avoidance," 385.
11. Daniel Ellsberg, *Papers on the War* (New York: Simon and Schuster, 1972), 97. There is significant debate over Kennedy's actual intentions, with even the most credible sources on the topic rife with contradictions. Accordingly, this quote is provided as illustration of a concept, not as evidence. See Mark Moyar, *Triumph Forsaken: The Vietnam War, 1954–1965* (New York: Cambridge

University Press, 2009), 277–8. Consistent with O'Donnell's recollection, Kennedy is also said to have told reporters at an off-the-record news conference in July 1963, "We don't have a prayer of staying in Vietnam... But I can't give up a piece of territory like that to the Communists and get the American people to reelect me." Quoted in Jeffrey Record, *The Wrong War: Why We Lost in Vietnam* (Naval Institute Press, 1998), https://www.nytimes.com/books/first/r/record-war.html (accessed April 11, 2015).

12. Darren Filson and Suzanne Werner, "Sensitivity to Costs of Fighting versus Sensitivity to Losing the Conflict: Implications for War Onset, Duration, and Outcomes," *Journal of Conflict Resolution* 51, no. 5 (2007): 691.
13. Sarah Croco, "The Decider's Dilemma: Leader Culpability, War Outcomes, and Domestic Punishment," *American Political Science Review* 105, no. 3 (2011): 459–60; Bueno de Mesquita, Siverson, and Woller, "War and the Fate of Regimes," 640.
14. Kuldip S. Ludra, *Operation 'Pawan'* (Chandigarh: Strategic Research Centre, 1999), 48; Manik de Silva, "The Lesser Evil: India Pulls Out, Leaving Tamil Issue Unresolved," *Far Eastern Economic Review* 148, no. 14 (1990): 10.
15. Adopted from Charles Fair, *From the Jaws of Victory* (New York: Simon and Schuster, 1971).
16. Douglas Porch, *The Portuguese Armed Forces and the Revolution*, Hoover Institution Publication 188 (London: Croom Helm; Hoover Institution Press, 1977), 84.
17. Harold MacMillan, *Riding the Storm, 1956–1959* (New York: Harper & Row, 1971), 226; Robert Holland, *Britain and the Revolt in Cyprus, 1954–59* (Oxford: Oxford University Press, 1998), 100.
18. MacMillan, *Riding the Storm, 1956–1959*, 661.
19. Holland, *Britain and the Revolt in Cyprus, 1954–59*, 302.
20. Emile Simpson, *War from the Ground Up: Twenty-First Century Combat as Politics* (Oxford: Oxford University Press, 2012), 207–10; Walter Fisher, *Human Communication as Narration: Toward a Philosophy of Reason, Value, and Action* (Columbia: University of South Carolina Press, 1995).
21. See Douglas L. Kriner, *After the Rubicon: Congress, Presidents, and the Politics of Waging War*, Chicago Series on International & Domestic Institutions (Chicago: University of Chicago Press, 2010), 9; Jack L. Snyder, *Myths of Empire: Domestic Politics and International Ambition*, Cornell Studies in Security Affairs (Ithaca, NY: Cornell University Press, 1991), 35.
22. Joshua W. Busby, *Moral Movements and Foreign Policy*, Cambridge Studies in International Relations (New York: Cambridge University Press, 2010), 59, 127. See also Joe D. Hagan et al., "Foreign Policy by Coalition: Deadlock, Compromise, Anarchy," *International Studies Review* 3, no. 2 (2001); Yoram Peri, *Generals in the Cabinet Room: How the Military Shapes Israeli Policy* (Washington DC: United States Institute of Peace Press, 2006).
23. Simpson, *War from the Ground Up*, 207. Robert D. Benford and David A. Snow, "Framing Processes and Social Movements: An Overview and Assessment," *Annual Review of Sociology* 26(2000): 619–22.

24. Robert Pierson, "The Epistemic Authority of Expertise," *Proceedings of the Biennial Meeting of the Philosophy of Science Association* 1(1994).
25. Kobi Michael, "Military Knowledge and Weak Civilian Control in the Reality of Low Intensity Conflict: The Israeli Case," *Israel Studies* 12, no. 1 (2007): 29–32.
26. Peter Feaver, *Armed Servants: Agency, Oversight, and Civil-Military Relations* (Cambridge, MA: Harvard University Press, 2003), 71–2.
27. Simpson, *War from the Ground Up*, 205–12.
28. S. E. Finer, *The Man on Horseback: The Role of the Military in Politics*, 2nd enlarged ed., Peregrine Books (Baltimore: Penguin, 1976), 5. Michael C. Desch, *Civilian Control of the Military: The Changing Security Environment* (Baltimore: Johns Hopkins University Press, 1999); Risa Brooks, *Shaping Strategy: The Civil-Military Politics of Strategic Assessment* (Princeton, NJ: Princeton University Press, 2008).
29. See Miles Kahler, *Decolonization in Britain and France: The Domestic Consequences of International Relations* (Princeton, NJ: Princeton University Press, 1984), 27–32. Also see Michael Stohl, *War and Domestic Political Violence: The American Capacity for Repression and Reaction*, Sage Library of Social Research V. 30 (Beverly Hills, CA: Sage Publications, 1976). Stein, *The Nation at War*, 10, 38–40.
30. John E. Mueller, *War, Presidents, and Public Opinion* (New York: Wiley, 1973), 229.
31. Robert Buzzanco, *Masters of War: Military Dissent and Politics in the Vietnam Era* (New York: Cambridge University Press, 1996), 327.
32. Ellsberg, *Papers on the War*, 91.
33. Ibid., 89–90.
34. William A. Boettcher and Michael D. Cobb, "Echoes of Vietnam? Casualty Framing and Public Perceptions of Success and Failure in Iraq," *Journal of Conflict Resolution* 50, no. 6 (2006): 833–4.
35. Iklé, *Every War Must End*, 96.
36. A. J. P. Taylor, *The Origins of the Second World War* (London: Hamilton, 1961), 92. Note: Taylor is referring to the initiation of wars, but this logic also applies to the continuation and termination of wars.
37. Christopher Gelpi, Peter Feaver, and Jason Aaron Reifler, *Paying the Human Costs of War: American Public Opinion and Casualties in Military Conflicts* (Princeton: Princeton University Press, 2009), 11–14.
38. William A. Boettcher, "Don't Let Them Die in Vain: Casualty Frames and Public Tolerance for Escalating Commitment in Iraq," *Journal of Conflict Resolution* 53, no. 5 (2009): 677–9; Patricia L. Sullivan, "Sustaining the Fight: A Cross-Sectional Time-Series Analysis of Public Support for Ongoing Military Interventions," *Conflict Management and Peace Science* 25(2008): 116–7.
39. Thomas Kelly, "Sunk Costs, Rationality, and Acting for the Sake of the Past," *NOUS* 38, no. 1 (2004): 62.
40. Boettcher, "Don't Let Them Die in Vain," 677–9.

41. Kelly, "Sunk Costs, Rationality, and Acting for the Sake of the Past," 62.
42. Gerhard Ritter, *The Sword and the Scepter: The Problem of Militarism in Germany, Volume 3* (Coral Gables, FL: University of Miami Press, 1972), 237.
43. Ibid., 188, 205.
44. See H. E. Goemans, *War and Punishment: The Causes of War Termination and the First World War*, Princeton Studies in International History and Politics (Princeton, NJ: Princeton University Press, 2000), 116.
45. Gerhard Ritter, *The Sword and the Scepter: The Problem of Militarism in Germany, Volume 4* (Coral Gables, FL: University of Miami Press, 1973), 53.
46. In the summer of 1944, several members of the Finnish government as well as a number of other prominent politicians appealed to Marshal Mannerheim to take the lead role in negotiating an end to the war. And in this case, they actually pushed for Mannerheim to accept the Presidency with the explicit goal of facilitating a settlement given a wide consensus he was the only person in Finland with the prestige and reputation needed to gain domestic acquiescence for what would likely be relatively harsh peace terms. Mannerheim was at first reluctant to take on this role but eventually agreed after repeated entreaties. See Carl Gustaf von Mannerheim, *The Memoirs of Marshal Mannerheim* (London: E. P. Dutton & Company Ltd., 1953), 491–2.
47. Kelly McHugh, "Understanding Congress's Role in Terminating Unpopular Wars: A Comparison of the Vietnam and Iraq Wars," *Democracy and Security* 10, no. 3 (2014): 192.
48. Ibid., 197.
49. Peter D. Feaver, "Anatomy of the Surge," *Commentary* 125, no. 4 (2008): 27.
50. Thomas E. Ricks, *The Gamble: General David Petraeus and the American Military Adventure in Iraq, 2006–2008* (New York: Penguin Press, 2009), 244. William G. Howell and Jon C. Pevehouse, "When Congress Stops Wars: Partisan Politics and Presidential Power," *Foreign Affairs* 86, no. 5 (2007).
51. Ricks, *The Gamble*, 79.
52. Duncan MacRae, *Parliament, Parties, and Society in France, 1946–1958* (New York: St. Martin's Press, 1967), 125. Philippe Devillers and Jean Lacouture, *End of a War: Indochina, 1954* (New York: Praeger, 1969), 67.
53. Based on Polity IV scores. See http://www.systemicpeace.org/polity/polity4.htm.
54. Diamantino P. Machado, *The Structure of Portuguese Society: The Failure of Fascism* (New York: Praeger, 1991), 167.
55. Marcello Caetano, *Depoimento* (Rio de Janeiro: Distribuidora Record, 1974), 196.
56. Norrie MacQueen, *The Decolonization of Portuguese Africa: Metropolitan Revolution and the Dissolution of Empire* (New York: Longman, 1997), 73.
57. See Al J. Venter, *The Terror Fighters: A Profile of Guerrilla Warfare in Southern Africa* (Cape Town, Johannesburg: Purnell, 1969), 89; Basil Davidson, *The Liberation of Guiné: Aspects of an African Revolution*, Penguin African Library Ap 27 (Harmondsworth: Penguin, 1969), 108. Interestingly, General Spinola

had a previous reputation as being the only Portuguese commander in Africa willing to speak regularly to journalists. See Al J. Venter, *Portugal's Guerrilla War: The Campaign for Africa* (Cape Town: J. Malherbe, 1973), 198.

58. Porch, *The Portuguese Armed Forces and the Revolution*, 83.
59. Antonio R. Bandeira, *Military Interventions in Portuguese Politics: Antecedents of the Armed Forces Movement* (Toronto: Brazilian Studies, 1975), 3. Also see MacQueen, *The Decolonization of Portuguese Africa*, 52.
60. W. G. Clarence-Smith, *The Third Portuguese Empire, 1825–1975: A Study in Economic Imperialism* (Manchester, UK; Dover, NH: Manchester University Press, 1985), 212. Also see Tom Gallagher, *Portugal: A Twentieth-Century Interpretation* (Manchester: Manchester University Press, 1983), 183–4.
61. MacQueen, *The Decolonization of Portuguese Africa*, 73.
62. Machado, *The Structure of Portuguese Society*, 167; Phillipe C. Schmitter, "Liberation by Golpe: Retrospective Thoughts on the Demise of Authoritarian Rule in Portugal," *Armed Forces and Society* 2, no. 1 (1975).
63. Machado, *The Structure of Portuguese Society*, 162.
64. George W. Downs and David M. Rocke, "Conflict, Agency, and Gambling for Resurrection: The Principal-Agent Problem Goes to War," *American Journal of Political Science* 38, no. 2 (1994).
65. Julian Jackson, *Charles De Gaulle*, Life & Times (London: Haus, 2003), 80.
66. Robert Baldick, *The Siege of Paris* (New York: Macmillan, 1964), 208.
67. Alistair Horne, *The Fall of Paris: The Siege and the Commune, 1870–71* (New York: St Martins Press, 1965), 224.
68. Maurice d'Irisson d' Hérisson, *Journel d'un Officier d'Ordnonnace, Julliet 1870-Fevrier 1871* (Paris: Paul Ollendorff, 1885), 308.
69. J. de Bouteiller, "The Workmen of Paris During the Siege," *Fraser's Magazine* 7, no. 87 (1873): 733.
70. Melvin Kranzberg, *The Siege of Paris, 1870–1871: A Political and Social History* (Westport, CT: Greenwood Press, 1971), 150–1. Note: Admittedly, the Battle of Buzenval anecdote does not fully align with this book's argument in that professional military leadership generally sided with the government in viewing the war as a lost cause while the National Guard, made up primarily of citizen-soldiers, exhibited a more obstructionist stance. Still, more than half of the soldiers sent to fight and die at Buzenval were part of the professional army. And overall, the anecdote is useful for providing illustration of a government ostensibly "bleeding" its army to demonstrate to the domestic audience the necessity of bringing the war to a close.
71. Weaver, "The Politics of Blame Avoidance," 385.
72. Croco, "The Decider's Dilemma," 460.
73. See Patricia L. Sullivan and Michael T. Koch, "Military Intervention by Powerful States, 1945–2003," *Journal of Peace Research* 46, no. 5 (2009). Also, Larisa Deriglazova, *Great Powers, Small Wars: Asymmetric Conflict since 1945* (Baltimore: The Johns Hopkins University Press, 2014). Note: In order to be consistent with the relevant literature, I treat Portugal's three overlapping wars in Africa (Angola, Mozambique, and Guinea-Bissau) separately. I do

the same for France's three overlapping wars in Africa (Tunisia, Algeria, and Cameroon).

74. In determining what constitutes a "success" or "failure" for the powerful state in each case, I weigh outcomes versus war aims but generally employ codings from the existing literature unless there is good reason to do otherwise.
75. As both precedent and model for delineating and coding civil-military bargaining across cases and over time within cases, see Feaver, *Armed Servants* and Brooks, *Shaping Strategy*. I draw upon each of these works for my coding methodology.
76. Jason Lyall and Isaiah Wilson, "Rage against the Machines: Explaining Outcomes in Counterinsurgency Wars," *International Organization* 63, Winter (2009): 70. Ivan Arreguin-Toft, "How the Weak Win Wars: A Theory of Asymmetric Conflict," *International Security* 26, no. 1 (2001).
77. Although this finding is relevant, one should not read too much into it given the blurred direction of causation. Failure in war is likely just as much a cause of civil-military conflict as it is an outcome associated with civil-military conflict.
78. Note: As an attempt to better capture variation in the timing of withdrawal, I also assessed the relationship between civil-military bargaining and political leadership behavior (new leaders) by dividing political leader observations into two-year time slices. This increased the number of observations (and thus makes the findings appear more robust) but had little impact on the direction of the findings.

4 Israel in Lebanon (1982–1985)

1. Neill Lochery, *The Israeli Labour Party: In the Shadow of the Likud* (Reading, Berkshire: Ithaca Press, 1997), 102. See also "An Israeli Pullout: The Obstacles in the Way," *New York Times*, September 25, 1984; Yael Yishai, "Hawkish Proletariat: The Case of Israel," *Journal of Political and Military Sociology* 13(1985): 56. David Shipler, "A Divided Israel," *New York Times*, July 7, 1984.
2. Avraham Tamir and Joan Comay, *A Soldier in Search of Peace: An inside Look at Israel's Strategy*, 1st American ed. (New York: Harper & Row, 1988), 127.
3. See Avner Yaniv, *Dilemmas of Security: Politics, Strategy, and the Israeli Experience in Lebanon* (New York: Oxford University Press, 1987), 193, 218, 51. Zeev Schiff, Ehud Yaari, and Ina Friedman, *Israel's Lebanon War* (New York: Simon and Schuster, 1984), 230. David Shipler, "A Quagmire for Israelis," *New York Times*, September 17, 1982; Dan Bavly and Eliahu Salpeter, *Fire in Beirut: Israel's War in Lebanon with the P.L.O.* (Briarcliff Manor, NY: Stein and Day, 1984), 172.
4. See "Israel's Victory in Lebanon," *The Washington Post*, January 18, 1985.
5. Avner Yaniv and Robert J. Lieber, "Personal Whim or Strategic Imperative? The Israeli Invasion of Lebanon," *International Security* 8, no. 2 (1983): 131.

"At Home Abroad: Looking for an Exit," *New York Times*, November 5, 1984; Amos Perlmutter, "Begin's Rhetoric and Sharon's Tactics," *Foreign Affairs* 60, no. 1 (1982); Robert W. Tucker, "Lebanon: The Case for the War," *Commentary* 74, no. 4 (1982).

6. See "Israelis Cut Off West Beirut, Trapping P.L.O. Leaders," *New York Times*, June 15, 1982.
7. Ariel Sharon and David Chanoff, *Warrior: The Autobiography of Ariel Sharon* (New York: Simon and Schuster, 1989), 469. See also "Israel Proclaims Tough Proposals for Ending War," *New York Times*, June 28, 1982.
8. Sharon and Chanoff, *Warrior: The Autobiography of Ariel Sharon*, 480. See also "New Battles Shatter Lebanon Cease-Fire," *New York Times*, June 14, 1982.
9. "Israelis Assert P.L.O. Is Fortifying Its Military and Political Positions," *New York Times*, July 13, 1982.
10. Itamar Rabinovich, *The War for Lebanon, 1970–1985*, rev. ed., Cornell Paperbacks (Ithaca: Cornell University Press, 1985), 139. See also David Shipler, "For Israelis, the Taste of Victory Starts to Turn Sour," *New York Times*, July 25, 1982.
11. Thomas L. Friedman, "P.L.O.'S Decision to Leave," *New York Times*, August 11, 1982; "Egypt and Syria Reported Opening Doors to the P.L.O.," *New York Times*, August 8, 1982. "Israeli Official Says Pullout Moves at a Satisfactory Pace," *New York Times*, August 30, 1982. "Israelis Accept Plan to End Beirut Siege; Goal Is to Begin P.L.O. Pullout Tomorrow," *New York Times*, August 20, 1982; "Last Guerillas Quit West Beirut," *New York Times*, September 2, 1982; "Syrian-Led Force Quits West Beirut," *New York Times*, August 28, 1982.
12. "Gemayel Is Buried as Political Leaders Call for Calm in Lebanon," *New York Times*, September 16, 1982.
13. "Excerpts from Testimony at Inquiry on Massacre," *New York Times*, October 26, 1982.
14. "Massacre in Beirut: The Evidence from Four Shameful Days," *The Times*, September 24, 1982.
15. Elie Adib Salem, *Violence and Diplomacy in Lebanon: The Troubled Years, 1982–1988* (London; New York: I. B. Tauris, Distributed by St. Martin's Press, 1995), 33; "Lebanon Says Pullout Talks with Israel May Start This Week," *New York Times*, December 22, 1982.
16. "Israeli Foreign Minister Says He Expects Pullout from Lebanon This Year," *New York Times*, October 3, 1982; "Israeli Statement on Pullout," *New York Times*, October 11, 1982; "Israel Is Said to Link Pullout Talks with Normalizing Lebanon Ties," *New York Times*, November 10, 1982; "Impasse on Troop Pullout: Israel Seeks a Peace Treaty," *New York Times*, December 6, 1982; "A Prior P.L.O. Pullout Is Demanded by Israelis," *New York Times*, October 6, 1982.
17. Rabinovich, *The War for Lebanon, 1970–1985*, 193. See also "Israel and Lebanon Sign Agreement at Two Ceremonies," *New York Times*, May 18, 1983.

18. "Scrapping of Accord with Israel Hastens Partition of Lebanon," *The Times*, March 6, 1984.
19. See "Israel Votes Lebanon Pact in Principle, but a Pullout Awaits Talks with Syrians," *New York Times*, May 7, 1983; "Lebanon: The Hawks Come Home to Roost," *The Times*, February 8, 1984; "Syria Fights Israeli Pullout Terms," *New York Times*, May 3, 1983; "Lebanese-Israeli Pullout Pact: Only Ink and Paper Unless Syrians Go Along," *New York Times*, May 18, 1983.
20. Rabinovich, *The War for Lebanon, 1970–1985*, 192. Also, see David Shipler, "A Retreat by Israel," *New York Times*, September 5, 1983.
21. "Shamir's Lebanon Plan Shows Typical Caution," *Los Angeles Times*, October 17, 1983. Roberto Suro, Johanna McGeary, and James Kelly, "Middle East: A House Divided," *Time*, August 8 1983.
22. Tamir and Comay, *A Soldier in Search of Peace*, 157–8. See also "Israel to Speed up Lebanon Pullout," *New York Times*, March 27, 1985.
23. "Israel Starts First Stage of Its Lebanon Pullout," *New York Times*, January 21, 1985. "Peres Sets June 6 for Lebanon Troop Pullout," *New York Times*, June 3, 1985.
24. Shai Feldman and Heda Rechnitz-Kijner, *Deception, Consensus and War: Israel in Lebanon*, vol. no. 27 (Tel Aviv: Jaffee Center for Strategic Studies, 1984), 50.
25. Quoted in Richard A. Gabriel, *Operation Peace for Galilee: The Israeli-PLO War in Lebanon* (New York: Hill and Wang, 1984), 184.
26. "Balking at Tank Attack on Beirut Ended Career of Young Israeli Colonel: Military, Political, Moral Objections," *The Washington Post*, April 20, 1985.
27. Gil Merom, *How Democracies Lose Small Wars: State, Society, and the Failures of France in Algeria, Israel in Lebanon, and the United States in Vietnam* (Cambridge, UK; New York: Cambridge University Press, 2003), 198.
28. Feldman and Rechnitz-Kijner, *Deception, Consensus and War*, 60.
29. Schiff, Yaari, and Friedman, *Israel's Lebanon War*, 281.
30. See Dominic D. P. Johnson and Dominic Tierney, *Failing to Win: Perceptions of Victory and Defeat in International Politics* (Cambridge, MA: Harvard University Press, 2006), 168–72.
31. Yitzhak Rabin, *The Rabin Memoirs*, expanded ed. (Berkeley: University of California Press, 1996), 238.
32. Merom, *How Democracies Lose Small Wars*, 189.
33. "Report of the Commission of Inquiry into the Events at the Refugee Camps in Beirut (the Kahan Commission)," http://www.jewishvirtuallibrary.org/jsource/History/kahan.html.
34. "Beirut Massacre Inquiry: Army Chief Was Reluctant to Use Phalangists," *The Times*, November 1, 1982.
35. Gabriel, *Operation Peace for Galilee*, 221. Also Amir Bar-or, "The Link Between the Government and the IDF," in *Military, State, and Society in Israel: Theoretical & Comparative Perspectives*, ed. Daniel Maman, Eyal Ben-Ari, and Zeev Rosenhek (New Brunswick, NJ: Transaction Publishers, 2001), 329.

36. See Merom, *How Democracies Lose Small Wars*, 189.
37. Yaniv, *Dilemmas of Security*, 195–9.
38. Ibid., 198.
39. "Israeli Document Asks Lebanon Exit," *New York Times*, January 11, 1984.
40. Yaniv, *Dilemmas of Security*, 261.
41. Ibid., 245.
42. Quoted in "Lebanon Has Sapped Israel's Army: Now It Is Smaller, Less Well Trained, More Dependent on U.S.," *The Washington Post*, April 20, 1985.
43. Ibid.
44. Ibid.
45. See Yaniv, *Dilemmas of Security*, 257.
46. "Lebanon Has Sapped Israel's Army," *The Washington Post.*
47. See Yaniv, *Dilemmas of Security*, 257.
48. Amos Perlmutter, "Begin's Rhetoric and Sharon's Tactics," *Foreign Affairs* 60, no. 1 (1982): 71. See also Ilan Peleg, "The Foreign Policy of Herut and the Likud," in *Israeli National Security: Political Actors and Perspectives*, ed. Bernard Reich and Gershon R. Kieval (New York: Greenwood Press, 1988), 65–7.
49. Perlmutter, "Begin's Rhetoric and Sharon's Tactics," 67–71. See also Avi Shlaim and Avner Yaniv, "Politics and Foreign Policy in Israel," *International Affairs* 56, no. 2 (1980): 246–55.
50. Ilan Peleg, *Begin's Foreign Policy, 1977–1983: Israel's Move to the Right*, Contributions in Political Science, (New York: Greenwood Press, 1987), 148.
51. Yaniv, *Dilemmas of Security*, 262. See also "Israeli Election: Likud May Live to Lament Lebanon," *The Times*, July 12, 1984.
52. Yaniv, *Dilemmas of Security*, 262. See also Bernard Reich, "Israeli National Security Policy: Issues and Actors," in *Israeli National Security: Political Actors and Perspectives*, ed. Bernard Reich and Gershon R. Kieval (New York: Greenwood Press, 1988), 7.
53. "Shamir's Lebanon Plan Shows Typical Caution," *Los Angeles Times.*
54. See "Peres Pledges Pullout from Lebanon If He Wins Vote," *New York Times*, June 23, 1984; Shimon Peres and David Landau, *Battling for Peace: A Memoir* (New York: Random House, 1995), 232.
55. See Yair Evron, *War and Intervention in Lebanon: The Israeli-Syrian Deterrence Dialogue* (Baltimore: Johns Hopkins University Press, 1987), 167; Marver H. Bernstein, "Coping with Turbulence: The First Two Years of the National Unity Government under Peres," in *Israeli National Security: Political Actors and Perspectives*, ed. Bernard Reich and Gershon R. Kieval (New York: Greenwood Press, 1988), 212; Gershon R. Kieval, "The Foreign Policy of the Labor Party," in *Israeli National Security: Political Actors and Perspectives*, ed. Bernard Reich and Gershon R. Kieval (New York: Greenwood Press, 1988), 41.
56. As evidence of this trend, see "Scrapping of Accord with Israel Hastens Partition of Lebanon," *The Times*; "Israelis Say Redeployment Isn't Withdrawal," *New York Times*, January 7, 1984.
57. Yaniv, *Dilemmas of Security*, 205.
58. "Withdrawal Plan Denied by Israeli," *New York Times*, January 9, 1984.

59. Ibid.
60. "Israeli Document Asks Lebanon Exit," *New York Times.*
61. Yaniv, *Dilemmas of Security*, 261.
62. "Israeli Document Asks Lebanon Exit," *New York Times.*
63. See "Israel Determined to Keep out of Lebanon Chaos," *The Times*, February 7, 1984; "Israeli Cabinet in Second Crisis Meeting on Lebanon," *The Times*, February 13, 1984.
64. See "Sidon Hq Handover: Israel May Pull Back Further," *The Times*, May 16, 1984; "Israelis Plan New Lebanon Strategy," *The Times*, March 7, 1984; "Israel Denies Preparing for Lebanon Pullback," *The Times*, March 12, 1984; "Cabinet Undecided on Pullout," *The Times*, March 13, 1984; "Israelis May Quit Lebanon before Syria Does," *New York Times*, January 7, 1984.
65. Peres and Landau, *Battling for Peace: A Memoir*, 234; Bernstein, "Coping with Turbulence," 209–10.
66. Evron, *War and Intervention in Lebanon*. See also Michael Bar-Zohar, *Shimon Peres: The Biography*, 1st American ed. (New York: Random House, 2007), 365.
67. Yaniv, *Dilemmas of Security*, 280. See also "Israeli Visits a Worried Border Town," *New York Times*, April 26, 1985.
68. Bernard Avishai, *A New Israel: Democracy in Crisis, 1973–1988: Essays* (New York: Ticknor & Fields, 1990), 153.
69. Lochery, *The Israeli Labour Party*, 121.
70. Richard A. Gabriel, *Correspondence with Author, April-June 2011*. "Peres Hints at Lebanon Withdrawal," *The Times*, October 12, 1984; "Israeli Officers Present Lebanon Pullout Plan," *New York Times*, August 12, 1984.
71. See "Lebanon Pullout Agreed by Israel," *The Times*, January 15, 1985.
72. Lochery, *The Israeli Labour Party*, 121.
73. "The Israeli Withdrawal: Peres Says Army Will Be Home from Lebanon by Summer," *The Times*, January 16, 1985.
74. See Elizbeth Hann Hastings and Philip K. Hastings, eds., *Index to International Public Opinion, 1985–1986, Prepared by Survey Research Consultants International, Inc.* (New York: Greenwood Press), 221. "Israeli Cabinet Approves Second Stage of Troop Pullout from Lebanon," *New York Times*, March 4, 1985.
75. "Israelis Complete Step Two of Pullout," *New York Times*, April 30, 1985; "Car Bomb Hits an Israeli Convoy in Southern Lebanon, Killing 12," *New York Times*, March 11, 1985.
76. Merom, *How Democracies Lose Small Wars*, 15–24.
77. Ibid., 15–16.
78. Original claims cited 400,000 participants, and this event is still often referred to as the "400,000 rally." Later estimates came in around 200,000 and even organizers of the event eventually conceded that the original number was vastly overstated. See Warchawski, "Inside the Anti-Occupation Camp," *The Link (Americans for Middle East Understanding)* 39, no. 2 (2006). It is also important to note that the size of this protest reflected public dissatisfaction with the government's handling of the Sabra and Shatilla incident, not necessarily dissatisfaction with the war as a whole.

79. Yaniv, *Dilemmas of Security*, 246.
80. Elizbeth Hann Hastings and Philip K. Hastings, eds., *Index to International Public Opinion, 1982–1983, Prepared by Survey Research Consultants International, Inc.* (New York: Greenwood Press), 232–4; ———, eds., *Index to International Public Opinion, 1983–1984, Prepared by Survey Research Consultants International, Inc.* (New York: Greenwood Press), 92; ———, eds., *Index to International Public Opinion, 1984–1985, Prepared by Survey Research Consultants International, Inc.* (New York: Greenwood Press), 225–6.
81. Referenced in Yaniv, *Dilemmas of Security*, 196.
82. Hastings and Hastings, eds., *Index to International Public Opinion, 1982–1983, Prepared by Survey Research Consultants International, Inc.*, 377; ———, eds., *Index to International Public Opinion, 1983–1984, Prepared by Survey Research Consultants International, Inc.*, 383.
83. See Gad Barzilai, *Wars, Internal Conflicts, and Political Order: A Jewish Democracy in the Middle East*, Suny Series in Israeli Studies (Albany: State University of New York Press, 1996), 147.
84. Daniel Judah Elazar, "Begin's Two-Year Government," in *Israel at the Polls, 1981: A Study of the Knesset Elections*, ed. Howard Rae Penniman and Daniel Judah Elazar (Washington: American Enterprise Institute for Public Policy Research, 1986), 249.
85. Yaniv, *Dilemmas of Security*, 156.
86. Elazar, "Begin's Two-Year Government," 249.
87. Yaniv, *Dilemmas of Security*, 156.
88. See Ned Temko, *To Win or to Die: A Personal Portrait of Menachem Begin* (New York: W. Morrow, 1987), 288.
89. Bavly and Salpeter, *Fire in Beirut*, 171. Also see Hastings and Hastings, eds., *Index to International Public Opinion, 1982–1983, Prepared by Survey Research Consultants International, Inc.*, 221–22.
90. From The *Jerusalem Post*, cited in Yaniv, *Dilemmas of Security*, 250.
91. Gabriel, *Operation Peace for Galilee*, 220.
92. The Shi'ite takeover of West Beirut, the collapse of the Lebanese government, and Amin's revoking of the May 17 Agreement were widely perceived as serious blows to Israel's Lebanon policy, but this series of events did not begin until February 1984.
93. Feldman and Rechnitz-Kijner, *Deception, Consensus and War*, 53; Yoram Peri, "Intractable Conflict and the Media," *Israel Studies* 12, no. 1 (2007): 83.
94. Quoted in Feldman and Rechnitz-Kijner, *Deception, Consensus and War*, 53.
95. Ibid.

5 The Netherlands in Indonesia (1946–1949)

1. Arend Lijphart, *The Politics of Accommodation: Pluralism and Democracy in the Netherlands* (Berkeley: University of California Press, 1968), 77, 101.
2. Marc Frey, "Dutch Elites and Decolonization," in *Elites and Decolonization in the Twentieth Century*, ed. Jost Dülffer and Marc Frey (New York: Palgrave

Macmillan, 2011), 58; "The Ambassador in the Netherlands (Baruch) to the Secretary of State, May 28, 1948," in *F.R.U.S., 1948, Volume 6*, 188; "Department of External Affairs to Kirby, January 3, 1948," in *Documents on Australian Foreign Policy, 1948, Volume 13*.

3. "Events in Indonesia 1939–48, Foreign Office Research Department Memorandum, June 16, 1948," in *British Documents on Foreign Affairs: Reports and Papers from the Foreign Office Confidential Print, Part 4, Series E, Asia 1948, Volume 6* (2001), 75; "The Acting Secretary of State to the Consulate General at Batavia, November 18, 1948," in *F.R.U.S., 1948, Volume 6*, 493.
4. "The Ambassador in the Netherlands (Baruch) to the Secretary of State, June 17, 1949," in *F.R.U.S., 1949, Volume 7*, 443–5.
5. "Dispute between the Netherlands and Indonesia, Sir P. Nichols to Mr. Attlee, December 1, 1949," in *British Documents on Foreign Affairs: Reports and Papers from the Foreign Office Confidential Print, Part 4, Series E, Asia 1949, Volume 9* (2001), 252.
6. "Events in Indonesia 1939–48, Foreign Office Research Department Memorandum, June 16, 1948," 67. Also see Hong Lee Oey, *War and Diplomacy in Indonesia, 1945–50*, South-East Asian Monograph Series, (Townsville, Australia: Committee of South-East Asian Studies, James Cook University of North Queensland, 1981), 10; "The Consul General at Batavia (Livengood) to the Secretary of State, November 17, 1947," in *F.R.U.S., 1947, Volume 6*, 1072.
7. "Basic Dutch-Indonesian Issues and the Linggadjati Agreement," (United States Central Intelligence Group, 9 June 1947), 3. "Lord Killearn to Mr. Bevin, May 11, 1946," in *British Documents on Foreign Affairs: Reports and Papers from the Foreign Office Confidential Print, Part 4, Series E, Asia 1946, Volume 1* (2001), 455.
8. "Political Developments within the Indonesian Republic, Consul-General Sir F. Shepherd to Mr. Bevin, September 30, 1948," in *British Documents on Foreign Affairs: Reports and Papers from the Foreign Office Confidential Print, Part 4, Series E, Asia 1948, Volume 6* (2001).
9. "Events in Indonesia 1939–48, Foreign Office Research Department Memorandum, June 16, 1948," 68.
10. Ibid. Also see J. Leimena, *The Dutch-Indonesian Conflict* (Jakarta 1949), 2.
11. *The Netherlands Commonwealth and the Future: Important Statements of H. M. Queen Wilhelmina on Post-War Aims, Together with Statements by the Netherlands Government, the Dutch Press, as well as Some American Comments*, (New York: The Netherlands Information Bureau, 1945), 21, 35.
12. "Summary of Proposals Leading to the Present Negotiations between the Dutch and Indonesians, E. Lambert, March 23, 1946," in *British Documents on Foreign Affairs: Reports and Papers from the Foreign Office Confidential Print, Part 4, Series E, Asia 1946, Volume 1* (2001), 282.
13. "Sir Nevile Bland to Mr. Bevin, August 6, 1946," in *British Documents on Foreign Affairs: Reports and Papers from the Foreign Office Confidential Print, Part 4, Series E, Asia 1946, Volume 2* (2001), 166.

14. "The Consul General at Batavia (Foote) to the Secretary of State, May 30, 1946," in *F.R.U.S., 1946, Volume 8*, 825. "Ballard to Evatt, January 6, 1947," in *Documents on Australian Foreign Policy, 1947, Volume 11*. "Summary of Events in Java, Mr. Sterndale Bennett to Mr. Wright, February 6, 1946," in *British Documents on Foreign Affairs: Reports and Papers from the Foreign Office Confidential Print, Part 4, Series E, Asia 1946, Volume 1* (2001), 278–9.
15. "Consul-General Mackereth to Mr. Bevin, April 17, 1946," in *British Documents on Foreign Affairs: Reports and Papers from the Foreign Office Confidential Print, Part 4, Series E, Asia 1946, Volume 1* (2001), 441. See also "Dutch-Indonesian Relations: Interpretation of Linggadjati Agreement Deadlock, Mr. Grey to Mr. Bevin, June 9, 1947," in *British Documents on Foreign Affairs: Reports and Papers from the Foreign Office Confidential Print, Part 4, Series E, Asia 1947, Volume 4* (2001), 236–7; "Gilchrist to Burton, July 21, 1947," in *Documents on Australian Foreign Policy, 1947, Volume 11*.
16. "The Consul General at Batavia (Foote) to the Secretary of State, July 25, 1947," in *F.R.U.S., 1947, Volume 6*, 989. "Eastern Sumatra: Netherlands-Indonesian Hostilities: Political-Military Developments, Acting-Consul Roberts to Consul-General Mitcheson (Batavia), July 26, 1947," in *British Documents on Foreign Affairs: Reports and Papers from the Foreign Office Confidential Print, Part 4, Series E, Asia 1947, Volume 4* (2001), 244. "Netherlands-Indonesian Relations, Mr. Gage to Mr. Bevin, July 20, 1947," in *British Documents on Foreign Affairs: Reports and Papers from the Foreign Office Confidential Print, Part 4, Series E, Asia 1947, Volume 4* (2001), 238. Also see "The Ambassador in the Netherlands (Baruch) to the Secretary of State, July 20, 1947," in *F.R.U.S., 1947, Volume 6*, 982.
17. "Sumatra: Netherlands-Indonesian Hostilities: Political-Military Developments, Acting-Consul Roberts to Mr. Mitcheson (Batavia), August 2, 1947," in *British Documents on Foreign Affairs: Reports and Papers from the Foreign Office Confidential Print, Part 4, Series E, Asia 1947, Volume 4* (2001), 249.
18. "Sumatra: Netherlands-Indonesian Hostilities: Political-Military Developments, Acting Consul Roberts to Consul-General Mitcheson (Batavia), 9 August, 1947," in *British Documents on Foreign Affairs: Reports and Papers from the Foreign Office Confidential Print, Part 4, Series E, Asia 1947, Volume 4* (2001), 250. See also "East Sumatra: Military-Political Situation, Acting Consul Roberts to Consul-General Mitcheson (Batavia), August 23, 1947," in *British Documents on Foreign Affairs: Reports and Papers from the Foreign Office Confidential Print, Part 4, Series E, Asia 1947, Volume 4* (2001), 257.
19. "Situation in Indonesia: Truce Agreement and Renville Principles, Consul-General Shepherd to Mr. Bevin, January 21, 1948," in *British Documents on Foreign Affairs: Reports and Papers from the Foreign Office Confidential Print, Part 4, Series E, Asia 1948, Volume 6* (2001), 33; "Kirby to Burton, January 9, 1948," in *Documents on Australian Foreign Policy, 1948, Volume 13*.
20. "Situation in Indonesia, Sir P. Nichols to Mr. Bevin, December 18, 1948," in *British Documents on Foreign Affairs: Reports and Papers from the Foreign Office Confidential Print, Part 4, Series E, Asia 1948, Volume 6* (2001), 115. Also see

P. M. H. Groen, "Dutch Armed Forces and the Decolonization of Indonesia: The Second Police Action (1948–1949), a Pandora's Box," *War and Society* 4, no. 1 (1986): 82.

21. "The Consul General at Batavia (Livengood) to the Secretary of State, December 18, 1948," in *F.R.U.S., 1948, Volume 6*, 581. "Situation in Indonesia, Consul-General Sir F. Shepherd to Mr. Bevin, March 28, 1949," in *British Documents on Foreign Affairs: Reports and Papers from the Foreign Office Confidential Print, Part 4, Series E, Asia 1949, Volume 9* (2001), 166–7. "Cutts to Department of External Affairs, December 19, 1948," in *Documents on Australian Foreign Policy, 1948, Volume 13.*
22. "The Acting Secretary of State to the Acting United States Representative at the United Nations (Jessup) at Paris, December 23, 1948," in *F.R.U.S., 1948, Volume 6*, 597–600; "Memorandum by the Director of the Office of Far Eastern Affairs (Butterworth) to the Counselor of the Department (Bohlen), January 17, 1949," in *F.R.U.S., 1949, Volume 7*, 136.
23. "Hodgson to Department of External Affairs, December 24, 1948," in *Documents on Australian Foreign Policy, 1948, Volume 13.*
24. "The Consul General at Batavia (Livengood) to the Secretary of State, November 11, 1948," in *F.R.U.S., 1948, Volume 6*, 483; "Memorandum of Conversation by the Acting Secretary of State, December 20, 1948," in *F.R.U.S., 1948, Volume 6*, 591.
25. Dirk U. Stikker, *Men of Responsibility: A Memoir* (New York: Harper & Row, 1966), 146; "The Ambassador in Belgium (Kirk) to the Secretary of State, February 9, 1949," in *F.R.U.S., 1949, Volume 7*, 217–22. "The Acting Secretary of State to the Consulate General at Batavia, November 18, 1948," 492.
26. Lucian Ashworth, "The 1945–1949 Dutch-Indonesian Conflict: Lessons and Perspectives in the Study of Insurgency," *Conflict Quarterly* Winter (1990): 41.
27. "The Ambassador in the Netherlands (Baruch) to the Secretary of State, June 17, 1949," 443–5.
28. J. A. A. Van Doorn, *The Soldier and Social Change: Comparative Studies in the History and Sociology of the Military*, Sage Series on Armed Forces and Society V. 7 (Beverly Hills, CA: Sage Publications, 1975), 129.
29. Rob Kroes, "Decolonization and the Military: The Case of the Netherlands, a Study in Political Reaction," in *On Military Intervention*, ed. Morris Janowitz and J. A. A. van Doorn (Rotterdam: Rotterdam University Press, 1971), 110.
30. Martin Thomas, Bob Moore, and L. J. Butler, *Crises of Empire: Decolonization and Europe's Imperial States, 1918–1975* (London: Hodder Education, 2008), 322.
31. J. Hoogenboezem, *Correspondence with Author, August-October 2011.*
32. Ibid.
33. P. M. H. Groen, "Militant Response: The Dutch Use of Military Force and the Decolonization of the Dutch East Indies, 1945–50," *Journal of Imperial and Commonwealth History* 21, no. 3 (1993): 35.
34. Hoogenboezem, *Correspondence with Author, August-October 2011.*

35. Jan R. Schoeman, "Netherlands," in *The Political Role of the Military: An International Handbook*, ed. Constantine P. Danopoulos and Cynthia Watson (London: Greenwood Press, 1996), 285.
36. Van Doorn, *The Soldier and Social Change*, 124.
37. P. M. H. Groen, *Correspondence with Author, August 2011.*
38. J. A. A. Van Doorn, "Justifying Military Action," in *On Military Ideology*, ed. Morris Janowitz and J. A. A. Van Doorn (Rotterdam: Rotterdam University Press, 1971).
39. "The Acting United States Representative at the United Nations (Jessup) to the Acting Secretary of State, January 17, 1949," in *F.R.U.S., 1949, Volume 7*, 162.
40. "Dispute between the Netherlands and Indonesia, Sir P. Nichols to Mr. Attlee, December 1, 1949," 251.
41. "Netherlands: The Indonesian Problem: Programme of the Dutch Labour Party, Sir N. Bland to Mr. Bevin, September 11, 1947," in *British Documents on Foreign Affairs: Reports and Papers from the Foreign Office Confidential Print, Part 4, Series E, Asia 1947, Volume 4* (2001), 259–60.
42. J. J. C. Voorhoeve, *Peace, Profits and Principles: A Study of Dutch Foreign Policy* (The Hague: Martinus Nijhoff, 1979), 60; R. B. Andeweg and Galen A. Irwin, *Dutch Government and Politics* (New York: St. Martin's Press, 1993), 37; Arend Lijphart, *Patterns of Democracy: Government Forms and Performance in Thirty-Six Countries* (New Haven: Yale University Press, 1999), 31–47.
43. Stikker, *Men of Responsibility*, 119.
44. "The Ambassador in the Netherlands (Baruch) to the Secretary of State, March 10, 1949," in *F.R.U.S., 1949, Volume 7*, 310; "Situation in Indonesia: Debate in the Netherlands Second Chamber, Sir P. Nichols to Mr. Bevin, May 19, 1949," in *British Documents on Foreign Affairs: Reports and Papers from the Foreign Office Confidential Print, Part 4, Series E, Asia 1949, Volume 9* (2001), 169–71; "The Chargé in the Netherlands (Steere) to the Secretary of State, July 18, 1949," in *F.R.U.S., 1949, Volume 7*, 460.
45. "The Ambassador in the Netherlands (Baruch) to the Secretary of State, December 21, 1948," in *F.R.U.S., 1948, Volume 6*, 596. "Situation in Indonesia: Events Leading up to Resumption of Police Action by the Netherlands Government, Consul-General Sir F. Shepherd to Mr. Bevin, December 22, 1948," in *British Documents on Foreign Affairs: Reports and Papers from the Foreign Office Confidential Print, Part 4, Series E, Asia 1949, Volume 9* (2001), 158–60.
46. Groen, "Militant Response," 34; "The Ambassador in the Netherlands (Baruch) to the Secretary of State, December 21, 1948," 596.
47. "Quinn to Hood, December 2, 1948," in *Documents on Australian Foreign Policy, 1948, Volume 13.*
48. "The Consul General at Batavia (Livengood) to the Secretary of State, November 25, 1948," in *F.R.U.S., 1948, Volume 6*, 500.
49. Frey, "Dutch Elites and Decolonization," 59.

50. "Netherlands: The Indonesian Problem: Programme of the Dutch Labour Party, Sir N. Bland to Mr. Bevin, September 11, 1947," 259–60; "Conversation between the Secretary of State and the Netherlands Minister for Foreign Affairs, Mr. Bevin to Mr. Gage (the Hague), October 1, 1948," in *British Documents on Foreign Affairs: Reports and Papers from the Foreign Office Confidential Print, Part 4, Series E, Asia 1948, Volume 6*, 104.
51. "Dispute between the Netherlands and Indonesia, Sir P. Nichols to Mr. Attlee, December 1, 1949," 253. Also see "The Ambassador in Belgium (Kirk) to the Secretary of State, February 9, 1949," 217–22.
52. "Netherlands: The Indonesian Problem: Programme of the Dutch Labour Party, Sir N. Bland to Mr. Bevin, September 11, 1947," 259–60.
53. Kroes, "Decolonization and the Military," 103. Also see Schoeman, "Netherlands," 283.
54. Groen, "Militant Response," 42. "Sumatra: Political-Military Situation in East Coast, Acting Consul Roberts to Consul-General Mitcheson (Batavia), May 22, 1947," in *British Documents on Foreign Affairs: Reports and Papers from the Foreign Office Confidential Print, Part 4, Series E, Asia 1947, Volume 4* (2001), 233–4.
55. "The Consul General at Batavia (Foote) to the Secretary of State, July 22, 1947," in *F.R.U.S., 1947, Volume 6*, 985; "Makin to Department of External Affairs, July 30, 1947," in *Documents on Australian Foreign Policy, 1947, Volume 11.*
56. Stikker, *Men of Responsibility: A Memoir*, 121.
57. "The Consul General at Batavia (Livengood) to the Secretary of State, July 21, 1948," in *F.R.U.S., 1948, Volume 6*, 287. "The Netherlands-Indonesian Problem: Views of Professor Schermerhorn, Sir N. Bland to Mr. Bevin, August 8, 1947," in *British Documents on Foreign Affairs: Reports and Papers from the Foreign Office Confidential Print, Part 4, Series E, Asia 1947, Volume 4* (2001), 245. There is also evidence that military leaders weighed in on the economic consequences of ceding Indonesia to the Republic. See "Consul-General Mackereth to Mr. Bevin, April 24, 1946," in *British Documents on Foreign Affairs: Reports and Papers from the Foreign Office Confidential Print, Part 4, Series E, Asia 1946, Volume 1* (2001), 442–3.
58. "Consul-General Mackereth to Mr. Bevin, April 24, 1946," 442–3.
59. See "The Ambassador in the Netherlands (Baruch) to the Secretary of State, October 8, 1948," in *F.R.U.S., 1948, Volume 6*, 398.
60. "The Ambassador in the Netherlands (Baruch) to the Secretary of State, October 30, 1948," in *F.R.U.S., 1948, Volume 6*, 442. Also see "Quinn to Evatt, March 1, 1949," in *Documents on Australian Foreign Policy, 1949, Volume 15.*
61. "The Consul General at Batavia (Livengood) to the Secretary of State, January 20, 1949," in *F.R.U.S., 1949, Volume 7*, 185–6.
62. "Consul-General Mackereth to Mr. Bevin, April 24, 1946," 442–3.
63. See Van Doorn, *The Soldier and Social Change*, 123. Also Arend Lijphart, *The Trauma of Decolonization: The Dutch and West New Guinea*, Yale Studies in Political Science, 17 (New Haven: Yale University Press, 1966), 122–5.

64. Frey, "Dutch Elites and Decolonization," 58. Also see "Quinn to Burton, December 22, 1948," in *Documents on Australian Foreign Policy, 1948, Volume 13*; "Quinn to Department of External Affairs, December 30, 1948," in *Documents on Australian Foreign Policy, 1948, Volume 13.*
65. "Political Situation in Indonesia, Consul-General Shepherd to Mr. Bevin, November 13, 1947," in *British Documents on Foreign Affairs: Reports and Papers from the Foreign Office Confidential Print, Part 4, Series E, Asia 1947, Volume 4* (2001), 293; "The Consul General at Batavia (Livengood) to the Secretary of State, January 20, 1949," 185–6.
66. Stikker, *Men of Responsibility*, 144.
67. "The Consul General at Batavia (Livengood) to the Secretary of State, January 7, 1948," in *F.R.U.S., 1948, Volume 6*, 65. "Lord Killearn to Mr. Bevin, May 27, 1946," in *British Documents on Foreign Affairs: Reports and Papers from the Foreign Office Confidential Print, Part 4, Series E, Asia 1946, Volume 1* (2001), 467.
68. "The Consul General at Batavia (Livengood) to the Secretary of State, October 13, 1948," in *F.R.U.S., 1948, Volume 6*, 416–17. "Mr. Bevin to Sir N. Bland, April 29, 1946," in *British Documents on Foreign Affairs: Reports and Papers from the Foreign Office Confidential Print, Part 4, Series E, Asia 1946, Volume 1* (2001), 448. Also "Lord Killearn to Mr. Bevin, October 13, 1946," in *British Documents on Foreign Affairs: Reports and Papers from the Foreign Office Confidential Print, Part 4, Series E, Asia 1946, Volume 2* (2001), 392.
69. Attributed to Vice Admiral Pinke. See "The Consul General at Batavia (Livengood) to the Secretary of State, November 11, 1948," 482. Also see "The Consul General at Batavia (Livengood) to the Secretary of State, November 7, 1948," in *F.R.U.S., 1948, Volume 6*, 471.
70. "The Consul General at Batavia (Livengood) to the Secretary of State, November 11, 1948," 482.
71. "The Consul General at Batavia (Livengood) to the Secretary of State, November 25, 1948," 500.
72. "The Secretary of State to the Embassy in the Netherlands, January 31, 1949," in *F.R.U.S., 1949, Volume 7*, 197.
73. "The Consul General at Batavia (Livengood) to the Secretary of State, January 3, 1949," in *F.R.U.S., 1949, Volume 7*, 120.
74. Groen, *Correspondence with Author, August 2011.*
75. "The Ambassador in the United Kingdom (Douglas) to the Secretary of State, February 18, 1949," in *F.R.U.S., 1949, Volume 7*, 243.
76. Thomas, Moore, and Butler, *Crises of Empire*, 331.
77. "The Ambassador in Belgium (Kirk) to the Secretary of State, February 9, 1949," 217–22. See also "The Acting Secretary of State to the Consulate General at Batavia, November 18, 1948," 492. "The Consul General at Batavia (Livengood) to the Secretary of State, December 2, 1948," in *F.R.U.S., 1948, Volume 6*, 508.
78. Groen, "Militant Response," 41.
79. Daniel Ellsberg, *Papers on the War* (New York: Simon and Schuster, 1972), 91.

80. See Groen, "Militant Response," 34.
81. Thomas, Moore, and Butler, *Crises of Empire*, 326. "Situation in the East Coast of Sumatra, Acting Consul Roberts to Consul-General Shepherd, November 17, 1947," in *British Documents on Foreign Affairs: Reports and Papers from the Foreign Office Confidential Print, Part 4, Series E, Asia 1947, Volume 4* (2001), 294.
82. Thomas, Moore, and Butler, *Crises of Empire*, 331.
83. Pierre Van der Eng, "Marshall Aid as Catalyst in the Decolonization of Indonesia, 1947–49," in *The Decolonization Reader*, ed. James D. Le Sueur (New York: Routledge, 2003), 131.
84. See George McTurnan Kahin, *Nationalism and Revolution in Indonesia*, Studies on Southeast Asia No. 35 (Ithaca, NY: Southeast Asia Program Publications, Cornell University, 2003), 406.
85. "Situation in Indonesia: Debate in the Netherlands Second Chamber, Sir P. Nichols to Mr. Bevin, May 19, 1949," 169–71; "High Commission in London to Department of External Affairs, February 18, 1949," in *Documents on Australian Foreign Policy, 1949, Volume 15*.
86. "The Ambassador in the United Kingdom (Douglas) to the Secretary of State, February 18, 1949," 243.
87. "The Consul General at Batavia (Livengood) to the Secretary of State, January 23, 1949," in *F.R.U.S., 1949, Volume 7*, 190; "The Ambassador in Belgium (Kirk) to the Secretary of State, February 9, 1949," 213.
88. "The Consul General at Batavia (Livengood) to the Secretary of State, March 8, 1949," in *F.R.U.S., 1949, Volume 7*, 307.
89. "The Consul General at Batavia (Livengood) to the Secretary of State, May 25, 1949," in *F.R.U.S., 1949, Volume 7*, 413; "The Consul General at Batavia (Livengood) to the Secretary of State, May 26, 1949," in *F.R.U.S., 1949, Volume 7*, 414.
90. Lijphart, *The Trauma of Decolonization: The Dutch and West New Guinea*, 122.

6 South Africa in Namibia (1966–1989)

1. Quoted in Willem Steenkamp, *South Africa's Border War, 1966–1989* (Gibraltar: Ashanti Pub., 1989), 145.
2. Chester A. Crocker, *High Noon in Southern Africa: Making Peace in a Rough Neighborhood* (New York: W.W. Norton, 1992), 353.
3. The Orange River defines a portion of the boundary between South Africa and Namibia.
4. See Robert I. Rotberg, "Namibia: The Regional Stalemate," in *South Africa and Its Neighbors: Regional Security and Self-Interest*, ed. Robert I. Rotberg et al. (Lexington, MA: Lexington Books, 1985), 147.
5. Robert S. Jaster, *The Defence of White Power: South African Foreign Policy under Pressure* (New York: St. Martin's Press, 1989), 19.

6. Crocker, *High Noon in Southern Africa: Making Peace in a Rough Neighborhood*, 362–3. Lieneke Eloff de Visser, "Winning Hearts and Minds in the Namibian Border War," *Scientia Militaria, South African Journal of Military Studies* 39, no. 1 (2011): 88; Hilton Hamann, *Correspondence with Author, August 2011.*
7. See Richard Leonard, *South Africa at War: White Power and the Crisis in Southern Africa* (Westport, CT: L. Hill, 1983), 61–3; P. Longmire, "Land and Labour in the Namibian Economy," in *Studies in the Economic History of Southern Africa*, ed. Zbigniew A. Konczacki, Jane L. Parpart, and Timothy M. Shaw (Savage, MD: F. Cass, 1990), 208; R. Dale, "The Armed Forces as an Instrument of South African Policy in Namibia," *Journal of Modern African Studies* 18, no. 1 (1980): 64. UNESCO, *Racism and Apartheid in Southern Africa: South Africa and Namibia* (Paris: U.N.E.S.C.O. Press, 1974). "Paper Prepared by the National Security Counicl Interdepartmental Group for Africa, Response to N.S.S.M. 89: South West Africa, April 2, 1970," in *F.R.U.S., 1969–1976, Volume 28*; "Memorandum from the President's Assistanct for National Security Affairs (Kissinger) to President Nixon, South West Africa (Namibia): Response to N.S.S.M. 89, April 15, 1970," in *F.R.U.S., 1969–1976, Volume 28.*
8. *United Nations, Resolution 2145, "Question of South West Africa,"* (United Nations General Assembly, Twenty-First Session, 27 October 1966).
9. Crocker, *High Noon in Southern Africa*, 159; Steenkamp, *South Africa's Border War, 1966–1989*, 29; H. R. Heitman, *War in Angola: The Final South African Phase* (Gibraltar: Ashanti Pub., 1990), 24–5.
10. Brian Pottinger, *The Imperial Presidency: P. W. Botha, the First 10 Years* (Johannesburg: Southern Book Publishers, 1988), 209–12; "Intelligence Note Prepared in the Bureau of Intelligence and Research, South West Africa: Enough South African-Waldheim Progress? May 10, 1973," in *F.R.U.S., 1969–1976, Volume 28.*
11. *Namibian Independence and Cuban Troop Withdrawal* (Pretoria, Republic of South Africa: Department of Foreign Affairs, 1989), 1; Robert M. Price, "Pretoria's Southern African Strategy," in *Exporting Apartheid: Foreign Policies in Southern Africa, 1978–1988*, ed. Stephen Chan (New York: St. Martin's Press, 1990), 166.
12. "Agreement among the People's Republic of Angola, the Republic of Cuba, and the Republic of South Africa, 22 December 1988," in *Namibian Independence and Cuban Troop Withdrawal* (Pretoria, Republic of South Africa: Department of Foreign Affairs, 1989).
13. "Intelligence Note from the Director of the Bureau of Intelligence and Research (Hughes) to Secretary of State Rogers, South Africa: The Indivisible Government, June 24, 1969," in *F.R.U.S., 1969–1976, Volume 28.* Robert I. Rotberg, "Decision Making and the Military in South Africa," in *South Africa and Its Neighbors: Regional Security and Self-Interest*, ed. Robert I. Rotberg et al. (Lexington, MA: Lexington Books, 1985), 15.
14. Quoted in Hilton Hamann, *Days of the Generals: The Untold Story of South Africa's Apartheid-Era Military Generals* (Cape Town: Zebra, 2001), 7.

15. Leonard, *South Africa at War*, 14; Rotberg, "Decision Making and the Military in South Africa," 17.
16. Steenkamp, *South Africa's Border War, 1966–1989*, 43. For an alternative perspective of Van den Bergh's views concerning Angola, see James Michael Roherty, *State Security in South Africa: Civil-Military Relations under P.W. Botha* (Armonk, NY: M. E. Sharpe, 1992), 73.
17. Quoted in Hamann, *Days of the Generals*, 53.
18. Philip H. Frankel, *Pretoria's Praetorians: Civil-Military Relations in South Africa* (New York: Cambridge University Press, 1984), 35. Also see Robert Davies and Dan O'Meara, "Total Strategy in Southern Africa—an Analysis of South African Regional Policy since 1978," in *Exporting Apartheid: Foreign Policies in Southern Africa, 1978–1988*, ed. Stephen Chan (New York: St. Martin's Press, 1990), 193.
19. Frankel, *Pretoria's Praetorians*, 152.
20. Mark Phillips, "The Nuts and Bolts of Military Power: The Structure of the S.A.D.F.," in *Society at War: The Militarisation of South Africa*, ed. Jacklyn Cock and Laurie Nathan (New York: St. Martin's Press, 1989), 25. James Selfe, "South Africa's National Management System," in *Society at War: The Militarisation of South Africa*, ed. Jacklyn Cock and Laurie Nathan (New York: St. Martin's Press, 1989), 150–3.
21. Pottinger, *The Imperial Presidency*, 48, 334–5.
22. Quoted in P. W. Botha and Pieter-Dirk Uys, *P. W. Botha in His Own Words* (New York: Penguin, 1987), 63–5. On Botha's demands for Cuban troop withdrawal, see also *United Nations Security Council, S/18767, Further Report of the Secretary General Concerning the Implementation of Security Council Resolutions 435 (1978) and 439 (1978) Concerning the Question of Namibia*, (March 31, 1987).
23. "White Paper on Defence and Armaments Supply, 1979," (Department of Defence, Republic of South Africa).
24. Hamann, *Correspondence with Author, August 2011.*
25. Kenneth W. Grundy, *The Militarization of South African Politics* (Bloomington: Indiana University Press, 1986), 94.
26. Crocker, *High Noon in Southern Africa*, 281.
27. Frankel, *Pretoria's Praetorians*, 72–3.
28. Daniel Conway, "Somewhere on the Border—of Credibility: The Cultural Construction and Contestation of the Border in White South African Society," in *Beyond the Border War: New Perspectives on Southern Africa's Late-Cold War Conflicts*, ed. Gary F. Baines and Peter C. J. Vale (South Africa: Unisa Press, 2008), 79.
29. See William Cobbett, "Apartheid's Army and the Arms Embargo," in *Society at War: The Militarisation of South Africa*, ed. Jacklyn Cock and Laurie Nathan (New York: St. Martin's Press, 1989), 232; Peter H. Katjavivi, *A History of Resistance in Namibia*, Apartheid & Society (London: Unesco Press, 1988), 110–11.

30. "Report of the Commission of Inquiry into Reporting on Security Matters Regarding the South African Defence Force and the South African Police Force" (Pretoria, Republic of South Africa, 1980), 61–2. Chester A. Crocker and Georgetown University. Center for Strategic and International Studies., *South Africa's Defense Posture: Coping with Vulnerability*, The Washington Papers (Beverly Hills: Published for the Center for Strategic and International Studies, Georgetown University by Sage Publications, 1981), 28–9.
31. Gil Merom, *How Democracies Lose Small Wars: State, Society, and the Failures of France in Algeria, Israel in Lebanon, and the United States in Vietnam* (Cambridge, UK; New York: Cambridge University Press, 2003), 21.
32. Christopher Coker, *South Africa's Security Dilemmas*, The Washington Papers (New York: Praeger, 1987), 16.
33. *Out of Step: War Resistance in South Africa* (London: Catholic Institute for International Relations, 1989), 80. See also Harald E. Winkler and Laurie Nathan, "Waging Peace: Church Resistance to Militarisation," in *Marching to a Different Beat: The History of the End Conscription Campaign*, ed. Jacklyn Cock and Laurie Nathan (New York: St. Martin's Press, 1989), 325–31.
34. *Out of Step: War Resistance in South Africa*, 88–9. Also see Conway, "Somewhere on the Border—of Credibility," 81–2; Laurie Nathan, "Marching to a Different Beat: The History of the End Conscription Campaign," in *Society at War: The Militarisation of South Africa*, ed. Jacklyn Cock and Laurie Nathan (New York: St. Martin's Press, 1989).
35. See Conway, "Somewhere on the Border—of Credibility," 82.
36. Nathan, "Marching to a Different Beat," 312–14.
37. South African Institute of International Affairs., "What Do We Think?" in *Geleentheidspublikasie/ die Suid-Afrikaanse Instituut van Internasionale Aangeleenthede* (Braamfontein, South Africa: South African Institute of International Affairs, 1982); J. J. Van Wyk, *Elite Opinions on South African Foreign Policy*, occasional paper/ Research Project on South Africa's Foreign Relations (Johannesburg: J. J. van Wyk, 1984).
38. For example, see *United Nations, Report of the Secretary General 8357, Addendum 1, "Question of South West Africa,"* (United Nations Security Council, January 25, 1968).
39. Helen E. Purkitt and Stephen Franklin Burgess, *South Africa's Weapons of Mass Destruction* (Bloomington, IN: Indiana University Press, 2005), 50–4.
40. See *United Nations Security Council Resolution 435*, (September 29, 1978). Note: The arms embargo was directed primarily at South Africa's apartheid policies but was at least in part justified by South Africa's illegal occupation of Namibia. See *United Nations Security Council Resolution 418* (November 4, 1977); Cobbett, "Apartheid's Army and the Arms Embargo," 232.
41. *United Nations Security Council Resolution 539* (28 October 1983).
42. Tore Linné Eriksen, *Norway and National Liberation in Southern Africa* (Uppsala, Sweden: Nordic Institute of African Studies, 1999), 89.
43. From *Rand Daily Mail*, May 10, 1978, quoted in Tony Weaver, "The South African Defence Force in Namibia," in *Society at War: The Militarisation of*

South Africa, ed. Jacklyn Cock and Laurie Nathan (New York: St. Martin's Press, 1989), 94.

44. Willem Steenkamp, *Borderstrike! South Africa into Angola* (Pretoria: Woburn Butterworths, 1983), 11.
45. Conway, "Somewhere on the Border—of Credibility," 75.
46. South African Institute of International Affairs, "What Do We Think?"; Van Wyk, *Elite Opinions on South African Foreign Policy.*
47. Frankel, *Pretoria's Praetorians*, 97; Pottinger, *The Imperial Presidency*, 425; Grundy, *The Militarization of South African Politics*, 59–60.
48. Gary F. Baines, "Introduction: Challenging the Boundaries, Breaking the Silences," in *Beyond the Border War: New Perspectives on Southern Africa's Late-Cold War Conflicts*, ed. Gary F. Baines and Peter C. J. Vale (South Africa: Unisa Press, 2008), 9–10.
49. Pottinger, *The Imperial Presidency: P.W. Botha, the First 10 Years*, 426.
50. Grundy, *The Militarization of South African Politics*, 64.
51. *Out of Step: War Resistance in South Africa*, 115.
52. Conway, "Somewhere on the Border—of Credibility," 82, 90. Also, see Daniel Conway, "The Masculine State in Crisis: State Response to War Resistance in Apartheid South Africa," *Men and Masculinities* 10, no. 4 (2008): 424.
53. Nathan, "Marching to a Different Beat: The History of the End Conscription Campaign," 308.
54. Daniel Conway, *Correspondence with Author, August-October 2011.*
55. Frankel, *Pretoria's Praetorians.*
56. Quoted in *Out of Step: War Resistance in South Africa*, 116.
57. Conway, *Correspondence with Author, August-October 2011.*
58. Johann Van Rooyen, *Hard Right: The New White Power in South Africa* (London I. B. Tauris, 1994), 121; Roherty, *State Security in South Africa*, 17–18.
59. Frankel, *Pretoria's Praetorians*, 155.
60. Crocker, *High Noon in Southern Africa*, 363.
61. Ibid., 368.
62. Brian Wood, "Preventing the Vacuum: Determinants of the Namibia Settlement," *Journal of Southern African Studies* 17, no. 4 (1991): 755.
63. Ibid., 755–65. Also see André Du Pisani, *SWA/Namibia, the Politics of Continuity and Change* (Johannesburg: J. Ball Publishers, 1985).
64. Crocker, *High Noon in Southern Africa*, 41. Jaster, *The Defence of White Power*, 23; Leonard, *South Africa at War*, 96.
65. Crocker, *High Noon in Southern Africa*, 381.
66. Ibid., 379–80.
67. Ibid., 380.
68. Frankel, *Pretoria's Praetorians*, 155.
69. Thula Simpson, *Correspondence with Author, August 2011.*
70. Quoted in Hamann, *Days of the Generals: The Untold Story of South Africa's Apartheid-Era Military Generals*, 55.
71. Chester A. Crocker, *Correspondence with Author, March 2015.* Conway, "Somewhere on the Border—of Credibility," 75, 84–8.

72. Conway, "Somewhere on the Border—of Credibility," 90; ———, *Correspondence with Author, August-October 2011.*
73. Crocker, *Correspondence with Author, March 2015.*
74. Ibid.
75. ———, *High Noon in Southern Africa*, 406–7.
76. Ibid., 408.
77. Ibid., 399.
78. Ibid., 408.
79. Crocker, *Correspondence with Author, March 2015.*
80. John A. Marcum, "Retrenchment and Recalculation: South Africa and the Angola-Namibia Agreements," in *Disengagement from Southwest Africa*, ed. Owen Ellison Kahn (London: Transaction Publishers, 1991), 136.
81. Jannie Geldenhuys, *At the Front: A General's Account of South Africa's Border War*, 2nd ed. (Jeppestown: Jonathan Ball, 2009), 101. Also see Hamann, *Days of the Generals*, 332–5.
82. Quoted in Hamann, *Days of the Generals*, 95.
83. Ian Liebenberg, "Through the Mirage: Retracing Moments of a War 'Up There,'" *Scientia Militaria, South African Journal of Military Studies* 38, no. 2 (2010): 144.

7 Conclusion

1. Stephen Walt, "Top Ten Reasons Why Wars Last Too Long," http://walt.foreignpolicy.com/posts/2010/09/01/ (accessed March 29, 2015).
2. Richard Andres, Craig Willis, and Thomas Griffith, "Winning with Allies: The Strategic Value of the Afghan Model," *International Security* 30, no. 3 (2005/2006).
3. Thomas E. Ricks, *The Gamble: General David Petraeus and the American Military Adventure in Iraq, 2006–2008* (New York: Penguin Press, 2009), 79.
4. To put this in perspective, Elizabeth Stanley claims her leadership change theory emphasizing coalition shifts accounts for 41 percent of interstate war endings since 1945; with this success rate, she proposes the theory "greatly improves our understanding of war duration and war termination." See Elizabeth A. Stanley, *Paths to Peace: Domestic Coalition Shifts, War Termination and the Korean War* (Stanford, CA: Stanford University Press, 2009), 9.
5. See Risa Brooks, *Shaping Strategy: The Civil-Military Politics of Strategic Assessment* (Princeton, NJ: Princeton University Press, 2008); Erica Chenoweth and Maria J. Stephan, *Why Civil Resistance Works: The Strategic Logic of Nonviolent Conflict* (New York: Columbia University Press, 2012).
6. Gil Merom, *How Democracies Lose Small Wars: State, Society, and the Failures of France in Algeria, Israel in Lebanon, and the United States in Vietnam* (Cambridge, UK; New York: Cambridge University Press, 2003), 15. See also Bradley N. Nelson, "Regime Type and the Persistence of Costly Small Wars" (PhD dissertation, The Ohio State University, 2008).

7. Allen Weiss and Erin Anderson, "Perceptions of Legitimacy as a Motive to Change Inter-Organizational Relations" (Research Paper #1175, Graduate School of Business, Stanford University, November 1991), 1.
8. Stephen Van Evera, "Causes of War" (PhD dissertation, Unversity of California, Berkeley, 1984), 206–7.
9. Douglas L. Wheeler, "The Military and the Portuguese Dictatorship, 1926–1974," in *Contemporary Portugal: The Revolution and Its Antecedents*, ed. Lawrence S. Graham and Harry M. Makler (Austin: University of Texas Press, 1979), 191.
10. Douglas Porch, *The Portuguese Armed Forces and the Revolution*, Hoover Institution Publication 188 (London: Croom Helm; Hoover Institution Press, 1977), 83.
11. For example, see Gareth Porter, "U.S.: Fears of Blame for Defeat Shadow Afghan War Meetings," Inter Press Service News Agency, http://www.ipsnews.net/2009/09/ (accessed November 20, 2014); Sara Carter, "Former Afghan Official: John Kerry Has 'Prepared the Ground for Absolving the Obama Administration' on Afghanistan," The Blaze, http://www.theblaze.com/stories/2014/08/01 (accessed November 20, 2014); Daniel Greenfield, "Hillary Clinton Already Shifting Blame to Obama for Afghanistan Disaster," Frontpage Mag, http://www.frontpagemag.com/2013/dgreenfield/ (accessed November 20, 2014); "Steele Blames Afghan War on Obama, Drawing Calls to Resign," http://www.foxnews.com/politics/2010/07/02/ (accessed November 20, 2014); Jean Mackenzie, "Is Obama to Blame for the Mess in Afghanistan?" GlobalPost, http://www.salon.com/2013/03/14 (accessed November 20, 2014); Con Coughlin, "If the Taliban Retake Control of Afghanistan, Blame Obama," http://blogs.telegraph.co.uk/news/concoughlin/100253464/ (accessed November 20, 2014); Hrafnkell Haraldsson, "The Republicans Are Still Blaming Obama for Iraq and Afghanistan," PoliticusUSA, http://www.politicususa.com/2013/12/02/ (accessed November 20, 2014).
12. Matthew Rosenberg and Mark Mazzetti, "U.S. May Stay in Afghanistan after '16," *New York Times*, http://www.nytimes.com/2015/03/21/world/asia/us-may-stay-in-afghanistan-after-16 (accessed March 29, 2015).
13. Quoted in Mark Landler, "U.S. Troops to Leave Afghanistan by End of 2016," *The New York Times*, http://www.nytimes.com/2014/05/28/world/asia/us-to-complete-afghan-pullout-by-end-of-2016-obama-to-say (accessed December 9, 2014).
14. Helene Cooper and David E. Sanger, "Obama Says Afghan Policy Won't Change after Dismissal," http://www.nytimes.com/2010/06/24/us/politics/24mcchrystal (accessed March 29, 2015).
15. Mark Mazzetti and Eric Schmitt, "In a Shift, Obama Extends U.S. Role in Afghan Combat," *New York Times*, http://www.nytimes.com/2014/11/22/us/politics/in-secret-obama-extends-us-role-in-afghan-combat (accessed March 29, 2015). Note: This discussion of the current administration and its war policy is purely descriptive, laying out elements of the domestic debate as widely reported by the media. This is in no way an expression of the author's

opinion and is not meant as any form of critique. The author remains completely neutral and agnostic on all related matters.

16. Ibid.
17. Ibid.
18. Arshad Mohammed, David Rohde, and Phil Steward, "U.S. Likely to Delay Planned Closure of Two Afghanistan Bases," http://www.reuters.com/article/2015/03/19/us-afghanistan-usa-bases (accessed March 29, 2015).
19. See Matthew Rosenberg and Mark Mazzetti, "More U.S. Troops Seen Staying in Afghanistan," *New York Times*, http://www.nytimes.com/2015/03/20/world/asia/more-us-troops-seen-staying-in-afghanistan (accessed March 29, 2015); Greg Jaffe and David Nakamura, "Obama Agrees to Slow U.S. Troop Withdrawal from Afghanistan," http://www.washingtonpost.com/politics/ (accessed April 1, 2015); Mary Bruce, "President Obama Announces Slowdown of Troop Withdrawal from Afghanistan," http://abcnews.go.com (accessed April 1, 2015).
20. Landler, "U.S. Troops to Leave Afghanistan by End of 2016."
21. Fred Charles Iklé, *Every War Must End*, Columbia Paperback (New York: Columbia University Press, 1971), 85.

References

Abrahamsson, Bengt. *Military Professionalism and Political Power.* London: Sage Publications, 1972.

"The Acting Secretary of State to the Acting United States Representative at the United Nations (Jessup) at Paris, December 23, 1948." In *F.R.U.S., 1948, Volume 6.*

"The Acting Secretary of State to the Consulate General at Batavia, November 18, 1948." In *F.R.U.S., 1948, Volume 6.*

"The Acting United States Representative at the United Nations (Jessup) to the Acting Secretary of State, January 17, 1949." In *F.R.U.S., 1949, Volume 7.*

"Agreement among the People's Republic of Angola, the Republic of Cuba, and the Republic of South Africa, 22 December 1988." In *Namibian Independence and Cuban Troop Withdrawal.* Pretoria, Republic of South Africa: Department of Foreign Affairs, 1989.

Alicke, Mark D. "Culpable Control and the Psychology of Blame." *Psychological Bulletin* 126, no. 4 (2000): 556–74.

Allison, Graham T., and Morton H. Halperin. "Bureacratic Politcs: A Paradigm and Some Policy Implications." *World Politics* 24 (1972): 40–79.

Allison, Graham T., and Philip Zelikow. *Essence of Decision: Explaining the Cuban Missile Crisis.* 2nd ed. New York: Longman, 1999.

"The Ambassador in Belgium (Kirk) to the Secretary of State, February 9, 1949." In *F.R.U.S., 1949, Volume 7.*

"The Ambassador in the Netherlands (Baruch) to the Secretary of State, December 21, 1948." In *F.R.U.S., 1948, Volume 6.*

"The Ambassador in the Netherlands (Baruch) to the Secretary of State, July 20, 1947." In *F.R.U.S., 1947, Volume 6.*

"The Ambassador in the Netherlands (Baruch) to the Secretary of State, June 17, 1949." In *F.R.U.S., 1949, Volume 7.*

"The Ambassador in the Netherlands (Baruch) to the Secretary of State, March 10, 1949." In *F.R.U.S., 1949, Volume 7.*

"The Ambassador in the Netherlands (Baruch) to the Secretary of State, May 28, 1948." In *F.R.U.S., 1948, Volume 6.*

"The Ambassador in the Netherlands (Baruch) to the Secretary of State, October 8, 1948." In *F.R.U.S., 1948, Volume 6.*

"The Ambassador in the Netherlands (Baruch) to the Secretary of State, October 30, 1948." In *F.R.U.S., 1948, Volume 6.*

"The Ambassador in the United Kingdom (Douglas) to the Secretary of State, February 18, 1949." In *F.R.U.S., 1949, Volume 7.*

Ambler, John S. *The French Army in Politics, 1945–1962.* Columbus: Ohio State University Press, 1966.

Andeweg, R. B., and Galen A. Irwin. *Dutch Government and Politics.* New York: St. Martin's Press, 1993.

Andres, Richard, Craig Willis, and Thomas Griffith. "Winning with Allies: The Strategic Value of the Afghan Model." *International Security* 30, no. 3 (2005/2006): 124–60.

Andrews, William George. *French Politics and Algeria: The Process of Policy Formation, 1954–1962*, Current Political Problems. New York: Appleton-Century-Crofts, 1962.

Anheier, Helmut K. *When Things Go Wrong: Organizational Failures and Breakdowns.* Thousand Oaks, CA: Sage Publications, 1999.

Arnold, Anthony. *The Fateful Pebble: Afghanistan's Role in the Fall of the Soviet Empire.* Novato, CA: Presidio, 1993.

Arreguin-Toft, Ivan. "How the Weak Win Wars: A Theory of Asymmetric Conflict." *International Security* 26, no. 1 (2001): 93–128.

Ashforth, Blake E., and Barrie W. Gibbs. "The Double-Edge of Organizational Legitimation." *Organization Science* 1, no. 2 (1990): 177–94.

Ashworth, Lucian. "The 1945–1949 Dutch-Indonesian Conflict: Lessons and Perspectives in the Study of Insurgency." *Conflict Quarterly* Winter (1990): 34–45.

Avant, Deborah D. *Political Institutions and Military Change: Lessons from Peripheral Wars*, Cornell Studies in Security Affairs. Ithaca: Cornell University Press, 1994.

Avishai, Bernard. *A New Israel: Democracy in Crisis, 1973–1988: Essays.* New York: Ticknor & Fields, 1990.

Baines, Gary F. "Introduction: Challenging the Boundaries, Breaking the Silences." In *Beyond the Border War: New Perspectives on Southern Africa's Late-Cold War Conflicts*, edited by Gary F. Baines and Peter C. J. Vale, 1–21. South Africa: Unisa Press, 2008.

Baldick, Robert. *The Siege of Paris.* New York: Macmillan, 1964.

"Balking at Tank Attack on Beirut Ended Career of Young Israeli Colonel: Military, Political, Moral Objections." *The Washington Post*, April 20, 1985.

"Ballard to Evatt, January 6, 1947." In *Documents on Australian Foreign Policy, 1947, Volume 11.*

Bandeira, Antonio R. *Military Interventions in Portuguese Politics: Antecedents of the Armed Forces Movement.* Toronto: Brazilian Studies, 1975.

Baron, R. M., and D. A. Kenny. "The Moderator-Mediator Variable Distinction in Social Psychology Research: Conceptual, Strategic, and Statisitical Considerations." *Journal of Personality and Social Psychology* 51, no. 6 (1986): 1173–82.

Barylski, Robert V. *The Soldier in Russian Politics: Duty, Dictatorship and Democracy under Gorbachev and Yeltsin.* New Brunswick, NJ: Transaction Publishers, 1998.

Barzilai, Gad. *Wars, Internal Conflicts, and Political Order: A Jewish Democracy in the Middle East*, Suny Series in Israeli Studies. Albany: State University of New York Press, 1996.

"Basic Dutch-Indonesian Issues and the Linggadjati Agreement." United States Central Intelligence Group, June 9, 1947.

Baum, Matthew A. "Going Private: Public Opinion, Presidential Rhetoric, and the Domestic Politics of Audience Costs in U.S. Foreign Policy Crises." *Journal of Conflict Resolution* 48, no. 5 (2004): 603–31.

Bavly, Dan, and Eliahu Salpeter. *Fire in Beirut: Israel's War in Lebanon with the P.L.O.* Briarcliff Manor, NY: Stein and Day, 1984.

"Beirut Massacre Inquiry: Army Chief Was Reluctant to Use Phalangists." *The Times*, November 1, 1982.

Benedetti, Charles, and Charles Chatfield. *An American Ordeal: The Antiwar Movement of the Vietnam War.* Syracuse: Syracuse University Press, 1990.

Benford, Robert D., and David A. Snow. "Framing Processes and Social Movements: An Overview and Assessment." *Annual Review of Sociology* 26 (2000): 611–39.

Bernstein, Marver H. "Coping with Turbulence: The First Two Years of the National Unity Government under Peres." In *Israeli National Security: Political Actors and Perspectives*, edited by Bernard Reich and Gershon R. Kieval, 207–24. New York: Greenwood Press, 1988.

Betts, Richard K. *Soldiers, Statesmen, and Cold War Crises.* Cambridge: Harvard University Press, 1977.

Bhasin, Avtar Singh. *India-Sri Lanka Relations and Sri Lanka's Ethnic Conflict Documents, 1947–2000, Volume 4.* New Delhi: Indian Research Press, 2001.

Boettcher, William A. "Don't Let Them Die in Vain: Casualty Frames and Public Tolerance for Escalating Commitment in Iraq." *Journal of Conflict Resolution* 53, no. 5 (2009): 677–97.

Boettcher, William A., and Michael D. Cobb. "Echoes of Vietnam? Casualty Framing and Public Perceptions of Success and Failure in Iraq." *Journal of Conflict Resolution* 50, no. 6 (2006): 831–54.

Boot, Max. *The Savage Wars of Peace: Small Wars and the Rise of American Power.* 1st paperback ed. New York: Basic Books, 2003.

Botha, P. W., and Pieter-Dirk Uys. *P. W. Botha in His Own Words.* New York: Penguin, 1987.

Bouteiller, J. de. "The Workmen of Paris During the Siege." *Fraser's Magazine* 7, no. 87 (1873): 728–37.

Brannon, Robert. *Russian Civil-Military Relations*, Military Strategy and Operational Art. Farnham, England; Burlington, VT: Ashgate Pub., 2009.

Bredow, Wilfried von. "The Order of Violence: Norms, Rules, and Taboos of Organized Violence and the De-Legitimization of the Military." In *Handbook of the Sociology of the Military*, edited by Giuseppe Caforio, 87–98. New York: Kluwer Academic/Plenum Publishers, 2003.

Brehm, John O., and Scott Gates. *Working, Shirking, and Sabotage: Bureaucratic Response to a Democratic Public*. Ann Arbor: University of Michigan Press, 1997.

Brooks, Risa. *Shaping Strategy: The Civil-Military Politics of Strategic Assessment*. Princeton, NJ: Princeton University Press, 2008.

Bruce, Mary. "President Obama Announces Slowdown of Troop Withdrawal from Afghanistan." http://abcnews.go.com (accessed April 1, 2015).

Bruneau, Thomas C. *Politics and Nationhood: Post-Revolutionary Portugal*. New York, NY: Praeger, 1984.

Bueno de Mesquita, Bruce. *The Logic of Political Survival*. Cambridge, MA: MIT Press, 2003.

Bueno de Mesquita, Bruce, and Randolph M. Siverson. "War and the Survival of Political Leaders: A Comparative Study of Regime Types and Political Accountability." *American Political Science Review* 89, no. 4 (1995): 841–55.

Bueno de Mesquita, Bruce, Randolph M. Siverson, and Gary Woller. "War and the Fate of Regimes: A Comparative Analysis." *American Political Science Review* 86, no. 3 (1992): 638–46.

Burk, James. "Expertise, Jurisdiction and Legitimacy of the Military Profession." In *The Future of the Army Profession*, edited by Don M. Snider and Lloyd Matthews. Boston: McGraw-Hill, 2005.

———. "The Public and the Military." *Javnost – The Public* 1, no. 4 (1994): 13–27.

Busby, Joshua W. *Moral Movements and Foreign Policy*, Cambridge Studies in International Relations. New York: Cambridge University Press, 2010.

Buzzanco, Robert. "The American Military's Rationale against the Vietnam War." *Political Science Quarterly* 101, no. 4 (1986): 559–76.

———. "Hawks as Doves: Military Dissent in Vietnam and Iraq." Colonel John B. Mckinney Lecture, Unpublished Manuscript, University of Tennessee, 2006.

———. *Masters of War: Military Dissent and Politics in the Vietnam Era*. New York: Cambridge University Press, 1996.

"C.P.S.U. C.C. Politburo Meeting Minutes, 13 November 1986." In *Cold War International History Project*.

"Cabinet Undecided on Pullout." *The Times*, March 13, 1984.

Caetano, Marcello. *Depoimento*. Rio de Janeiro: Distribuidora Record, 1974.

Calahan, H. A. *What Makes a War End?* New York: The Vanguard Press, 1944.

Callwell, C. E. *Small Wars: Their Principles and Practice*. Lincoln, NE: University of Nebraska Press, 1996.

Cann, John P. *Counterinsurgency in Africa: The Portuguese Way of War, 1961–1974*, Contributions in Military Studies. Westport, CT: Greenwood Press, 1997.

"Car Bomb Hits an Israeli Convoy in Southern Lebanon, Killing 12." *New York Times*, March 11, 1985.

Carter, Sara. "Former Afghan Official: John Kerry Has 'Prepared the Ground for Absolving the Obama Administration' on Afghanistan." The Blaze, http://www.theblaze.com/stories/2014/08/01 (accessed November 20, 2014).

Chaffard, Georges. *Les Carnets Secrets de la Décolonisation, Volume 2*. Paris: Calmann-Lévy, 1965.

"The Chargé in the Netherlands (Steere) to the Secretary of State, July 18, 1949." In *F.R.U.S., 1949, Volume 7.*

Chari, P. R. "The I.P.K.F. Experience in Sri Lanka." *ACDIS Occasional Paper* (February 1994).

Chenoweth, Erica, and Maria J. Stephan. *Why Civil Resistance Works: The Strategic Logic of Nonviolent Conflict.* New York: Columbia University Press, 2012.

Clarence-Smith, W. G. *The Third Portuguese Empire, 1825–1975: A Study in Economic Imperialism.* Manchester, UK; Dover, NH: Manchester University Press, 1985.

Clayton, Anthony. *The Wars of French Decolonization,* Modern Wars in Perspective. London; New York: Longman, 1994.

Cobbett, William. "Apartheid's Army and the Arms Embargo." In *Society at War: The Militarisation of South Africa,* edited by Jacklyn Cock and Laurie Nathan, 232–43. New York: St. Martin's Press, 1989.

Cochran, Shawn T. "The Civil-Military Divide in Protracted Small War: An Alternative View of Military Leadership Preferences and War Termination." *Armed Forces & Society* 40, no. 1 (2014): 71–95.

Cohen, Eliot A. "Constraints on America's Conduct of Small Wars." *International Security* 9, no. 2 (1984): 151–81.

Cohen, Stuart A. "Why Do They Quarrel? Civil-Military Tensions in LIC Situations." In *Democracies and Small Wars,* edited by Efraim Inbar, 21–40. London: Frank Cass, 2003.

Coker, Christopher. *South Africa's Security Dilemmas,* The Washington Papers. New York: Praeger, 1987.

Coletta, Damon, and Peter Feaver. "Civilian Monitoring of U.S. Military Operations in the Information Age." *Armed Forces & Society* 33, no. 1 (2006): 106–26.

Colton, Timothy J. "Perspectives on Civil-Military Relations in the Soviet Union." In *Soldiers and the Soviet State: Civil-Military Relations from Brezhnev to Gorbachev,* edited by Timothy J. Colton and Thane Gustafson, 3–43. Princeton: Princeton University Press, 1990.

"Consul-General Mackereth to Mr. Bevin, April 17, 1946." In *British Documents on Foreign Affairs: Reports and Papers from the Foreign Office Confidential Print, Part 4, Series E, Asia 1946, Volume 1,* 2001.

"Consul-General Mackereth to Mr. Bevin, April 24, 1946." In *British Documents on Foreign Affairs: Reports and Papers from the Foreign Office Confidential Print, Part 4, Series E, Asia 1946, Volume 1,* 2001.

"The Consul General at Batavia (Foote) to the Secretary of State, July 22, 1947." In *F.R.U.S., 1947, Volume 6.*

"The Consul General at Batavia (Foote) to the Secretary of State, July 25, 1947." In *F.R.U.S., 1947, Volume 6.*

"The Consul General at Batavia (Foote) to the Secretary of State, May 30, 1946." In *F.R.U.S., 1946, Volume 8.*

"The Consul General at Batavia (Livengood) to the Secretary of State, December 2, 1948." In *F.R.U.S., 1948, Volume 6.*

"The Consul General at Batavia (Livengood) to the Secretary of State, December 18, 1948." In *F.R.U.S., 1948, Volume 6.*
"The Consul General at Batavia (Livengood) to the Secretary of State, January 3, 1949." In *F.R.U.S., 1949, Volume 7.*
"The Consul General at Batavia (Livengood) to the Secretary of State, January 7, 1948." In *F.R.U.S., 1948, Volume 6.*
"The Consul General at Batavia (Livengood) to the Secretary of State, January 20, 1949." In *F.R.U.S., 1949, Volume 7.*
"The Consul General at Batavia (Livengood) to the Secretary of State, January 23, 1949." In *F.R.U.S., 1949, Volume 7.*
"The Consul General at Batavia (Livengood) to the Secretary of State, July 21, 1948." In *F.R.U.S., 1948, Volume 6.*
"The Consul General at Batavia (Livengood) to the Secretary of State, March 8, 1949." In *F.R.U.S., 1949, Volume 7.*
"The Consul General at Batavia (Livengood) to the Secretary of State, May 25, 1949." In *F.R.U.S., 1949, Volume 7.*
"The Consul General at Batavia (Livengood) to the Secretary of State, May 26, 1949." In *F.R.U.S., 1949, Volume 7.*
"The Consul General at Batavia (Livengood) to the Secretary of State, November 7, 1948." In *F.R.U.S., 1948, Volume 6.*
"The Consul General at Batavia (Livengood) to the Secretary of State, November 11, 1948." In *F.R.U.S., 1948, Volume 6.*
"The Consul General at Batavia (Livengood) to the Secretary of State, November 17, 1947." In *F.R.U.S., 1947, Volume 6.*
"The Consul General at Batavia (Livengood) to the Secretary of State, November 25, 1948." In *F.R.U.S., 1948, Volume 6.*
"The Consul General at Batavia (Livengood) to the Secretary of State, October 13, 1948." In *F.R.U.S., 1948, Volume 6.*
"Conversation between the Secretary of State and the Netherlands Minister for Foreign Affairs, Mr. Bevin to Mr. Gage (the Hague), October 1, 1948." In *British Documents on Foreign Affairs: Reports and Papers from the Foreign Office Confidential Print, Part 4, Series E, Asia 1948, Volume 6.*
Conway, Daniel. *Correspondence with Author, August-October 2011.*
———. "The Masculine State in Crisis: State Response to War Resistance in Apartheid South Africa." *Men and Masculinities* 10, no. 4 (2008): 422–39.
———. "Somewhere on the Border—of Credibility: The Cultural Construction and Contestation of the Border in White South African Society." In *Beyond the Border War: New Perspectives on Southern Africa's Late-Cold War Conflicts*, edited by Gary F. Baines and Peter C. J. Vale, 75–93. South Africa: Unisa Press, 2008.
Cooper, Helene, and David E. Sanger. "Obama Says Afghan Policy Won't Change after Dismissal." http://www.nytimes.com/2010/06/24/us/politics/24mcchrystal (accessed March 29, 2015).
Corson, William R. *Consequences of Failure.* New York: Norton, 1973.

Coughlin, Con. "If the Taliban Retake Control of Afghanistan, Blame Obama." http://blogs.telegraph.co.uk/news/concoughlin/100253464/ (accessed November 20, 2014).

Crocker, Chester A. *Correspondence with Author, March 2015.*

———. *High Noon in Southern Africa: Making Peace in a Rough Neighborhood.* New York: W. W. Norton, 1992.

Crocker, Chester A., and Georgetown University. Center for Strategic and International Studies. *South Africa's Defense Posture: Coping with Vulnerability*, The Washington Papers. Beverly Hills: Published for the Center for Strategic and International Studies, Georgetown University by Sage Publications, 1981.

Croco, Sarah. "The Decider's Dilemma: Leader Culpability, War Outcomes, and Domestic Punishment." *American Political Science Review* 105, no. 3 (2011): 457–77.

Crozier, Brian. *De Gaulle.* New York: Scribner, 1973.

"Cutts to Department of External Affairs, December 19, 1948." In *Documents on Australian Foreign Policy, 1948, Volume 13.*

Dale, R. "The Armed Forces as an Instrument of South African Policy in Namibia." *Journal of Modern African Studies* 18, no. 1 (1980): 57–71.

Davidson, Basil. *The Liberation of Guiné: Aspects of an African Revolution*, Penguin African Library Ap 27. Harmondsworth: Penguin, 1969.

Davies, J. E. *Constructive Engagement? Chester Crocker & American Policy in South Africa, Namibia & Angola, 1981–8.* Athens, OH: Ohio University Press, 2007.

Davies, Robert, and Dan O'Meara. "Total Strategy in Southern Africa—an Analysis of South African Regional Policy since 1978." In *Exporting Apartheid: Foreign Policies in Southern Africa, 1978–1988*, edited by Stephen Chan, 179–218. New York: St. Martin's Press, 1990.

De Gaulle, Charles. *Memoirs of Hope: Renewal and Endeavor.* New York: Simon and Schuster, 1971.

"Department of External Affairs to Kirby, January 3, 1948." In *Documents on Australian Foreign Policy, 1948, Volume 13.*

Deriglazova, Larisa. *Great Powers, Small Wars: Asymmetric Conflict since 1945.* Baltimore: The Johns Hopkins University Press, 2014.

Desch, Michael C. *Civilian Control of the Military: The Changing Security Environment.* Baltimore: Johns Hopkins University Press, 1999.

Devillers, Philippe, and Jean Lacouture. *End of a War: Indochina, 1954.* New York: Praeger, 1969.

"Dispute between the Netherlands and Indonesia, Sir P. Nichols to Mr. Attlee, December 1, 1949." In *British Documents on Foreign Affairs: Reports and Papers from the Foreign Office Confidential Print, Part 4, Series E, Asia 1949, Volume 9*, 2001.

Donnelly, Thomas, and Frederick W. Kagan. *Lessons for a Long War: How America Can Win on New Battlefields.* Washington, DC: AEI Press, 2010.

Downs, George W. "The Lessons of Disengagement." In *The Dynamics of Foreign Military Intervention*, edited by Ariel Levite, Bruce W. Jentleson, and Ilan Berman. New York: Columbia University Press, 1992.

Downs, George W., and David M. Rocke. "Conflict, Agency, and Gambling for Resurrection: The Principal-Agent Problem Goes to War." *American Journal of Political Science* 38, no. 2 (1994): 362–80.

Doyle, Kevin. "Vietnam's Forgotten Cambodian War." http://www.bbc.com/news/world-asia-29106034 (accessed March 31, 2015).

Druckman, James N., and Arthur Lupia. "Preference Formation." *Annual Review of Political Science* 3 (2000): 1–24.

Du Pisani, André. *SWA/Namibia, the Politics of Continuity and Change.* Johannesburg: J. Ball Publishers, 1985.

"Dutch-Indonesian Relations: Interpretation of Linggadjati Agreement Deadlock, Mr. Grey to Mr. Bevin, June 9, 1947." In *British Documents on Foreign Affairs: Reports and Papers from the Foreign Office Confidential Print, Part 4, Series E, Asia 1947, Volume 4*, 2001.

"East Sumatra: Military-Political Situation, Acting Consul Roberts to Consul-General Mitcheson (Batavia), August 23, 1947." In *British Documents on Foreign Affairs: Reports and Papers from the Foreign Office Confidential Print, Part 4, Series E, Asia 1947, Volume 4*, 2001.

"Eastern Sumatra: Netherlands-Indonesian Hostilities: Political-Military Developments, Acting-Consul Roberts to Consul-General Mitcheson (Batavia), July 26, 1947." In *British Documents on Foreign Affairs: Reports and Papers from the Foreign Office Confidential Print, Part 4, Series E, Asia 1947, Volume 4*, 2001.

"Egypt and Syria Reported Opening Doors to the P.L.O." *New York Times*, August 8, 1982.

Elazar, Daniel Judah. "Begin's Two-Year Government." In *Israel at the Polls, 1981: A Study of the Knesset Elections*, edited by Howard Rae Penniman and Daniel Judah Elazar, 244–65. Washington: American Enterprise Institute for Public Policy Research, 1986.

Ellis, Richard. *Presidential Lightning Rods: The Politics of Blame Avoidance*, Studies in Government and Public Policy. Lawrence, KS: University Press of Kansas, 1994.

Ellsberg, Daniel. *Papers on the War.* New York: Simon and Schuster, 1972.

Elster, Jon. *Explaining Social Behavior: More Nuts and Bolts for the Social Sciences.* Cambridge; New York: Cambridge University Press, 2007.

———. "A Plea for Mechanisms." In *Social Mechanisms: An Analytical Approach to Social Theory*, edited by Peter Hedström and Richard Swedberg, 45–73. New York: Cambridge University Press, 1998.

Englehardt, Michael J. "Democracies, Dictatorships and Counterinsurgency: Does Regime Type Really Matter?" *Conflict Quarterly* Spring (1992).

Eriksen, Tore Linné. *Norway and National Liberation in Southern Africa.* Uppsala, Sweden: Nordic Institute of African Studies, 1999.

Evans, Rowland, and Robert D. Novak. *Nixon in the White House: The Frustration of Power.* New York: Random House, 1971.

"Events in Indonesia 1939–48, Foreign Office Research Department Memorandum, June 16, 1948." In *British Documents on Foreign Affairs: Reports and Papers from the Foreign Office Confidential Print, Part 4, Series E, Asia 1948, Volume 6*, 2001.

Evron, Yair. *War and Intervention in Lebanon: The Israeli-Syrian Deterrence Dialogue*. Baltimore: Johns Hopkins University Press, 1987.

"Excerpts from Testimony at Inquiry on Massacre." *New York Times*, October 26, 1982.

Fair, Charles. *From the Jaws of Victory*. New York: Simon and Schuster, 1971.

Falleti, Tulia G., and Julia F. Lynch. "Context and Causal Mechanisms in Political Analysis." *Comparative Political Studies* 42, no. 9 (2009): 1143–66.

Feaver, Peter. *Armed Servants: Agency, Oversight, and Civil-Military Relations*. Cambridge, MA: Harvard University Press, 2003.

———. "Anatomy of the Surge." *Commentary* 125, no. 4 (2008): 24–8.

Feaver, Peter, and Christopher Gelpi. *Choosing Your Battles: American Civil-Military Relations and the Use of Force*. Princeton: Princeton University Press, 2004.

Fehrenbach, T. R. *This Kind of War: The Classic Korean War History*. London: Brassey's, 1994.

Feit, Edward. *The Armed Bureaucrats: Military-Administrative Regimes and Political Development*. Boston: Houghton Mifflin, 1972.

Feldman, Shai, and Heda Rechnitz-Kijner. *Deception, Consensus and War: Israel in Lebanon*. Paper No. 27. Tel Aviv: Jaffee Center for Strategic Studies, 1984.

Felgenhauer, Pavel. "Russian Military Reform: Ten Years of Failure." In *Russian Defense Policy Towards the Year 2000*, edited by Elizabeth Skinner and Mikhail Tsypkin. Naval Postgraduate School, Monterey, CA, 1997.

Filson, Darren, and Suzanne Werner. "Sensitivity to Costs of Fighting versus Sensitivity to Losing the Conflict: Implications for War Onset, Duration, and Outcomes." *Journal of Conflict Resolution* 51, no. 5 (2007): 691–714.

Finer, S. E. *The Man on Horseback: The Role of the Military in Politics*. 2nd enlarged ed., Peregrine Books. Baltimore: Penguin, 1976.

Fisher, Walter. *Human Communication as Narration: Toward a Philosophy of Reason, Value, and Action*. Columbia: University of South Carolina Press, 1995.

Flores, A. Quiroz. "A Competing Risks Model of War Termination and Leader Change." *International Studies Quarterly* 56, no. 4 (2012): 809–19.

Forster, Anthony. "The Military Covenant and British Civil-Military Relations: Letting the Genie out of the Bottle." *Armed Forces and Society* 38, no. 2 (2012): 273–90.

"France: The Juin Affair." *Time*, April 12, 1954.

Frankel, Philip H. *Pretoria's Praetorians: Civil-Military Relations in South Africa*. New York: Cambridge University Press, 1984.

Frey, Marc. "Dutch Elites and Decolonization." In *Elites and Decolonization in the Twentieth Century*, edited by Jost Dülffer and Marc Frey, 56–73. New York: Palgrave Macmillan, 2011.

Friedman, Thomas L. "P.L.O.'S Decision to Leave." *New York Times*, August 11, 1982.

Furniss, Edgar Stephenson. *De Gaulle and the French Army: A Crisis in Civil-Military Relations*. New York: Twentieth Century Fund, 1964.

Gabriel, Richard A. *Correspondence with Author, April-June 2011.*

———. *Operation Peace for Galilee: The Israeli-PLO War in Lebanon.* New York: Hill and Wang, 1984.

Gal, Reuven. "Limits of Military Legitimacy and Its Relation to Military Commitment." In *Legitimacy and Commitment in the Military*, edited by Thomas C. Wyatt and Reuven Gal. New York: Greenwood Press, 1990.

Galeotti, Mark. *Afghanistan, the Soviet Union's Last War.* London, England; Portland, OR: Frank Cass, 1995.

Gall, Carlotta, and Thomas De Waal. *Chechnya: Calamity in the Caucasus.* New York: New York University Press, 1998.

Gallagher, Tom. *Portugal: A Twentieth-Century Interpretation.* Manchester: Manchester University Press, 1983.

Geldenhuys, Jannie. *At the Front: A General's Account of South Africa's Border War.* 2nd ed. Jeppestown: Jonathan Ball, 2009.

Gelpi, Christopher, Peter Feaver, and Jason Aaron Reifler. *Paying the Human Costs of War: American Public Opinion and Casualties in Military Conflicts.* Princeton: Princeton University Press, 2009.

"Gemayel Is Buried as Political Leaders Call for Calm in Lebanon." *New York Times*, September 16, 1982.

George, Alexander L., and Andrew Bennett. *Case Studies and Theory Development in the Social Sciences*, B.C.S.I.A. Studies in International Security. Cambridge, MA: MIT Press, 2005.

"Gilchrist to Burton, July 21, 1947." In *Documents on Australian Foreign Policy, 1947, Volume 11.*

Giles, Frank. *The Locust Years: The Story of the Fourth French Republic, 1946–1958.* London: Secker & Warburg, 1991.

Goemans, H. E. *War and Punishment: The Causes of War Termination and the First World War*, Princeton Studies in International History and Politics. Princeton, NJ: Princeton University Press, 2000.

Greenfield, Daniel. "Hillary Clinton Already Shifting Blame to Obama for Afghanistan Disaster." Frontpage Mag, http://www.frontpagemag.com/2013/dgreenfield/ (accessed November 20, 2014).

Greenstein, Fred I., and Nelson W. Polsby. *Strategies of Inquiry*, Handbook of Political Science V. 7. Reading, MA: Addison-Wesley Pub. Co., 1975.

Groen, P. M. H. *Correspondence with Author, August 2011.*

———. "Dutch Armed Forces and the Decolonization of Indonesia: The Second Police Action (1948–1949), a Pandora's Box." *War and Society* 4, no. 1 (1986): 79–104.

———. "Militant Response: The Dutch Use of Military Force and the Decolonization of the Dutch East Indies, 1945–50." *Journal of Imperial and Commonwealth History* 21, no. 3 (1993): 30–44.

Grundy, Kenneth W. *The Militarization of South African Politics.* Bloomington: Indiana University Press, 1986.

Hagan, Joe D., Philip Everts, Harhiro Fukui, and John D. Stempel. "Foreign Policy by Coalition: Deadlock, Compromise, Anarchy." *International Studies Review* 3, no. 2 (2001): 169–216.

Halperin, Morton H. "War Termination as a Problem in Civil-Military Relations." *The Annals of the American Academy of Political and Social Sciences* 392 (1970): 86–95.

Halperin, Morton H., Priscilla Clapp, and Arnold Kanter. *Bureaucratic Politics and Foreign Policy.* Washington: The Brookings Institution, 1974.

Hamann, Hilton. *Correspondence with Author, August 2011.*

———. *Days of the Generals: The Untold Story of South Africa's Apartheid-Era Military Generals.* Cape Town: Zebra, 2001.

Handel, Michael I. *War Termination, a Critical Survey,* Jerusalem Papers on Peace Problems. Jerusalem Hebrew University, Leonard Davis Institute for International Relations, 1978.

Haraldsson, Hrafnkell. "The Republicans Are Still Blaming Obama for Iraq and Afghanistan." PoliticusUSA, http://www.politicususa.com/2013/12/02/ (accessed November 20, 2014).

Harries-Jenkins, Gwyn. "Legitimacy and the Problem of Order." In *The Military and the Problem of Legitimacy,* edited by J. A. A. Van Doorn and Gwyn Harries-Jenkins, 41–58. London: Sage Publishers, 1976.

Harrison, Alexander. *Challenging De Gaulle: The O.A.S. and the Counterrevolution in Algeria, 1954–1962.* New York: Praeger, 1989.

Hastings, Elizbeth Hann, and Philip K. Hastings, eds. *Index to International Public Opinion, 1982–1983, Prepared by Survey Research Consultants International, Inc.* New York: Greenwood Press.

———, eds. *Index to International Public Opinion, 1983–1984, Prepared by Survey Research Consultants International, Inc.* New York: Greenwood Press.

———, eds. *Index to International Public Opinion, 1984–1985, Prepared by Survey Research Consultants International, Inc.* New York: Greenwood Press.

———, eds. *Index to International Public Opinion, 1985–1986, Prepared by Survey Research Consultants International, Inc.* New York: Greenwood Press.

Hauner, Milan. *The Soviet War in Afghanistan: Patterns of Russian Imperialism.* Philadelphia, PA: University Press of America, 1991.

Heitman, H. R. *War in Angola: The Final South African Phase.* Gibraltar: Ashanti Pub., 1990.

Hérisson, Maurice d'Irisson d'. *Journel d'un Officier d'Ordnonnace, Julliet 1870-Fevrier 1871.* Paris: Paul Ollendorff, 1885.

Herspring, Dale R. *The Kremlin & the High Command: Presidential Impact on the Russian Military from Gorbachev to Putin*, Modern War Studies. Lawrence: University Press of Kansas, 2006.

———. *The Pentagon and the Presidency: Civil-Military Relations from FDR to George W. Bush*, Modern War Studies. Lawrence: University Press of Kansas, 2005.

"High Commission in London to Department of External Affairs, February 18, 1949." In *Documents on Australian Foreign Policy, 1949, Volume 15.*

"Hodgson to Department of External Affairs, December 24, 1948." In *Documents on Australian Foreign Policy, 1948, Volume 13.*

Holland, Robert. *Britain and the Revolt in Cyprus, 1954–59.* Oxford: Oxford University Press, 1998.

Hood, Christopher. *The Blame Game: Spin, Bureaucracy, and Self-Preservation in Government.* Princeton: Princeton University Press, 2011.

Hoogenboezem, J. *Correspondence with Author, August-October 2011.*

Horne, Alistair. *The Fall of Paris: The Siege and the Commune, 1870–71.* New York: St Martins Press, 1965.

———. *The French Army and Politics, 1870–1970.* 1st American ed. New York: Peter Bedrick Books: Distributed in the United States by Harper & Row, 1984.

Howell, William G., and Jon C. Pevehouse. "When Congress Stops Wars: Partisan Politics and Presidential Power." *Foreign Affairs* 86, no. 5 (2007): 95–107.

Huntington, Samuel P. *The Soldier and the State: The Theory and Politics of Civil-Military Relations.* Cambridge: Belknap Press of Harvard University Press, 1957.

Iklé, Fred Charles. *Every War Must End*, Columbia paperback. New York: Columbia University Press, 1971.

"Impasse on Troop Pullout: Israel Seeks a Peace Treaty." *New York Times*, December 6, 1982.

"Intelligence Note from the Director of the Bureau of Intelligence and Research (Hughes) to Secretary of State Rogers, South Africa: The Indivisible Government, June 24, 1969." In *F.R.U.S., 1969–1976, Volume 28.*

"Intelligence Note Prepared in the Bureau of Intelligence and Research, South West Africa: Enough South African-Waldheim Progress?, May 10, 1973." In *F.R.U.S., 1969–1976, Volume 28.*

Ion, A. Hamish, and Elizabeth Jane Errington. *Great Powers and Little Wars: The Limits of Power.* Westport, CT: Praeger, 1993.

"Israel's Victory in Lebanon." *The Washington Post*, January 18, 1985.

"Israel and Lebanon Sign Agreement at Two Ceremonies." *New York Times*, May 18, 1983.

"Israel Denies Preparing for Lebanon Pullback." *The Times*, March 12, 1984.

"Israel Determined to Keep out of Lebanon Chaos." *The Times*, February 7, 1984.

"Israel Is Said to Link Pullout Talks with Normalizing Lebanon Ties." *New York Times*, November 10, 1982.

"Israel Proclaims Tough Proposals for Ending War." *New York Times*, June 28, 1982.

"Israel Starts First Stage of Its Lebanon Pullout." *New York Times*, January 21, 1985.

"Israel to Speed up Lebanon Pullout." *New York Times*, March 27, 1985.

"Israel Votes Lebanon Pact in Principle, but a Pullout Awaits Talks with Syrians." *New York Times*, May 7, 1983.

"Israeli Cabinet Approves Second Stage of Troop Pullout from Lebanon." *New York Times*, March 4, 1985.

"Israeli Cabinet in Second Crisis Meeting on Lebanon." *The Times*, February 13, 1984.

"Israeli Document Asks Lebanon Exit." *New York Times*, January 11, 1984.

"Israeli Election: Likud May Live to Lament Lebanon." *The Times*, July 12, 1984.

"Israeli Foreign Minister Says He Expects Pullout from Lebanon This Year." *New York Times*, October 3, 1982.

"Israeli Officers Present Lebanon Pullout Plan." *New York Times*, August 12, 1984.
"Israeli Official Says Pullout Moves at a Satisfactory Pace." *New York Times*, August 30, 1982.
"An Israeli Pullout: The Obstacles in the Way." *New York Times*, September 25, 1984.
"Israeli Statement on Pullout." *New York Times*, October 11, 1982.
"Israeli Visits a Worried Border Town." *New York Times*, April 26, 1985.
"The Israeli Withdrawal: Peres Says Army Will Be Home from Lebanon by Summer." *The Times*, January 16, 1985.
"Israelis Accept Plan to End Beirut Siege; Goal Is to Begin P.L.O. Pullout Tomorrow." *New York Times*, August 20, 1982.
"Israelis Assert P.L.O. Is Fortifying Its Military and Political Positions." *New York Times*, July 13, 1982.
"Israelis Complete Step Two of Pullout." *New York Times*, April 30, 1985.
"Israelis Cut Off West Beirut, Trapping P.L.O. Leaders." *New York Times*, June 15, 1982.
"Israelis May Quit Lebanon before Syria Does." *New York Times*, January 7, 1984.
"Israelis Plan New Lebanon Strategy." *The Times*, March 7, 1984.
"Israelis Say Redeployment Isn't Withdrawal." *New York Times*, January 7, 1984.
Jackson, Julian. *Charles De Gaulle*, Life & Times. London: Haus, 2003.
Jaffe, Greg, and David Nakamura. "Obama Agrees to Slow U.S. Troop Withdrawal from Afghanistan." http://www.washingtonpost.com/politics/ (accessed April 1, 2015).
Jaster, Robert S. *The Defence of White Power: South African Foreign Policy under Pressure*. New York: St. Martin's Press, 1989.
Javeline, Debra. *Protest and the Politics of Blame: The Russian Response to Unpaid Wages*, Interests, Identities, and Institutions in Comparative Politics. Ann Arbor: University of Michigan Press, 2003.
Johnson, Dominic D. P., and Dominic Tierney. *Failing to Win: Perceptions of Victory and Defeat in International Politics*. Cambridge, MA: Harvard University Press, 2006.
Kahin, George McTurnan. *Nationalism and Revolution in Indonesia*, Studies on Southeast Asia No. 35. Ithaca, NY: Southeast Asia Program Publications, Cornell University, 2003.
Kahler, Miles. *Decolonization in Britain and France: The Domestic Consequences of International Relations*. Princeton, NJ: Princeton University Press, 1984.
Karnow, Stanley. *Vietnam, a History*. Rev. and updated ed. New York, NY: Viking, 1991.
Katjavivi, Peter H. *A History of Resistance in Namibia*, Apartheid & Society. London: Unesco Press, 1988.
Kelly, George Armstrong. *Lost Soldiers: The French Army and Empire in Crisis, 1947–1962*. Cambridge, MA: M.I.T. Press, 1965.
Kelly, Thomas. "Sunk Costs, Rationality, and Acting for the Sake of the Past." *NOUS* 38, no. 1 (2004): 60–85.

Kettle, Michael. *De Gaulle and Algeria 1940–60: From Mers El-Kebir to the Algiers Barricades*. London: Quartet Books, 1993.

Kieval, Gershon R. "The Foreign Policy of the Labor Party." In *Israeli National Security: Political Actors and Perspectives*, edited by Bernard Reich and Gershon R. Kieval, 19–54. New York: Greenwood Press, 1988.

Kimball, Jeffrey. "The Stab-in-the-Back-Legend and the Vietnam War." *Armed Forces and Society* 14, no. Spring (1988): 433–58.

"Kirby to Burton, January 9, 1948." In *Documents on Australian Foreign Policy, 1948, Volume 13*.

Kissinger, Henry, and Clare Boothe Luce. *White House Years*. Boston: Little, Brown, 1979.

Koch, Michael T., and Patricia L. Sullivan. "Should I Stay or Should I Go Now? Partisan Approval and the Duration of Major Power Democratic Military Interventions." *Journal of Politics* 72, no. 3 (2010): 616–29.

Kodikara, Shelton U., W. B. Dorakumbure, and Bandaranaike Centre for International Studies. *Domestic Politics and Diplomacy: A Study of Linkage Politics in Indo-Sri Lanka Relations*. Colombo: Bandaranaike Centre for International Studies, 2008.

Kranzberg, Melvin. *The Siege of Paris, 1870–1871: A Political and Social History*. Westport, CT: Greenwood Press, 1971.

Kriner, Douglas L. *After the Rubicon: Congress, Presidents, and the Politics of Waging War*, Chicago Series on International & Domestic Institutions. Chicago: University of Chicago Press, 2010.

Kroes, Rob. "Decolonization and the Military: The Case of the Netherlands, a Study in Political Reaction." In *On Military Intervention*, edited by Morris Janowitz and J. A. A. van Doorn, 93–116. Rotterdam: Rotterdam University Press, 1971.

———. *Soldiers and Students: A Study of Right- and Left-Wing Radicals*, International Library of Sociology. London; Boston: Routledge & K. Paul, 1975.

Landler, Mark. "U.S. Troops to Leave Afghanistan by End of 2016." *The New York Times*, http://www.nytimes.com/2014/05/28/world/asia/us-to-complete-afghan-pullout-by-end-of-2016-obama-to-say (accessed December 9, 2014).

"Last Guerillas Quit West Beirut." *New York Times*, September 2, 1982.

"Lebanese-Israeli Pullout Pact: Only Ink and Paper Unless Syrians Go Along." *New York Times*, May 18, 1983.

"Lebanon Has Sapped Israel's Army: Now It Is Smaller, Less Well Trained, More Dependent on U.S." *The Washington Post*, April 20, 1985.

"Lebanon Pullout Agreed by Israel." *The Times*, January 15, 1985.

"Lebanon Says Pullout Talks with Israel May Start This Week." *New York Times*, December 22, 1982.

"Lebanon: The Hawks Come Home to Roost." *The Times*, February 8, 1984.

Leimena, J. *The Dutch-Indonesian Conflict*. Jakarta 1949.

Leonard, Richard. *South Africa at War: White Power and the Crisis in Southern Africa*. Westport, CT: L. Hill, 1983.

"Letter from the Chief of the M.A.A.G. In Vietnam (McGarr) to the Chairman of the Joint Chiefs of Staff (Lemnitzer), Saigon, 12 October 1961." In *F.R.U.S., 1961–1963, Volume 1*, 347–59.

Liebenberg, Ian. "Through the Mirage: Retracing Moments of a War 'Up There.'" *Scientia Militaria, South African Journal of Military Studies* 38, no. 2 (2010): 131–49.

Lieven, Anatol. *Chechnya: Tombstone of Russian Power.* New Haven: Yale University Press, 1998.

Lijphart, Arend. *Patterns of Democracy: Government Forms and Performance in Thirty-Six Countries.* New Haven: Yale University Press, 1999.

———. *The Politics of Accommodation: Pluralism and Democracy in the Netherlands.* Berkeley: University of California Press, 1968.

———. *The Trauma of Decolonization: The Dutch and West New Guinea*, Yale Studies in Political Science, 17. New Haven: Yale University Press, 1966.

Ling, Nai-min. *Tibet, 1950–1967.* Hong Kong: Union Research Institute, 1968.

Lochery, Neill. *The Israeli Labour Party: In the Shadow of the Likud.* Reading, Berkshire: Ithaca Press, 1997.

Longmire, P. "Land and Labour in the Namibian Economy." In *Studies in the Economic History of Southern Africa*, edited by Zbigniew A. Konczacki, Jane L. Parpart, and Timothy M. Shaw. Savage, MD: F. Cass, 1990.

"Lord Killearn to Mr. Bevin, May 11, 1946." In *British Documents on Foreign Affairs: Reports and Papers from the Foreign Office Confidential Print, Part 4, Series E, Asia 1946, Volume 1*, 2001.

"Lord Killearn to Mr. Bevin, May 27, 1946." In *British Documents on Foreign Affairs: Reports and Papers from the Foreign Office Confidential Print, Part 4, Series E, Asia 1946, Volume 1*, 2001.

"Lord Killearn to Mr. Bevin, October 13, 1946." In *British Documents on Foreign Affairs: Reports and Papers from the Foreign Office Confidential Print, Part 4, Series E, Asia 1946, Volume 2*, 2001.

Ludra, Kuldip S. *Operation 'Pawan.'* Chandigarh: Strategic Research Centre, 1999.

Lukes, Steven. *Power: A Radical View.* 2nd ed. New York: Palgrave Macmillan, 2004.

Lyall, Jason, and Isaiah Wilson. "Rage against the Machines: Explaining Outcomes in Counterinsurgency Wars." *International Organization* 63, Winter (2009): 67–106.

Machado, Diamantino P. *The Structure of Portuguese Society: The Failure of Fascism.* New York: Praeger, 1991.

Mack, Andrew. "Why Big Nations Lose Small Wars: The Politics of Asymmetric Conflict." *World Politics* 27, no. 2 (1975): 170–200.

Mackenzie, Jean. "Is Obama to Blame for the Mess in Afghanistan?" GlobalPost, http://www.salon.com/2013/03/14 (accessed November 20, 2014).

Macleod, Jenny, ed. *Defeat and Memory: Cultural Histories of Military Defeat in the Modern Era.* New York: Palgrave Macmillan, 2008.

MacMillan, Harold. *Riding the Storm, 1956–1959*. New York: Harper & Row, Publishers, 1971.

MacQueen, Norrie. *The Decolonization of Portuguese Africa: Metropolitan Revolution and the Dissolution of Empire*. New York: Longman, 1997.

MacRae, Duncan. *Parliament, Parties, and Society in France, 1946–1958*. New York: St. Martin's Press, 1967.

"Makin to Department of External Affairs, July 30, 1947." In *Documents on Australian Foreign Policy, 1947, Volume 11*.

Maman, Daniel, Eyal Ben-Ari, and Zeev Rosenhek. *Military, State, and Society in Israel: Theoretical & Comparative Perspectives*. New Brunswick, NJ: Transaction Publishers, 2001.

Mannerheim, Carl Gustaf von. *The Memoirs of Marshal Mannerheim*. Translated by Count Eric Lewenhaupt. London: E. P. Dutton & Company, Ltd., 1953.

Maoz, Zeev, and Randolph M. Siverson. "Bargaining, Domestic Politics, and International Context in the Management of War: A Review Essay." *Conflict Management and Peace Science* 25 (2008): 171–89.

March, James G. *A Primer on Decision Making: How Decisions Happen*. New York: The Free Press, 1994.

Marcum, John A. "Retrenchment and Recalculation: South Africa and the Angola-Namibia Agreements." In *Disengagement from Southwest Africa*, edited by Owen Ellison Kahn, 131–48. London: Transaction Publishers, 1991.

Mason, Robert. *Richard Nixon and the Quest for a New Majority*. Chapel Hill: University of North Carolina Press, 2004.

"Massacre in Beirut: The Evidence from Four Shameful Days." *The Times*, September 24, 1982.

Mayer, Frederick W. "Managing Domestic Differences in International Negotiations: The Strategic Use of Internal Side-Payments." *International Organization* 46, no. 4 (1992): 793–818.

Mazzetti, Mark, and Eric Schmitt. "In a Shift, Obama Extends U.S. Role in Afghan Combat." *New York Times*, http://www.nytimes.com/2014/11/22/us/politics/in-secret-obama-extends-us-role-in-afghan-combat (accessed March 29, 2015).

McGraw, Kathleen M. "Managing Blame: An Experimental Test of the Effects of Political Accounts." *The American Political Science Review* 85, no. 4 (1991): 1133–57.

McHugh, Kelly. "Understanding Congress's Role in Terminating Unpopular Wars: A Comparison of the Vietnam and Iraq Wars." *Democracy and Security* 10, no. 3 (2014): 191–224.

McMichael, Scott R. *Stumbling Bear: Soviet Military Performance in Afghanistan*. London; Washington: Brassey's, 1991.

"Memorandum by the Director of the Office of Far Eastern Affairs (Butterworth) to the Counselor of the Department (Bohlen), January 17, 1949." In *F.R.U.S., 1949, Volume 7*.

"Memorandum from the President's Assistanct for National Security Affairs (Kissinger) to President Nixon, South West Africa (Namibia): Response to N.S.S.M. 89, April 15, 1970." In *F.R.U.S., 1969–1976, Volume 28*.

"Memorandum from the President's Assistant for National Security Affairs (Kissinger) to President Nixon, Coup in Portugal, April 29, 1974." In *F.R.U.S., 1969–1976, Volume 28.*

"Memorandum of Conversation by the Acting Secretary of State, December 20, 1948." In *F.R.U.S., 1948, Volume 6.*

"Memorandum, Gen. M. B. Ridgway for General and Flag-Officer Members of the U.N. Delegation, 7 July 1951." GHQ, UNC SGS files.

Merom, Gil. *How Democracies Lose Small Wars: State, Society, and the Failures of France in Algeria, Israel in Lebanon, and the United States in Vietnam.* Cambridge, UK; New York: Cambridge University Press, 2003.

Meyer, John W., and Brian Rowan. "Institutionalized Organizations: Formal Structures as Myth and Ceremony." *American Journal of Sociology* 83, no. 2 (1977): 340–63.

Michael, Kobi. "Military Knowledge and Weak Civilian Control in the Reality of Low Intensity Conflict: The Israeli Case." *Israel Studies* 12, no. 1 (2007): 28–52.

"Military Contests and Settlement." http://www.fsmitha.com/h2/ch24kor8.htm (accessed April 11, 2015).

Miskimmon, Alister, Ben O'Loughlin, and Laura Roselle. *Strategic Narratives: Communications and the New World Order.* London: Routledge, 2013.

Mohammed, Arshad, David Rohde, and Phil Steward. "U.S. Likely to Delay Planned Closure of Two Afghanistan Bases." http://www.reuters.com/article/2015/03/19/us-afghanistan-usa-bases (accessed March 29, 2015).

Moskos, Charles C. "From Institution to Occupation: Trends in Military Organization." *Armed Forces and Society* 41, no. 1 (1977): 41–50.

Moyar, Mark. *Triumph Forsaken: The Vietnam War, 1954–1965.* New York: Cambridge University Press, 2009.

"Mr. Bevin to Sir N. Bland, April 29, 1946." In *British Documents on Foreign Affairs: Reports and Papers from the Foreign Office Confidential Print, Part 4, Series E, Asia 1946, Volume 1,* 2001.

Mueller, John E. "War Has Almost Ceased to Exist: An Assessment." *Political Science Quarterly* 124, no. 2 (2009): 297–321.

———. *War, Presidents, and Public Opinion.* New York: Wiley, 1973.

Namibian Independence and Cuban Troop Withdrawal. Pretoria, Republic of South Africa: Department of Foreign Affairs, 1989.

Nathan, Laurie. "Marching to a Different Beat: The History of the End Conscription Campaign." In *Society at War: The Militarisation of South Africa,* edited by Jacklyn Cock and Laurie Nathan, 308–23. New York: St. Martin's Press, 1989.

Nelson, Bradley N. "Regime Type and the Persistence of Costly Small Wars." PhD dissertation, The Ohio State University, 2008.

"The Netherlands-Indonesian Problem: Views of Professor Schermerhorn, Sir N. Bland to Mr. Bevin, August 8, 1947." In *British Documents on Foreign Affairs: Reports and Papers from the Foreign Office Confidential Print, Part 4, Series E, Asia 1947, Volume 4,* 2001.

"Netherlands-Indonesian Relations, Mr. Gage to Mr. Bevin, July 20, 1947." In *British Documents on Foreign Affairs: Reports and Papers from the Foreign Office Confidential Print, Part 4, Series E, Asia 1947, Volume 4*, 2001.

The Netherlands Commonwealth and the Future: Important Statements of H. M. Queen Wilhelmina on Post-War Aims, Together with Statements by the Netherlands Government, the Dutch Press, as Well as Some American Comments. New York: The Netherlands Information Bureau, 1945.

"Netherlands: The Indonesian Problem: Programme of the Dutch Labour Party, Sir N. Bland to Mr. Bevin, September 11, 1947." In *British Documents on Foreign Affairs: Reports and Papers from the Foreign Office Confidential Print, Part 4, Series E, Asia 1947, Volume 4*, 2001.

Neustadt, Richard E. *Presidential Power, the Politics of Leadership.* New York: Wiley, 1960.

"New Battles Shatter Lebanon Cease-Fire." *New York Times*, June 14, 1982.

Nordlinger, Eric A. *Soldiers in Politics: Military Coups and Governments*, Prentice-Hall Contemporary Comparative Politics Series. Englewood Cliffs, NJ: Prentice-Hall, 1977.

Oey, Hong Lee. *War and Diplomacy in Indonesia, 1945–50*, South-East Asian Monograph Series. Townsville, Australia: Committee of South-East Asian Studies, James Cook University of North Queensland, 1981.

Out of Step: War Resistance in South Africa. London: Catholic Institute for International Relations, 1989.

"Paper Prepared by the National Security Counicl Interdepartmental Group for Africa, Response to N.S.S.M. 89: South West Africa, April 2, 1970." In *F.R.U.S., 1969–1976, Volume 28.*

Paul, T. V. *Asymmetric Conflicts: War Initiation by Weaker Powers*, Cambridge Studies in International Relations 33. Cambridge; New York, NY: Cambridge University Press, 1994.

Pearlman, Michael D. *Truman & Macarthur: Policy, Politics, and the Hunger for Honor and Renown.* Bloomington: Indiana University Press, 2008.

Peleg, Ilan. *Begin's Foreign Policy, 1977–1983: Israel's Move to the Right*, Contributions in Political Science. New York: Greenwood Press, 1987.

———. "The Foreign Policy of Herut and the Likud." In *Israeli National Security: Political Actors and Perspectives*, edited by Bernard Reich and Gershon R. Kieval, 55–78. New York: Greenwood Press, 1988.

"Peres Hints at Lebanon Withdrawal." *The Times*, October 12, 1984.

"Peres Pledges Pullout from Lebanon If He Wins Vote." *New York Times*, June 23, 1984.

"Peres Sets June 6 for Lebanon Troop Pullout." *New York Times*, June 3, 1985.

Peres, Shimon, and David Landau. *Battling for Peace: A Memoir.* New York: Random House, 1995.

Peri, Yoram. *Generals in the Cabinet Room: How the Military Shapes Israeli Policy.* Washington DC: United States Institute of Peace Press, 2006.

———. "Intractable Conflict and the Media." *Israel Studies* 12, no. 1 (2007): 79–102.

Perlmutter, Amos. "Begin's Rhetoric and Sharon's Tactics." *Foreign Affairs* 60, no. 1 (1982): 76–83.

Perlmutter, Amos, and Harvard University. Center for International Affairs. *The Military and Politics in Modern Times: On Professionals, Praetorians, and Revolutionary Soldiers.* New Haven: Yale University Press, 1977.

Perry, Mark. *Four Stars.* Boston: Houghton Mifflin, 1989.

Phillips, Mark. "The Nuts and Bolts of Military Power: The Structure of the S.A.D.F." In *Society at War: The Militarisation of South Africa*, edited by Jacklyn Cock and Laurie Nathan, 16–27. New York: St. Martin's Press, 1989.

Pierson, Robert. "The Epistemic Authority of Expertise." *Proceedings of the Biennial Meeting of the Philosophy of Science Association* 1 (1994): 398–405.

Pillar, Paul R. *Negotiating Peace: War Termination as a Bargaining Process.* Princeton: Princeton University Press, 1983.

Pognon, Edmond. *De Gaulle et l'Armée*, Collection Espoir. Paris: Plon, 1976.

"Political Developments within the Indonesian Republic, Consul-General Sir F. Shepherd to Mr. Bevin, September 30, 1948." In *British Documents on Foreign Affairs: Reports and Papers from the Foreign Office Confidential Print, Part 4, Series E, Asia 1948, Volume 6*, 2001.

"Political Situation in Indonesia, Consul-General Shepherd to Mr. Bevin, November 13, 1947." In *British Documents on Foreign Affairs: Reports and Papers from the Foreign Office Confidential Print, Part 4, Series E, Asia 1947, Volume 4*, 2001.

Porch, Douglas. *Correspondence with Author, February 2012.*

———. *The Portuguese Armed Forces and the Revolution*, Hoover Institution Publication 188. London: Croom Helm; Hoover Institution Press, 1977.

Porter, Bruce D. "The Military Abroad: Internal Consequences of External Expansion." In *Soldiers and the Soviet State: Civil-Military Relations from Brezhnev to Gorbachev*, edited by Timothy J. Colton and Thane Gustafson, 285–333. Princeton: Princeton University Press, 1990.

Porter, Gareth. "U.S.: Fears of Blame for Defeat Shadow Afghan War Meetings." Inter Press Service News Agency, http://www.ipsnews.net/2009/09/ (accessed November 20, 2014).

Posen, Barry. *The Sources of Military Doctrine: France, Britain, and Germany between the World Wars*, Cornell Studies in Security Affairs. Ithaca: Cornell University Press, 1984.

Pottinger, Brian. *The Imperial Presidency: P.W. Botha, the First 10 Years.* Johannesburg: Southern Book Publishers, 1988.

Powell, Robert. "Bargaining Theory and International Conflict." *Annual Review of Political Science* 5 (2002): 1–30.

Powell, Walter W., and Paul DiMaggio. *The New Institutionalism in Organizational Analysis.* Chicago: University of Chicago Press, 1991.

Price, Robert M. "Pretoria's Southern African Strategy." In *Exporting Apartheid: Foreign Policies in Southern Africa, 1978–1988*, edited by Stephen Chan, 145–69. New York: St. Martin's Press, 1990.

"A Prior P.L.O. Pullout Is Demanded by Israelis." *New York Times*, October 6, 1982.

Purkitt, Helen E., and Stephen Franklin Burgess. *South Africa's Weapons of Mass Destruction*. Bloomington, IN: Indiana University Press, 2005.

"Quinn to Burton, December 22, 1948." In *Documents on Australian Foreign Policy, 1948, Volume 13*.

"Quinn to Department of External Affairs, December 30, 1948." In *Documents on Australian Foreign Policy, 1948, Volume 13*.

"Quinn to Evatt, March 1, 1949." In *Documents on Australian Foreign Policy, 1949, Volume 15*.

"Quinn to Hood, December 2, 1948." In *Documents on Australian Foreign Policy, 1948, Volume 13*.

Rabin, Yitzhak. *The Rabin Memoirs*. Expanded ed. Berkeley: University of California Press, 1996.

Rabinovich, Itamar. *The War for Lebanon, 1970–1985*. Rev. ed., Cornell paperbacks. Ithaca: Cornell University Press, 1985.

Record, Jeffrey. "The Wrong War: Why We Lost in Vietnam." Naval Institute Press, 1998.

Reich, Bernard. "Israeli National Security Policy: Issues and Actors." In *Israeli National Security: Political Actors and Perspectives*, edited by Bernard Reich and Gershon R. Kieval, 1–18. New York: Greenwood Press, 1988.

Reiter, Dan. *How Wars End*. Princeton: Princeton University Press, 2009.

"Report of the Commission of Inquiry into Reporting on Security Matters Regarding the South African Defence Force and the South African Police Force." Pretoria, Republic of South Africa, 1980.

"Report of the Commission of Inquiry into the Events at the Refugee Camps in Beirut (the Kahan Commission)." http://www.jewishvirtuallibrary.org/jsource/History/kahan.html.

Ricks, Thomas E. *The Gamble: General David Petraeus and the American Military Adventure in Iraq, 2006–2008*. New York: Penguin Press, 2009.

Ritter, Gerhard. *The Sword and the Scepter: The Problem of Militarism in Germany, Volume 3*. Coral Gables, FL: University of Miami Press, 1972.

———. *The Sword and the Scepter: The Problem of Militarism in Germany, Volume 4*. Coral Gables, FL: University of Miami Press, 1973.

Roherty, James Michael. *State Security in South Africa: Civil-Military Relations under P.W. Botha*. Armonk, NY: M.E. Sharpe, 1992.

Rosenberg, Matthew, and Mark Mazzetti. "More U.S. Troops Seen Staying in Afghanistan." *New York Times*, http://www.nytimes.com/2015/03/20/world/asia/more-us-troops-seen-staying-in-afghanistan (accessed March 29, 2015).

———. "U.S. May Stay in Afghanistan after '16." *New York Times*, http://www.nytimes.com/2015/03/21/world/asia/us-may-stay-in-afghanistan-after-16 (accessed March 29, 2015).

Rotberg, Robert I. "Decision Making and the Military in South Africa." In *South Africa and Its Neighbors: Regional Security and Self-Interest*, edited by Robert I. Rotberg, Henry Bienen, Robert Legvold, and Gavin G. Maasdorp, 13–26. Lexington, MA: Lexington Books, 1985.

———. "Namibia: The Regional Stalemate." In *South Africa and Its Neighbors: Regional Security and Self-Interest*, edited by Robert I. Rotberg, Henry Bienen, Robert Legvold, and Gavin G. Maasdorp, 137–50. Lexington, MA: Lexington Books, 1985.

Rourke, Francis E. *Bureaucracy and Foreign Policy*, Studies in International Affairs. Baltimore: Johns Hopkins University Press, 1972.

Salem, Elie Adib. *Violence and Diplomacy in Lebanon: The Troubled Years, 1982–1988*. London; New York: I.B. Tauris, Distributed by St. Martin's Press, 1995.

Schiff, Zeev, Ehud Yaari, and Ina Friedman. *Israel's Lebanon War*. New York: Simon and Schuster, 1984.

Schivelbusch, Wolfgang. *The Culture of Defeat: On National Trauma, Mourning, and Recovery*. 1st American ed. New York: Metropolitan Books, 2003.

Schlenker, Barry R., Thomas W. Britt, John Pennington, Rodolfo Murphy, and Kevin Doherty. "The Triangle Model of Responsibility." *Psychological Review* 101, no. 4 (1994): 632–52.

Schmitter, Phillipe C. "Liberation by Golpe: Retrospective Thoughts on the Demise of Authoritarian Rule in Portugal." *Armed Forces and Society* 2, no. 1 (1975): 5–33.

Schnabel, James F., and Robert J. Watson. "The Korean War Part Two." In *The Joint Chiefs of Staff and National Policy, Vol 3, 1951–1953*. Washington DC: Office of the Chairman of the Joint Chiefs of Staff, 1998.

Schoeman, Jan R. "Netherlands." In *The Political Role of the Military: An International Handbook*, edited by Constantine P. Danopoulos and Cynthia Watson, 283–98. London: Greenwood Press, 1996.

Schwab, Orrin. *A Clash of Cultures: Civil-Military Relations During the Vietnam War*. In War and in Peace. Westport, CT: Praeger Security International, 2006.

Scott, W. Richard. *Institutions and Organizations*, Foundations for Organizational Science. Thousand Oaks: SAGE, 1995.

"Scrapping of Accord with Israel Hastens Partition of Lebanon." *The Times*, March 6, 1984.

"The Secretary of State to the Embassy in the Netherlands, January 31, 1949." In *F.R.U.S., 1949, Volume 7*.

Seawright, Jason, and John Gerring. "Case Selection Techniques in Case Study Research." *Political Research Quarterly* 61, no. 2 (2008): 294–308.

Selfe, James. "South Africa's National Management System." In *Society at War: The Militarisation of South Africa*, edited by Jacklyn Cock and Laurie Nathan, 149–58. New York: St. Martin's Press, 1989.

"Shamir's Lebanon Plan Shows Typical Caution." *Los Angeles Times*, October 17, 1983.

Sharon, Ariel, and David Chanoff. *Warrior: The Autobiography of Ariel Sharon*. New York: Simon and Schuster, 1989.

Shipler, David. "For Israelis, the Taste of Victory Starts to Turn Sour." *New York Times*, July 25, 1982.

———. "A Quagmire for Israelis." *New York Times*, September 17, 1982.

———. "A Retreat by Israel." *New York Times*, September 5, 1983.

Shlaim, Avi, and Avner Yaniv. "Politics and Foreign Policy in Israel." *International Affairs* 56, no. 2 (1980): 242–62.

"Sidon Hq Handover: Israel May Pull Back Further." *The Times*, May 16, 1984.

Silva, Manik de. "The Lesser Evil: India Pulls Out, Leaving Tamil Issue Unresolved." *Far Eastern Economic Review* 148, no. 14 (1990): 10–11.

Simpson, Emile. *War from the Ground Up: Twenty-First Century Combat as Politics.* Oxford: Oxford University Press, 2012.

Simpson, Thula. *Correspondence with Author, August 2011.*

"Sir Nevile Bland to Mr. Bevin, August 6, 1946." In *British Documents on Foreign Affairs: Reports and Papers from the Foreign Office Confidential Print, Part 4, Series E, Asia 1946, Volume 2*, 2001.

"Situation in Indonesia, Consul-General Sir F. Shepherd to Mr. Bevin, March 28, 1949." In *British Documents on Foreign Affairs: Reports and Papers from the Foreign Office Confidential Print, Part 4, Series E, Asia 1949, Volume 9*, 2001.

"Situation in Indonesia, Sir P. Nichols to Mr. Bevin, December 18, 1948." In *British Documents on Foreign Affairs: Reports and Papers from the Foreign Office Confidential Print, Part 4, Series E, Asia 1948, Volume 6*, 2001.

"Situation in Indonesia: Debate in the Netherlands Second Chamber, Sir P. Nichols to Mr. Bevin, May 19, 1949." In *British Documents on Foreign Affairs: Reports and Papers from the Foreign Office Confidential Print, Part 4, Series E, Asia 1949, Volume 9*, 2001.

"Situation in Indonesia: Events Leading up to Resumption of Police Action by the Netherlands Government, Consul-General Sir F. Shepherd to Mr. Bevin, December 22, 1948." In *British Documents on Foreign Affairs: Reports and Papers from the Foreign Office Confidential Print, Part 4, Series E, Asia 1949, Volume 9*, 2001.

"Situation in Indonesia: Truce Agreement and Renville Principles, Consul-General Shepherd to Mr. Bevin, January 21, 1948." In *British Documents on Foreign Affairs: Reports and Papers from the Foreign Office Confidential Print, Part 4, Series E, Asia 1948, Volume 6*, 2001.

"Situation in the East Coast of Sumatra, Acting Consul Roberts to Consul-General Shepherd, November 17, 1947." In *British Documents on Foreign Affairs: Reports and Papers from the Foreign Office Confidential Print, Part 4, Series E, Asia 1947, Volume 4*, 2001.

Smith, Sebastian. *Allah's Mountains: The Battle for Chechnya*. London; New York: TPP, 2006.

Snyder, Jack L. *Myths of Empire: Domestic Politics and International Ambition*, Cornell Studies in Security Affairs. Ithaca, NY: Cornell University Press, 1991.

South African Institute of International Affairs. "What Do We Think?" In *Geleentheidspublikasie/ die Suid-Afrikaanse Instituut van Internasionale Aangeleenthede*. Braamfontein, South Africa: South African Institute of International Affairs, 1982.

Sowers, Thomas. "Beyond the Soldier and the State: Contemporary Operations and Variance in Principal-Agent Relationships." *Armed Forces and Society* 31, no. 2 (2005): 385–409.

Spanier, John W. *The Truman-Macarthur Controversy and the Korean War.* Cambridge, MA: Belknap Press, 1959.

Spínola, António de. *País Sem Rumo: Contributo Para a História De Uma Revolução.* Lisboa: SCIRE, 1978.

———. *Portugal and the Future.* Johannesburg: Perskor Publishers, 1974.

Stanley, Elizabeth A. *Paths to Peace: Domestic Coalition Shifts, War Termination and the Korean War.* Stanford, CA: Stanford University Press, 2009.

"Steele Blames Afghan War on Obama, Drawing Calls to Resign." http://www.foxnews.com/politics/2010/07/02/ (accessed November 20, 2014).

Steenkamp, Willem. *Borderstrike! South Africa into Angola.* Pretoria: Woburn Butterworths, 1983.

———. *South Africa's Border War, 1966–1989.* Gibraltar: Ashanti Pub., 1989.

Stevenson, Charles A. *Warriors and Politicians: US Civil-Military Relations under Stress*, Cass Military Studies. London; New York: Routledge, 2006.

Stikker, Dirk U. *Men of Responsibility: A Memoir.* New York: Harper & Row, 1966.

Stohl, Michael. *War and Domestic Political Violence: The American Capacity for Repression and Reaction*, Sage Library of Social Research V. 30. Beverly Hills, CA: Sage Publications, 1976.

Suchman, Mark C. "Managing Legitimacy: Strategic and Institutional Approaches." *Academy of Management Review* 20, no. 3 (1995): 571–610.

Sulitzeanu-Kenan, Raanan, and Lior Sheffer. "A Formal Model of Social Blame in Political Context." Paper presented at the 69th Annual Midwest Political Science Association Conference, March 31-April 3, 2011. Chicago, IL.

Sullivan, Patricia L. "Sustaining the Fight: A Cross-Sectional Time-Series Analysis of Public Support for Ongoing Military Interventions." *Conflict Management and Peace Science* 25 (2008): 112–35.

Sullivan, Patricia L., and Michael T. Koch. "Military Intervention by Powerful States, 1945–2003." *Journal of Peace Research* 46, no. 5 (2009): 707–18.

Sulzberger, C. L. *The Test: De Gaulle and Algeria.* New York: Harcourt, 1962.

"Sumatra: Netherlands-Indonesian Hostilities: Political-Military Developments, Acting-Consul Roberts to Mr. Mitcheson (Batavia), August 2, 1947." In *British Documents on Foreign Affairs: Reports and Papers from the Foreign Office Confidential Print, Part 4, Series E, Asia 1947, Volume 4*, 2001.

"Sumatra: Netherlands-Indonesian Hostilities: Political-Military Developments, Acting Consul Roberts to Consul-General Mitcheson (Batavia), 9 August, 1947." In *British Documents on Foreign Affairs: Reports and Papers from the Foreign Office Confidential Print, Part 4, Series E, Asia 1947, Volume 4*, 2001.

"Sumatra: Political-Military Situation in East Coast, Acting Consul Roberts to Consul-General Mitcheson (Batavia), May 22, 1947." In *British Documents on Foreign Affairs: Reports and Papers from the Foreign Office Confidential Print, Part 4, Series E, Asia 1947, Volume 4*, 2001.

"Summary of Events in Java, Mr. Sterndale Bennett to Mr. Wright, February 6, 1946." In *British Documents on Foreign Affairs: Reports and Papers from the Foreign Office Confidential Print, Part 4, Series E, Asia 1946, Volume 1,* 2001.

"Summary of Proposals Leading to the Present Negotiations between the Dutch and Indonesians, E. Lambert, March 23, 1946." In *British Documents on Foreign Affairs: Reports and Papers from the Foreign Office Confidential Print, Part 4, Series E, Asia 1946, Volume 1,* 2001.

Suro, Roberto, Johanna McGeary, and James Kelly. "Middle East: A House Divided." *Time,* August 8 1983.

"Syria Fights Israeli Pullout Terms." *New York Times,* May 3, 1983.

"Syrian-Led Force Quits West Beirut." *New York Times,* August 28, 1982.

Tamir, Avraham, and Joan Comay. *A Soldier in Search of Peace: An Inside Look at Israel's Strategy.* 1st American ed. New York: Harper & Row, 1988.

Taylor, A. J. P. *The Origins of the Second World War.* London: Hamilton, 1961.

Temko, Ned. *To Win or to Die: A Personal Portrait of Menachem Begin.* New York: W. Morrow, 1987.

Thomas, Martin. *The French North African Crisis: Colonial Breakdown and Anglo-French Relations, 1945–62,* Studies in Military and Strategic History. New York: St. Martin's Press, 2000.

Thomas, Martin, Bob Moore, and L. J. Butler. *Crises of Empire: Decolonization and Europe's Imperial States, 1918–1975.* London: Hodder Education, 2008.

Tilly, Charles. *Credit and Blame.* Princeton: Princeton University Press, 2008.

UNESCO. *Racism and Apartheid in Southern Africa: South Africa and Namibia.* Paris: U.N.E.S.C.O. Press, 1974.

United Nations Security Council Resolution 418. November 4, 1977.

United Nations Security Council Resolution 435. September 29, 1978.

United Nations Security Council Resolution 539. October 28, 1983.

United Nations Security Council, S/18767, Further Report of the Secretary General Concerning the Implementation of Security Council Resolutions 435 (1978) and 439 (1978) Concerning the Question of Namibia. March 31, 1987.

United Nations, Report of the Secretary General 8357, Addendum 1, "Question of South West Africa." United Nations Security Council, January 25, 1968.

United Nations, Resolution 2145, "Question of South West Africa." United Nations General Assembly, Twenty-First Session, October 27, 1966.

Van der Eng, Pierre. "Marshall Aid as Catalyst in the Decolonization of Indonesia, 1947–49." In *The Decolonization Reader,* edited by James D. Le Sueur, 123–38. New York: Routledge, 2003.

Van Doorn, J. A. A. "Continuity and Discontinuity in Civil-Military Relations." In *The Military, Militarism, and the Polity: Essays in Honor of Morris Janowitz,* edited by Michel L. Martin and Ellen Stern McCrate, 35–49. New York: Free Press, 1984.

———. "Justifying Military Action." In *On Military Ideology,* edited by Morris Janowitz and J. A. A. Van Doorn, 75–96. Rotterdam: Rotterdam University Press, 1971.

———. "The Military and the Crisis of Legitimacy." In *The Military and the Problem of Legitimacy*, edited by J. A. A. Van Doorn and Gwyn Harries-Jenkins, 17–40. London: Sage Publications, 1976.

———. "The Officer Corps: A Fusion of Profession and Organization." *Journal of European Sociology* 6, no. 2 (1965): 262–82.

———. *The Soldier and Social Change: Comparative Studies in the History and Sociology of the Military*, Sage Series on Armed Forces and Society V. 7. Beverly Hills, CA: Sage Publications, 1975.

Van Evera, Stephen. "Causes of War." PhD dissertation, Unversity of California, Berkeley, 1984.

Van Rooyen, Johann. *Hard Right: The New White Power in South Africa*. London: I.B. Tauris, 1994.

Van Wyk, J. J. *Elite Opinions on South African Foreign Policy*, Occasional Paper/ Research Project on South Africa's Foreign Relations. Johannesburg: J. J. van Wyk, 1984.

Venter, Al J. *Portugal's Guerrilla War: The Campaign for Africa*. Cape Town: J. Malherbe, 1973.

———. *The Terror Fighters: A Profile of Guerrilla Warfare in Southern Africa*. Cape Town, Johannesburg: Purnell, 1969.

Visser, Lieneke Eloff de. "Winning Hearts and Minds in the Namibian Border War." *Scientia Militaria, South African Journal of Military Studies* 39, no. 1 (2011): 85–100.

Voorhoeve, J. J. C. *Peace, Profits and Principles: A Study of Dutch Foreign Policy*. The Hague: Martinus Nijhoff, 1979.

Walt, Stephen. "Top Ten Reasons Why Wars Last Too Long." http://walt.foreign-policy.com/posts/2010/09/01/ (accessed March 29, 2015).

Warchawski. "Inside the Anti-Occupation Camp." *The Link (Americans for Middle East Understanding)* 39, no. 2 (2006).

Weaver, R. Kent. "The Politics of Blame Avoidance." *Journal of Public Policy* 6, no. 4 (1986): 371–98.

Weaver, Tony. "The South African Defence Force in Namibia." In *Society at War: The Militarisation of South Africa*, edited by Jacklyn Cock and Laurie Nathan, 90–102. New York: St. Martin's Press, 1989.

Weeks, Jessica L. "Autocratic Audience Costs: Regime Type and Signaling Resolve." *International Organization* 62, no. 1 (2008): 35–64.

Weiss, Allen, and Erin Anderson. "Perceptions of Legitimacy as a Motive to Change Inter-Organizational Relations." Research Paper #1175, Graduate School of Business, Stanford University, November 1991.

Wheeler, Douglas L. "The Military and the Portuguese Dictatorship, 1926–1974." In *Contemporary Portugal: The Revolution and Its Antecedents*, edited by Lawrence S. Graham and Harry M. Makler, 191–220. Austin: University of Texas Press, 1979.

"White Paper on Defence and Armaments Supply, 1979." Department of Defence, Republic of South Africa.

Winkler, Harald E., and Laurie Nathan. "Waging Peace: Church Resistance to Militarisation." In *Marching to a Different Beat: The History of the End Conscription Campaign*, edited by Jacklyn Cock and Laurie Nathan, 324–37. New York: St. Martin's Press, 1989.

"Withdrawal Plan Denied by Israeli." *New York Times*, January 9, 1984.

Wood, Brian "Preventing the Vacuum: Determinants of the Namibia Settlement." *Journal of Southern African Studies* 17, no. 4 (1991): 742–69.

"Yalu Could've Been Taken in 1951: Ridgway Doubts Its Worth in Yank Lives." *Chicago Tribune* (21 February 1956), http://archives.chicagotribune.com/1956/02/21/page/37/article/yalu-couldve-been-taken-in-1951-ridgway (accessed April 11, 2015).

Yaniv, A. *Dilemmas of Security: Politics, Strategy, and the Israeli Experience in Lebanon*. New York: Oxford University Press, 1987.

Yaniv, Avner, and Robert J. Lieber. "Personal Whim or Strategic Imperative? The Israeli Invasion of Lebanon." *International Security* 8, no. 2 (1983): 117–42.

Yishai, Yael. "Hawkish Proletariat: The Case of Israel." *Journal of Political and Military Sociology* 13 (1985): 53–73.

"Zhukov Report on the Situation in Hungary, 4 November 1956." In *Cold War International History Project*.

Zucker, Lynne G. "Institutional Theories of Organization." *Annual Review of Sociology* 13 (1987): 443–64.

Index

CPSIA information can be obtained
at www.ICGtesting.com
Printed in the USA
LVOW04*1700110316
478793LV00013B/162/P

9 781137 527967